CHAMPIONS

Mike Walters

CHAMPIONS

The Golden Age of Darts from PRIESTLEY TO LITTLER

pitch

First published by Pitch Publishing, 2026
1

Pitch Publishing
9 Donnington Park, 85 Birdham Road
Chichester, West Sussex, PO20 7AJ
www.pitchpublishing.co.uk
info@pitchpublishing.co.uk

Set in Adobe Caslon 12/19pt

Typeset by Pitch Publishing

Cover design by Olner Design

Printed and bound in Great Britain by TJ Books, Padstow

The authorised representative in the EEA is Easy Access System Europe OÜ, Mustamäe tee 50, 10621 Tallinn, Estonia gpsr.requests@easproject.com

A CIP catalogue record for this book is available from the British Library

ISBN 978-1-83680-478-9

Papers used by Pitch Publishing are from well-managed forests and other responsible sources

MIX
Paper | Supporting responsible forestry
FSC® C013056

CONTENTS

For Jack, Oscar and Millie

FOREWORD

by JOHN McDONALD

IN ALL honesty, I thought my first assignment as master of ceremonies at the darts would be my last, and I couldn't get off the stage fast enough.

Little did I know that, over the next 20 years, I would introduce every Professional Darts Corporation World Champion to the arena and enjoy a front-row view of their genius in action.

'The Showdown' between Phil 'The Power' Taylor and Andy 'The Viking' Fordham at the Circus Tavern in Purfleet in November 2004 was a meeting of two empires, a clash between the reigning PDC and British Darts Organisation World Champions, billed as the greatest darts match on earth. Worth a tidy £100,000 to the winner, it was Sky Sports' first pay-per-view adventure in darts and, although I barely knew who they were, I got the job for presenting the equivalent of a prize fight between Marvin Hagler and Sugar Ray Leonard.

Taylor was leading 5-2 in sets, or by 19 legs to 13 for those who were counting, in a high-quality match when Fordham, a gentle giant who had been perspiring profusely under the stage lights, was taken ill backstage during the break. I knew enough first aid to know that he was in a bad way and he couldn't possibly carry on. After I took his pulse and phoned 999 for the first time in my life, Andy left in an ambulance and it was down to me to go back out on stage and declare that the contest was over.

When I walked out to face the punters, shaking my head, at first it all went dead quiet. A few seconds later, I was under fire for being the bearer of bad news. The fans, most of them backing Fordham, had paid good money for their tickets and they didn't like it. No sooner had I asked them to show their appreciation for both players, and declared Phil 'The Power' Taylor as the winner, than the flak started flying.

I had been an MC at many boxing promotions, snooker events and worked on Sky Sports productions at pool, fishing, tenpin bowling, you name it. But that night, I didn't think darts and me was a match made in heaven, especially if I was getting pelters and a hefty dry cleaning bill for something totally beyond my control.

I was invited back for another crack at darts, at the 2005 World Matchplay in Blackpool and 2006 Premier League before the PDC chairman Barry Hearn, who had always been able to turn lemons into lemonade, told me he wanted me to be the voice of the walk-on and pre-match formalities at major darts tournaments on television from 2007 onwards. Talk about being in the right place at the right time!

From my privileged place front of house, I've watched darts grow from Brick Lane to Park Lane, from pub qualifiers to deafening venues where the players are welcomed like rock stars. The Premier League has gone from provincial leisure centres to international arenas in Berlin or Rotterdam where the noise can make your dentures rattle.

And best of all, being master of ceremonies means I've been part of some of the greatest sporting stories you've welcomed into your living rooms every Christmas, when the PDC World Championship is now part of our festive culture like roast turkey and pulling crackers.

As I write, there have been 13 PDC World Champions – and it has been my pleasure, my honour, to welcome them all on stage at Alexandra Palace. Each has a great story to tell and it is my privilege to introduce them again in this book – just as I summoned them down the walkway at Ally Pally.

I owe so much to my wonderful wife, Sharon, my four sons and eight grandchildren (to date), who have put up with me being an absent husband, father and grandad before I hung up the microphone and retired in January 2026.

But from that inconspicuous debut at the Circus Tavern, darts gave me the best job in sport, the best ticket money couldn't buy and some of the best friends out of eight billion people on the planet, whether it was going for a walk with them on the morning of a big game or going out for a pizza at lunchtime thousands of miles from home.

Dennis Priestley: A trailblazer for the PDC who once made a seven-hour round trip from his home in Yorkshire to do an exhibition in Colchester for 3,000 troops who were being posted to Afghanistan the next day – and he did it for free. I once gave 'Dennis the Menace' my hotel room key during a Players Championship so he could grab a few hours' kip between matches and he used every teabag, leaving me a note saying, 'You have been Menaced.'

Phil Taylor: He was the greatest player who ever threw a dart because he left nothing to chance. Phil understood that to be the best, you had to make sacrifices – and he drove others to raise their standards. I didn't get the chance to see Muhammad Ali box or Pelé play football, but I'm so glad I got the chance to see Phil Taylor hit two nine-darters in a Premier League final. When I introduced him for the last time, at the 2018 World Championship final, he said, 'John, you made me cry.' I replied, 'That's OK, you deserve it.'

John Part: My first gig as MC at Ally Pally was the year John beat £5-an-hour sheet metal worker Kirk Shepherd in the final, which meant he had won World Championship titles in his 20s,

30s and 40s – quite a feat when everyone thought Phil Taylor was virtually unbeatable. He was methodical, meticulous, not really a pants-on-fire showman, but one of the greats.

Raymond van Barneveld: All the top players have a vogue following now, but the Barney Army had something magical about it. When I introduced him on stage at the first Premier League night in Rotterdam, the sea of orange looked like a fleet of EasyJet planes. Whatever Michael van Gerwen and all the terrific Netherlands players achieve, 'Barney' will always be the King of Holland.

Adrian Lewis: For me, the most naturally gifted player on earth. His no-look 180, where he's not even looking at the target when the third dart is on its way into the treble 20 bed, epitomises the showman he is. And the tale of how he acquired his 'Jackpot' nickname is one of the greatest hard-luck stories in sport.

Michael van Gerwen: Peak MVG was absolutely unplayable. I once travelled with him to a big exhibition in Australia and he had the PDC World Championship trophy with him on the flight to Melbourne. The carrier, Etihad, used to sponsor Formula 1 and had a special compartment in the cabin for the F1 trophy – Michael walked off the plane with this huge trophy as if it was his hand luggage.

Gary Anderson: Give him a coffee machine and he's the happiest man on the planet. When he beat Phil Taylor to win his first World Championship, he suffered an outrageous triple bounce-out at a key moment – the first two darts landed in the treble 20 bed and when the third one knocked them both out, all three landed on the floor. It would have killed the spirit in lesser men.

Rob Cross: One of the greatest underdog stories of my life was Rob coming from nowhere to qualify for the World Championship and win it at the first attempt. He used to get up at 4am to drive up to London from the Sussex coast and rewire circuits in embassies as an electrician. He became a champion for every white van man with a blue-collar day job.

Peter Wright: He is the ultimate Marvel character. By day, Peter is shy, quietly-spoken and as loud as a church mouse – but put him in the barber's chair for a couple of hours, let his wife Jo loose with the face paint and hair colouring, slip on a pair of mad trousers and he turns into a superhero. The story of how he became 'Snakebite' will make your heart soar.

Gerwyn Price: I once told Vic Wakeling, the head of Sky Sports, that we were missing a trick by not covering non-league football because it was a great spectacle. He told me, 'It doesn't matter who you are, if you do something brilliant but you turn round and there's hardly anyone watching, it's not the same.' Gezzy won the World Championship behind closed doors during the pandemic – he deserved to be roared on by a full house.

Michael Smith: Probably the most emotional of all the finals I've seen. 'Bully Boy' sank to his knees, then ran into his children's arms, after several near misses he was finally the World Champion. That perfect leg where Van Gerwen narrowly missed out on a nine-darter and then Smith completed his own was like two heavyweight boxers knocking each other out simultaneously.

Luke Humphries: The consummate professional – if anyone deserved to become a World Champion, Luke did. He used to work as a roofer with his dad, and it was a fantastic moment when he won and said the prize money meant his dad could retire instead of scrambling up ladders every day. A genuinely nice guy who reinvented himself to get in the best possible shape to succeed.

Luke Littler: We used to have a private joke during his walk-on about shaking hands in time to the chorus from his 'Greenlight' song 'Cos I'm ready to go oh, oh, oh.' If we missed the beat, we would both start laughing and one would tell the other, 'You're out of time.' Littler has always had an incredible belief in his own ability, going back to the JDC junior world championship final at a deserted Ally Pally, when I told him he would play one day in front of a packed crowd there. He replied, 'Yeah, you're right – I'll see you on Wednesday.' He had qualified for the main draw at the World Championship, he beat Christian Kist 3-0 on his debut… and the rest is history.

There you go – 13 great champions, now enjoy their 13 great stories. Working with these guys and living in the aura of their success was a treat. Now it's your turn.

John McDonald
Bexhill-on-Sea, April 2026

INTRODUCTION

DARKNESS HAD fallen like a curtain, but hours before the first shots were fired, touts were reportedly selling tickets on the black market for up to £1,000 a pop.

Hustlers can always smell a quick buck, and the cold night air had not deterred the 1st Battalion Del Boy Chancers. Outside on the steps, just yards from the VIP entrance, they were out in force.

Among the secondary ticket sharks, market forces were also rampant on the souvenir tat exchange. Half-and-half scarves, the preferred resort for hedging your bets, had been rustled up at fewer than 24 hours' notice and the least partisan fashion accessories in sport were fetching £20 a time if your pockets ran deeper than your IQ. Half-and-half scarves? They are monuments to naffness, like waiting for half-time in the Calcutta Cup before picking which side you want to win (unless one parent is Scottish and the other is English, in which case divided loyalties is an acceptable dilemma).

Every spare parking bay was occupied by outside broadcast trucks or mobile production units, some of them adorned with satellite dishes and cables like unruly portions of spaghetti, as every international news organisation worth its salt descended on the famous venue for a night of sporting history.

It was not just the biggest show in town on the back pages. All this commotion, all this hue and cry would dominate the news at ten. It would be the top story in all the bulletins at the top of the hour, not so much driving traffic on the worldwide web as virtually breaking the internet.

And it wasn't about football.

Forget about the overhyped Premier League, with its nit-picking VAR jobsworths, absurd kick-off times to make it as difficult as possible for loyal fans to follow their clubs home and away, its conniving cheats falling down at the merest breath of wind or poleaxed by passing insects, or its ludicrous transfer fees suggesting a portly left-back from a European backwater is somehow worth more than building a cancer hospital.

This stampede was all in the name of a darts match. A 16-year-old boy, Luke Littler, had started his maiden Professional Darts Corporation World Championship at Alexandra Palace ranked a lowly No.164 in the world and as a 66-1 outsider whose talent was a closely guarded secret outside a coterie in the know. Three weeks earlier, he could have crossed the high street in any town nationwide without anyone knowing who he was or what he was about to achieve.

Now, 18 days before his 17th birthday, he was facing the in-form Luke Humphries in the final for a jackpot prize of half a million pounds – and almost overnight, the world's media had been converted into darts experts.

At 16, Littler was not just within touching distance of becoming the youngest darts World Champion of all time. He was, potentially, a couple of hours away from being the youngest world champion at virtually anything. Boris Becker had won Wimbledon as an unseeded 17-year-old, Pelé had won the football World Cup with Brazil at the same age and Lester Piggott won his first Epsom Derby at 18.

But Littler's magic carpet ride at such a tender age was preposterous. No wonder television stations, radio outlets, wire services, news agencies, foreign correspondents and mainstream media had beaten a path to Ally Pally. Win or lose, Littler – who had beaten three former World Champions (Christian Kist, Raymond van Barneveld and Rob Cross) on his way to the final – was the name on everyone's lips. His opponent, Luke Humphries, was narrowly the bookies' favourite and in ominously good form, but tonight he was the 'other' bloke on stage, like Andrew Ridgeley's supporting act to George Michael in the eighties pop heyday of Wham!

For the darts cognoscenti, it was a lightbulb moment bringing their sport into the public eye like never before.

Just 12 months earlier, they had witnessed Michael Smith's nine-darter in the final against Michael van Gerwen, the most incredible leg of all time in which the Dutchman had missed his own shot at perfection before the 'Bully Boy' stepped up to complete the shortest journey from 501 to zero. Darts had enjoyed the boom years of Phil Taylor's record accumulation of 16 world titles in just 23 years – two of them under the original British Darts Organisation banner, the other 14 as flagship of the PDC armada – and the ultimate drama of his sudden-death final defeat by Van Barneveld in 2007. Then Fallon Sherrock's brief coup as Queen of the Palace in 2019, when her victories against Ted Evetts and Mensur Suljovic struck twin blows for the sisterhood in a male-dominated sport and exercised the admiration of sporting royalty including tennis legend Billie Jean King, proved darts was capable of exploring new frontiers.

But Littler's passage to his 'Lukes of Hazard' final against Humphries catapulted the sport into another solar system. The world was not enough – this feeding frenzy was more far-out than Pluto. A record 4.8 million viewers watched the pre-tournament long-shot's defeat, the biggest non-football audience in Sky Sports' 34-year history, and in 2024, more people searched online for Littler than the King or the Prime Minister.

Teenage celebrity opened doors rarely unlocked for a darts player. Littler was granted an audience with Sir Alex Ferguson – managerial royalty at his beloved Manchester United – went for a spin around Silverstone with future Formula 1 World Champion Lando Norris, and he was the star turn on a Christmas special of born-again game show *Bullseye*, although he went home to Cheshire without a speedboat or caravan.

Contrast the media circus and the trappings of fame with the ridicule and dilettante clumsiness of a sport which had struggled to discard its image as a pub game, with players allowed to smoke and drink alcohol on stage. In 1980, the culture was mocked in a sketch on the satirical BBC comedy show *Not The Nine O'Clock News*, with two overweight darts players squaring off in a drinking contest and casually lobbing darts in between sinking pints and shots of double vodka, triple Bacardi, or gin with ice and lemon.

Eric Bristow, whose 'Crafty Cockney' alter-ego as a likeable geezer had done so much to bring darts into our living rooms in a smouldering age, felt the sketch – with Rowan Atkinson's Geordie lilt obviously impersonating TV commentator Sid Waddell – only hardened the prejudices of 'luvvies who ruled the BBC and other channels' and did darts few favours. Others feared it reinforced the sport with its 'fat belly' image portrayed in the skit, and the Professional Darts Corporation has always been keen to distance the modern game from the derision of irreverent light entertainment.

But Littler's remarkable assault on the hilltop fortress of Ally Pally at 16 years of age was not just light years from the cheap shots of comic genius. It was a crowning glory of darts' climb from pubs to a fumigated phenomenon at the top of the news agenda, a celebration of teenage audacity opening the eyes of his contemporaries to the millions within their reach.

Twelve months after his noble defeat by Humphries, 'Luke the Nuke' made no mistake. His 7-3 demolition of Van Gerwen in the final confirmed that the boy who would be king had not missed his coronation: it had merely been deferred.

Littler became the 13th PDC World Champion before he was legally old enough to buy alcohol, vote or watch films containing graphic violence or explicit lust at the cinema. That, in itself, represents the consecration of a sport which has now become a part of the soundtrack to Christmas as much as 'Jingle Bells' or carol singers.

With every dart of the World Championship covered live on Sky Sports, nodding off on the sofa during the third tin of Quality Street, with the metronomic thud-thud-thud of arrows hitting the board in the background, has become a pagan ritual of the festive season. Darts has become embedded in our culture.

This tribute to PDC World Champions, from Dennis Priestley in 1994 to Littler reaching greatness before adulthood, is a baker's dozen painted in 13 shades of glory. We thank them for reliving their triumphs, confronting their ghosts and allowing the searchlight into corners of a champion's mind.

Each has been a credit to his sport, ushering in a golden age of darts. These are their stories.

DENNIS PRIESTLEY

BDO World Champion: 1991
PDC World Champion: 1994

HE IS the godfather of the Professional Darts Corporation, the 'Old King Coal' who led a mutiny that changed his sport forever.

Dennis Priestley was the first player to win World Championship titles on both sides of the divide between the British Darts Organisation and the PDC, wearing each crown at the first attempt by beating the greatest player of the 20th century, Eric Bristow, and the most decorated marksman since Robin Hood, Phil Taylor, in one-sided finals.

Synonymous with a red-and-black hooped shirt and his 'Dennis the Menace' nickname after the *Beano* comic character, Priestley's stand left the most indelible mark by an insurgent movement since Kerry Packer's rebel circus transformed cricket in the late 1970s. Where Packer's revolutionary coloured clothing, white ball, floodlights and razzmatazz effectively rinsed a sport of its starch, the advent of the PDC has taken darts from its hinterland in halls where the arrows pierced curtains of smoke to a multi-million-pound rolling maul in rock 'n' roll party atmospheres.

As a player, Priestley, a coal merchant by trade, would have won far more than two World Championship titles if his peak years had not coincided with the rise of Taylor, against whom he contested five of the first seven PDC World Championship finals.

But generations of gilded players today owe their affluence to the brave stand of a ringleader whose sotto voce Yorkshire tones concealed a steely determination to keep darts in the spotlight when TV companies were beginning to steer their broadcast artillery elsewhere. Priestley was born, raised and has lived all his life in the Yorkshire coalfields where Arthur Scargill was once king, and after his rebels' breakaway from the BDO was ratified by a Tomlin order in the courts, confirming their right to coexist, he deserves to be celebrated as a modern-day King Arthur who pulled a sword from the stone.

His trademark Groucho Marx moustache now bristles with more strands of salt than pepper, but the story of the coalman whose career only took off when he was the north side of 40 years old is enough to make your heart melt.

'I never wanted for anything as a kid – there was always food on the table and I don't remember ever going hungry – but after leaving school at 15 my dad, Maurice, got me a job as an apprentice bricklayer and I only lasted two weeks,' he says. 'I never saw a brick or trowel – just a sweeping brush and cups of tea – so I quit and ended up working at Park Gate iron and steelworks and then as a coal merchant.

'I didn't even throw a dart until I was in my mid-twenties. On a Monday night I started to play darts, dominoes and crib in a pub called the Miners Arms and I bought a set of 26g tungsten darts for £11.20, which was nearly half a week's wages in those days, after having a bet on Grundy to win the Derby in 1975 and it came in. But until I was into my thirties, I was more interested in feeding my family than taking darts seriously. What changed? Playing for Yorkshire, and travelling to places like Sweden and Canada to play in tournaments – all at your own expense, no sponsors – and my wife Jenny was very supportive. If you haven't got the backing of your partner at home, you're batting uphill all the time, but I was bringing home a few cheques.

'When I qualified for the Embassy (BDO World Championship) in 1991, Ladbrokes had me at 50-1 so I put £20 on myself and made a few bob. All my mates were smarter than me because they found Corals were offering me at 80-1, so even then I lost hundreds of pounds, but that's a Yorkshireman for you.'

Priestley's day job distributing sacks of fossil fuel was a hand-in-glove fit for where he lived in Mexborough, but the coal trade went through unprecedented turbulence before Margaret Thatcher drove it towards extinction, and the red lines he was most anxious not to cross were usually picket lines.

In the 1970s, with Edward Heath's Tory government unravelling, the Prime Minister imposed a three-day week on all but essential businesses to conserve electricity, which was in short supply because of industrial action by miners and railway workers. It was a bleak period, with Britain literally cast back into the dark ages during the early months of 1974 as power cuts left households running on candlelight and television companies were ordered to cease broadcasting after 10.30pm at night to conserve power.

Only services deemed essential to keep the country running on a skeletal basis – such as hospitals, supermarkets and newspaper printing presses – were exempt from the restrictions, and in the face of rampant inflation the National Union of Mineworkers was chasing a 35 per cent pay increase for its members, who produced most of Britain's electricity through a network of coal-burning power stations. For coal merchants like Priestley, distributing up to five tons of fuel in eight-stone sacks to domestic customers, it was critical to stay the right side of union directives.

He says: 'We had to tread very carefully because we didn't want to cause any trouble with the miners. My dad worked down the pits, so I was familiar with the working practices and what a dangerous, dirty industry it was. When the miners went on strike, it was never about something trivial, like not enough holes in their teabags. As a workforce, they had strong principles and whole communities were built on them.

'I lived almost bullseye in the middle of the Yorkshire coalfield – there were ten pits within a ten-minute drive of us, so when there was unrest, we were slap-bang at the centre of it.

'Around 1972-74, we had to play it strictly by the book,' he recalls. 'We had to call in at the social club where the miners' union were set up and collect tickets for permission to deliver bags to old age pensioners and families with small children. Then you would present these dockets to the coal yard, where you could fill up and be on your way. It was much simpler to be on the right side of the union than a scab.

'Industrial disputes could turn families against each other, but with my dad's background in the coal business I always felt I could find my way around. He had been a mechanic in the Army during the Second World War, and when the war was over they wanted to pay mechanics less than the lads who had been fighting. He went down the pit to earn a better living, and he worked down on the coalface by night and built up the family coal business by day.

'I was lucky – I saw plenty of the stuff, but fortunately it wasn't me who brought it to the surface. In hindsight, maybe I should have gone underground for a day just to see what the conditions were like, but by the time there was another miners' strike ten years later, I had sold the business in 1980 after contracting glandular tuberculosis. I thought there must be more to life than slogging bags of coal over your shoulder the far side of 40, and at one point I thought that glandular tuberculosis was going to be a death sentence, but I came through it.

'I started doing contract work, which gave me more time on my hands to practice my darts. When I sold up, I kept the scales and the van we used to deliver the sacks of coal. If I'd stayed in the coal game, there wouldn't be much of a living now, but from 1980 to 1990 I had a contract taking the miners' concessionary fuels out for delivery. I put a couple of guys on the wagon so I didn't have to go out on the rounds myself unless one of them let me down or was off sick. I used to lie awake at 5.45am hoping to hear the lorry start up – that's when I knew I wouldn't be getting a knock at the door and have to go out on the delivery myself.'

Priestley has lived in Mexborough all of his life – and now lives barely an oche length from the house where he was born on Church Street. The town has suffered since the demise of the coal industry and he observes: 'When the pits closed, they were effectively shutting down the local economy. It's so sad to see thriving local communities turn into ghost towns.

'At the time of the pit closures, the Tory government knew 99 per cent of the miners would spend their redundancy very quickly, which gave the economy a boost in the short term, but most of them had nothing to fall back on savings-wise, and it hit them hard. We used to have a busy, bustling town centre, but not anymore. I guess we came out of it with cleaner air and rivers, but they don't pay the bills.

'Darts changed my life and although success came relatively late, when you're getting older you don't want your body to be lifting sacks of coal in your forties when they are wet through, there's snow on the ground, the diesel is freezing in the cab and you're having to clean the jets out. I didn't miss being a coalman in the winter, that's for certain.'

Little realising that momentous times on the oche were lurking just around the corner, Priestley bought a newsagents in 1990, becoming a hub for distributing the news – and soon he was in the headlines himself.

Sleep was usually the first casualty when his two orbits of high street retail and tungsten collided.

'When my dad died, my mother wanted me to have the bungalow where we lived and the coal yard where I parked the lorry,' he says. 'I had bought some land down on Church Street to build a house for myself, so I sold the bungalow for £45,000 but, over the years, the money was dwindling away and I decided to buy into something before we had nothing left. That's when I hit upon the idea of running a newsagents, which we took over in August 1990, although I had no idea how hard it would be to run the business while my darts career was taking off.

"When I won the BDO World Championship in 1991, I was virtually commuting between Frimley Green and Mexborough, near enough a 400-mile round trip, and looking back I'm amazed I found the energy to do it. After beating Magnus Caris 3-0 in the first round, I had to drive straight home to be with the stock-takers in the newsagents until 10pm that night. I rushed back to beat Bob Sinnaeve of Canada, which set up a quarter-final against Phil Taylor, the defending champion, but more importantly reaching the last eight meant you were automatically invited back the following year.

'At 3-1 down against Phil, I was a sitting duck – but I came back to beat him 4-3, and it was obviously a proud moment when I beat Bob Anderson in the semis and Eric Bristow 6-0 in the final to win my first World Championship title, but it was hard graft.

'There was a lot going on 1991 – the Iraq war, the first one, was all over the news at the time, and that often made the papers late because they were extending their print deadlines. If I had known I was going to win the World Championship at the Lakeside, I wouldn't have bought the newsagents in the first place.

'I was getting back from tournaments or exhibitions at 2am and two or three hours later I would have to be up again. We managed to get shot of it about six months later or it would have killed us. Occasionally I wouldn't just be selling the papers – I'd be in them. I woke up one morning after winning the Isle of Man Open and there was a headline on the back page of the *Daily Mirror* about 'Dennis the Menace' being king of the Manx. I think it was only in that edition of the paper on the

Isle of Man, but those were different times when the back page was tailored to suit readers in a particular region.

'There was a lot more to running a newsagents than you might think. Apart from Christmas Day, you never get a day off – up before the crack of dawn seven days a week, taking delivery of the papers every morning, sorting out weekly and monthly magazines, bundling up the papers you didn't sell the day before, organising the paper rounds for delivery and jumping into the car to do the rounds yourself if the vans were late because of a delayed print run and the paper boys had to get off to school. It was a pain in the backside when that happened. I devised a method where the kids got a £1 bonus each week if they turned up every morning, so they were rewarded for not missing a round, but you couldn't make them late for school.

'I doubt if there are many other people who went from heaving sacks of coal to running a newsagents and becoming a darts World Champion, but I've had a good run.'

It's a subjective argument whether Priestley's finest hour with darts in hand was his dismantling of Bristow at the Lakeside in 1991 or demolition of Taylor in the inaugural PDC final (then operating under its fledgling banner as the World Darts Council) three years later. Unquestionably, however, the best result of his life was beating prostate cancer when he was diagnosed with one of the United Kingdom's most prolific diseases which, frighteningly, is currently expected to hit one in eight men.

There are, Priestley learned, 247 different types of cancer. More than 400,000 people are diagnosed with cancer in Britain every year, with 168,000 deaths attributed to the insidious disease annually, but survival rates are rising, with almost 50 per cent living ten or more years beyond diagnosis. With prostate cancer, that figure has climbed to 79 per cent – and the long-term prognosis is often excellent if the illness is treated promptly, without procrastination.

Luckily, 'Dennis the Menace' didn't hang about when he was concerned by a change in his nocturnal habits.

'Each case is different, and there are various signs that something's not right,' he says. 'I was getting up to go to the toilet four or five times in the night, so I decided to get checked out – and that's the biggest step, the most important step. Don't wait until it's too late, don't be shy, go and see your doctor. Prostate cancer can be beaten if you catch it early enough, so what are you waiting for? At first, I just thought I had a weak bladder, so when I found out I had cancer it was a shock, especially as I was away in Cyprus when I got the call.

'I was told the alternatives: Radiotherapy, surgery to have your prostate removed, or wait and see. The third one is not really an option because cancers don't get better by themselves. I asked the specialist about having radiotherapy first and, if that didn't work, to go for a full prostatectomy, but he warned me, "It doesn't work like that – the radiotherapy will shrivel it, so it's one or the other".

'Keyhole surgery was still a fairly new concept in cancer treatment in those days, so I had an operation which left a scar from my belly button to the top of my privates – and here I am, telling the tale almost 20 years later. Within a few weeks, I was back playing competitive darts and when I walked into the hall at my first tournament in Wigan, everyone started clapping. That was a nice reception, but I didn't really do anything apart from having the sense to flag it up in the first place. The real hero was my consultant urologist, a chap called Damien Greene. He was fantastic – I was only in hospital for one night. He said, "If you're feeling good, I'd rather send you home".

'I've never been one of those people who thinks a problem will go away if you just sweep it under the carpet. Prostate cancer surgery is a very intimate, personal thing to go through, but what's the point of dying instead of being shy about rubber gloves and fingers up your bum? And I'm not even sure they do that anymore.

'The best thing I ever did was to get it checked out. I was knocked out of the World Championship before Christmas in 2007, the first one played at Alexandra Palace. It was probably a mistake to try and play, but my heart was ruling my head and I wasn't quite ready for it. But after a biopsy, where they took five samples from one side of the prostate and three of them were cancerous, I had the surgery done early in 2008.

'It's marvellous that the World Championship became an extended advertisement for men to get themselves tested (for prostate cancer) when Paddy Power became tournament sponsor.

'Their pledge to donate £1,000 for every 180 scored was a great idea – I'm not sure they realised how much they would be paying out, but it raised more than £2 million in two years, and to have Sir Chris Hoy presenting the trophy sent out a really powerful message. If a super-fit cyclist who won six Olympic gold medals can be struck down by prostate cancer, nobody is safe from it.'

Priestley is keen to bang the drum for Prostate Cancer UK, and has become a prominent ambassador for the charity, because he believes innately in the cause and conviction is one of his best traits.

When the big split happened in 1993, and he led a platoon of 16 players on their breakaway from the BDO, he never swayed from his belief that it was the right thing to do – even when the legal pitfalls looked ominous and unappealing.

Like snooker, darts had enjoyed an unprecedented boom as a televised sport during the 1980s, with Eric Bristow's 'Crafty Cockney' marmite act gaining traction and his rivals Jocky Wilson, John Lowe, Bobby George, Keith Deller, Leighton Rees and Bob Anderson capturing the imagination of viewers. The consequent influx of sponsorship and prize money allowed many players to turn professional, but its shelf life proved finite. By the end of the decade, TV coverage had dropped to just one tournament, the BDO World Championship, and by 1993 the top players were disillusioned by the BDO's failure to reverse the decline in television revenue.

When they left the BDO to run their own tournaments, initially as the World Darts Council (WDC), the BDO responded by imposing a worldwide ban on the rebels and anyone who associated with them. A costly four-year legal battle ensued, culminating in the compromise Tomlin order in 1997. When the BDO lifted the ban, formally recognising the WDC and the right of players to participate in darts competitions outside their jurisdiction, market forces prevailed. In return, the WDC dropped its claim to being a world governing body and renamed itself the Professional Darts Corporation.

Priestley still reels off the names of the rebels like the daily roll call at Trumpton Fire Station: Taylor, Lowe, Bristow, Wilson, Anderson, Deller, Rod Harrington, Alan Warriner, Peter Evison, Jamie Harvey, Cliff Lazarenko, Ritchie Gardner, Kevin Spiolek, Mike Gregory and Chris Johns. They released a joint statement in January 1993, warning they would only participate in the following year's World Championship if it was under the WDC banner; the BDO responded by banning all 16 from their tournaments on British soil.

Worse still, the remaining BDO players and officials were banned from taking part in or even attending exhibitions featuring the 16 rebels. The late Sid Waddell, whose Geordie-intoned puns and pathos as a commentator belied his expertise on the Machiavellian machinations of darts, observed that the

BDO's appetite for outlawing the rebels became 'a licence for every little witch-finder in every nook and cranny of their organisation'. Pub teams were threatened with expulsion from competitions if their pubs hosted rebel exhibitions.

Although the outlaws secured a three-year TV deal with Sky Sports, worth a reported $1 million, to screen their rival version of the 1994 World Championship and other tournaments, their cause was hit when Gregory and Johns performed U-turns and 'defected' back to the BDO.

Priestley was convinced they had been 'leaned on' by BDO founder Olly Croft, but ultimately the collective sacrifice was vindicated. The commercial mammoth we see at Ally Pally now, which has become as much a part of our soundtrack to Christmas as 'Jingle Bells', took root in Croft's futile litigious squabbling.

The split also marked the genesis of a unique accord between Priestley and Taylor to pool their prize money – an arrangement which lasted six years – by the end of which 'The Power' was established as No.1 in the world and doing most of the heavy lifting in terms of earning power. If their alliance was based on an unbreakable bond of trust, 'Dennis the Menace' now has reservations about his part in helping to create the unstoppable winning machine that Taylor became.

'When I won the first PDC World Championship, I split the £26,000 prize money with Phil – now the winner at Ally Pally picks up £1 million,' he says. 'I hope modern players appreciate their earning power, and the risks we took that made it possible, but at times I'm not sure some of them do.

'What we went through around the time of the break-up took us to the brink of ruin. It was a traumatic time with all the blustering coming our way from the BDO about the consequences of a split. The two who went back had their reasons, but the feeling was they let the other players down. In the language of a miners' strike they would have been called scabs, although, to be fair, I think they were being leaned on. The BDO warned us we would have to sell our houses to pay the legal fees and we had discussed signing our homes over to family members so they couldn't take them off us.

'It became petty and nasty. I went to a county game at a pub five or six miles down the road just outside Doncaster, to hand back some of the trophies I'd won on the BDO circuit, and they wouldn't even let me in the building. They sent someone to collect the trophies from me in the car park. What made it worse is that when I opened the boot of the car, the trophies had been sliding all over the place and some of the glass cases were broken.

'I told the official, "Believe it or not, I have already repaired them once because they were damaged when I got them." I don't know whether he believed me, but apart from fragments of broken glass all over my car boot, it wasn't my problem. There was no goodwill, even when it was all settled.

'After the Tomlin order, I won the first tournament when both sides could compete against each other – the British Classic at the Norbreck Castle Hotel in Blackpool. I beat Andy Smith in the final and Olly Croft didn't like giving me the trophy, but he'd already had his pound of flesh.

'When the split happened I had just been picked to be England captain, which was a fantastic honour, but I was prevented from doing that and from playing for my beloved Yorkshire as well. Players left in the BDO were told they would be blacklisted if they appeared at exhibition nights with any of the so-called rebels and they tried to scare us into backing down. But when the breakaway was complete, we had just about all the best players in the world on our side. A lot of the lads left behind must have been clapping their hands and doing somersaults when we left. Imagine being ranked No.17 in the world and then, all of a sudden, the top 16 disappear and you are suddenly No.1 – just like that.

'The reason we decided to split was because we had lost nearly all the TV coverage and we were in danger of slipping back into obscurity. When we broke away, I was ranked No.1 in the world but I wasn't a 'big' name like Eric (Bristow) or Jocky (Wilson) and I'd reached an age where there wasn't much else I could do.

'It was Phil who suggested we could share prize money. It wasn't until the 2000 final that we agreed to split a certain amount and then, beyond that point, it was every man for himself.

'Friends told me I would play better if we didn't share. Phil knew what he was doing and, looking back, maybe I shouldn't have let him get as close to me. It would have made me more determined, but I never had the motivation to drive him into the ground because we got on so well.

'I don't have any regrets as such because we shared our money for all the right reasons, but given my time again, yes, I would have done things differently. I would have kept him more at arm's length. In a competitive setting Phil had a ruthless streak, he had that nastiness – I mean that as a compliment – but that mentality wasn't part of my make-up. I never went into a game with premeditated anger or wanting to rip the other guy's head off.

'I was always a better player if someone got my back up by trying to break my concentration, because focus and tunnel vision was a big part of my game, and when I was on the way down the mental side went before my throwing arm.

'By the time Phil was beginning to dominate darts in the way Eric had dominated in the 1980s – except Phil didn't just rule for a decade, he reigned for more than 20 years – he was virtually unplayable. It's only when you look at other sports that you realise how incredible Phil Taylor was because he stayed at the top for so long.

'Steve Davis ruled snooker for a decade, then along came Stephen Hendry and he took over for about the same length of time. In tennis, Pete Sampras was the best in the business for more or less a decade before Roger Federer took over. And when I won the Embassy (BDO) World Championship in 1991 I thought, "If I can get another ten years out of the game at this level, I'll be made for life" – and I didn't do too badly.

'But you have to look at Phil as the GOAT (Greatest Of All Time) because he was at the top for so long. Sir Alex Ferguson won his first trophy as Manchester United manager in 1990 and his last in 2013, a 23-year span that sets him apart from everyone else in football, but Phil reached his first World Championship final in 1990 and his last one in 2018 – he kept his standards for almost 30 years. That's absolutely incredible.

'Normally you look at a sport and if somebody has dominated it for a decade, more or less, they've had a great run, but to dominate for more than two decades shows the desire and the commitment of the man.

'When I beat him in the 1994 final, I had gone into the tournament without any great expectations because I hadn't been playing that well and it was a massive moment for me. Whether it's darts, a boxing world title or even on the athletics track, just being known as the World Champion is the pinnacle. It never even dawned on me how special it was until years later when people reminded me I was the first-ever PDC World Champion – nobody will ever be able to take that away from me – and the first player to win both versions of the World Championship title.

'It didn't register at the time, but to win my two titles I beat Eric Bristow and Phil Taylor. One was the greatest player in the BDO era and the other dominated for two decades in the PDC. That's not bad for a coal merchant.

'I've often said that I paid a heavy price for beating Phil 6-1 in that final because I turned him into the monster that he became – a winning machine that couldn't stop winning – and you have to admire what he went on to achieve. We met again in another four World Championship finals, and in 1996 I became the first player to record a 100-plus average in the final, but I lost all four.

'For a few years we were trying to hammer each other on the board but we were sharing our prize money because, for a few years after the breakaway, it wasn't always easy to make ends meet and there were some hard times. We had to go over to play in Canada and the United States, where the rebels weren't banned, to establish a rankings system, sometimes flying in on a Friday afternoon and playing the same night with jet lag.

'The prize money was often poor, maybe $1,000 or $2,000 depending on the format, and we had to reach the semis or finals to make it worth our while.

'It was a difficult time for all the players who stuck it out, but for me and Phil it was a working relationship where we agreed to do as well as we could, and make as much as we could, while the PDC (as it became known) got off the ground.

It was a big gamble, a huge gamble, but we trusted the people advising us.

'I was running all over the country, as chairman of our PDPA players' union, having meetings with manufacturers and players' management, all for no pay. Nothing coming into your bank account. So, yes, it was a big gamble – but fortunately it paid off.'

The small print in legal disputes is invariably buttock-clenchingly dull but it is important when it exonerates men of principle, and when the searchlight reveals Priestley's role in the birth of the PDC, it marks him out as one of the great men of darts.

At one point, the company who loaned the stage furniture and lighting for the World Championship went into receivership 48 hours before the tournament. Only Priestley and Taylor's selfless gesture of dipping their hands in their own pockets to prop up the ailing company, kept the show on the road.

'Many a time we had that problem,' says Priestley. 'We won prize money with the World Darts Council, but we didn't get paid. Me and Phil lent them nearly all our prize money, which is why we ended up with more shares (in the PDC) than other players.

'The partnership I had with Phil worked a treat because the arrangement was simple: whatever prize money we won, we would pool it and split it down the middle, so it gave us two chances of landing the winner's share. We used to get paid cash in the States, so we'd throw all these dollar bills on one of the beds in our twin room, count it out, see how much we'd got and share it.

'Sounds good in theory, but if we didn't make the semi-finals, we were normally out of pocket by the time we'd paid for our flights and hotels.

'Fair play to Phil: after I beat him comfortably in the 1994 World Championship, he dedicated himself to practising religiously to make sure he never got beat so comprehensively again. He sacrificed a hell of a lot, in terms of his family life, to make himself the best player in the world – and the harder he practised, the better he played.

'When I look back, I always wish we had been the same age. I was already giving him ten years when my desire was starting to wane as I got older, but I should have won more titles than I did. There was a few that went missing – for example, I never won the World Matchplay but reached the first three finals. I didn't do as well as I ought to have done. Phil probably didn't take over from me until 1996, and I won 12 tournaments in 1992 but came up short at the World Championship in January 1993… but that was the year that the dirt hit the fan and it was an upsetting tournament.

'I've always regarded that as the one that got away, but I kept going and did all right. Was it glory or money that kept me going? A bit of both – but a bit of money always helps.'

Priestley cheerfully plays along with the stereotypical myth about a Yorkshireman's pockets running deep, and on the PDC's *Darts Show Podcast*, hosted by Dan Dawson, he recounted the glorious tale of buying his house and refusing to pay the fee for transferring money electronically from his account to the bank. He withdrew a substantial sum, in bundles of notes, and delivered it to the branch handling his mortgage in a holdall, completing the short walk between banks in Doncaster looking over his shoulder every few steps.

'It's a true story,' confirms Priestley, drawing an imaginary rainbow arc with his index finger. 'I didn't trust money flying through the air just like that, so we transferred it in cash. It was well into multiple thousands.'

'Dennis the Menace' might have felt safer if his comic-strip accomplice, Abyssinian wire-haired tripe hound Gnasher, has been escorting him, but in truth 'Old King Coal' rarely deserted his methodical, diligent ways and resorted to the mischief of his alter ego from *The Beano*. Apart from his red and black top, Priestley was congenitally as far removed from his nickname as it was possible to be, but his many fans happily made the connection.

He says: 'I'm not sure if I was the first player to wear a shirt that became part of the act. Eric Bristow had a red top with his Crafty Cockney emblem on the back, and it served him well. I think he got his nickname from an English-themed pub in California, but everyone knew who he was.

'I thought, "If people can't remember my name, maybe they will remember me as the bloke who wore red-and-black hoops like the comic strip character". Fortunately, it caught on among darts fans, but *The Beano* publishers didn't like it.

'They rang me up from somewhere in Scotland and asked me to stop encouraging the Dennis the Menace image among spectators because they claimed it was bad for the comic. They asked me if I could tell my supporters not to wave those little dolls in red and black stripes. I told them I couldn't influence my fans in terms of what they wear, or what they bring to the darts, and if they want to turn up waving those red and black dolls, that's entirely up to them. You would have thought *The Beano* would be falling over themselves for all that free publicity.'

If Priestley didn't immediately appreciate the marketing opportunity his moniker represented, the same cannot be said for PDC president Barry Hearn, whose lifetime as a promoter turned the likes of Steve Davis, Chris Eubank and Phil Taylor into household names.

Hearn was a master salesman who could sell ice cubes to eskimos and sandcastles to bedouins in the Sahara, but he could always 'smell money' and spot an opportunity to turn a corner shop into a department store. When he acquired a majority stake in the Professional Darts Corporation in July 2001, that was the moment when a commercial powerhouse was born.

'I never expected the game to grow to the level it has,' admits Priestley. 'I thought when Phil walked away there may be a bit of a lull, but fair play to the youngsters and the other top professionals who have kept the game moving forwards. The game has gone from strength to strength. The PDC have always been one step ahead and they've kept evolving. It's absolutely marvellous.

'If I had the chance to do it all again, I would throw like Luke Littler, Luke Humphries or Adrian Lewis, who was maybe the first player to make it look so simple and fluid. The game is so much quicker now – much faster than me standing there trying to concentrate while my arm stopped shaking.

'They used to put a stopwatch on my throw and timed it at 17 seconds for me to release three darts where Phil took 13 seconds. I got it rammed down my throat so many times and admittedly it's not as quick as someone like Ricky Evans, who can hit 180 in about 2.2 seconds, but it wasn't a question of mind games or deliberately putting off your opponent. And what's four seconds between friends?

'I just hope the game continues to grow and the players are allowed to express themselves. We don't yet know what Littler is going to achieve, and how good he's going to be, because he's got another 20 or 30 years ahead of him if he wants it. If he's still going when he's 40, and he practises even half as much as Phil, the mind boggles. I once said that if he stays grounded, and he can be top of the tree for ten years, he could be worth more than David Beckham.

'Darts has already come a long way since Bob Anderson brought a horse into the Circus Tavern in December 1994 (because his nickname was the 'Limestone Cowboy') for his walk-on at the World Championship. It must have been the world's most placid horse – just imagine if it had kicked off or panicked. Health and safety officials now would have had a field day. They say you should never work with children and animals – remember what happened when they brought a baby elephant into the studio on *Blue Peter*?

'Fortunately, I think it was an ex-police horse, so it had probably been in more rowdy settings than a darts crowd. I think Bob was asked to ride it into the venue – but the ceiling was too low and he didn't like horses, which is a bit ironic given his nickname. There is a rumour that Barry was watching it live on TV and was so fascinated by the spectacle of a horse at a World Darts Championship that's when he decided it might be time to get involved.'

PHIL TAYLOR

BDO World Champion: 1990, 1992
PDC World Champion: 1995, 1996, 1997, 1998, 1999, 2000, 2001, 2002, 2004, 2005, 2006, 2009, 2010, 2013

THERE WAS a time, and it may still endure, when Phil Taylor could lay claim to being Britain's greatest living sportsman.

Even now, in a more crowded field, his achievements stack up, skyscraper-high, with the very best. One man's Empire State Building is another man's Burj Khalifa, but 16 World Championship titles and another five finals, spread across a 28-year span is not just an impressive body of work. It's a masterpiece in the Michelangelo class.

If Taylor's numbers alone are eye-wateringly impressive – 214 professional titles, including 87 televised majors and those 16 World Championship garlands – they hardly do justice to the application of a factory worker who was manufacturing ceramic toilet roll holders for a £52 a week before he morphed into the ultimate winning machine. By the time he retired at 57, 'The Power' had been so successful he could have trailed miles of gold-plated bog roll all over his Potteries kingdom from those earthenware accessories.

Peak Taylor took darts into orbits it had never explored before, like finishing runner-up in the BBC Sports Personality of the Year poll in 2010 behind jump jockey royalty Sir Tony McCoy, an astonishing feat when the Beeb did not even hold the rights to a minute of live PDC darts events.

In the same year, he had furnished a Premier League play-off final against James Wade with two perfect nine-darters. For the sake of equivalence, nobody has ever sunk two holes-in-one at a golf major, nor twin 147 maximum breaks at snooker's Crucible melting pot.

If Taylor is not our greatest living sportsman, it is not because his majesty has been overtaken or diminished. He has simply been joined in the pantheon by Sir Andy Murray, who conquered the strawberry fields of Wimbledon where platoons of his countrymen had failed for 77 years, and a peloton of cyclists led by Sir Jason Kenny and his wife Dame Laura Kenny, whose 12 Olympic gold medals combined means the arguments begin with the greatest athlete in their household, let alone their home nation. Those who consider Formula 1 to be exceptional sport, not a glorified trade fair or global pollutant, would add Sir Lewis Hamilton, a seven-times winner of the World Drivers' Championship, to the shortlist.

Cue deity Ronnie O'Sullivan, a player Taylor loves to cite when he turns name-dropping into an Olympic sport, and decathlon superstar Daley Thompson, whose back-to-back gold medals in Moscow and Los Angeles set the template for distinction when Taylor was a young thruster in Stoke-on-Trent's vibrant pub scene, would be his most prominent nominations for the accolade.

At heart, Taylor has never forsaken the upstart who took on county-standard players for cash and invested his winnings on home improvements. As a newlywed, he once took home £500 from a night ambushing the Staffordshire rank-and-file in licensed premises and the swag funded a shower unit. It was a luxurious upgrade for a working-class lad brought up in a dilapidated terrace house, sleeping downstairs because the upstairs accommodation was condemned, and male grooming began with a tin bath in the yard. 'A shower was like a status symbol,' he said. 'It was great – you'd have thought we were in Buckingham Palace.'

Once his mentor, Eric Bristow, had loaned him £10,000 to provide for his young family as he established himself on the professional circuit, the career Taylor unfurled beggars belief. His hunger for titles was ferocious and his appetite for more was voracious.

Just have a look at his scroll of honour in the six most prestigious events on the darts calendar and marvel at the application required to harvest so many trophies, so many titles, on a relentless conveyor belt of success.

World Championships – 16: From the night he dismantled Bristow 6-1 in the 1990 final, to lifting the Sid Waddell Trophy after a resilient comeback to beat rising star Michael van Gerwen 7-4 at Alexandra Palace 23 years later, Taylor was the closest thing to invincible.

World Matchplay – 16: Another sweet sixteen. To most visitors, Blackpool's promenade is a Golden Mile of seaside pomp, from the Big One rollercoaster at the Pleasure Beach fairground to saucy postcards, donkey rides, candy floss and the Eiffel Tower lookalike rising 518 feet above the shore. For Taylor, it's his favourite provincial fiefdom where he enjoyed 22 years of triumph at the Winter Gardens.

World Grand Prix – 11: The unique double-start format has proved a tripwire for many great players, but not for Taylor. Between 1998 and 2013, he made light of a mentally challenging hurdle. It was as if he turned Becher's Brook, the most feared fence on Aintree's Grand National course, into stepping off the kerb.

Premier League – 6: The advent of the Thursday night circus, up to 17 weeks of pin-balling between rock concert venues against the best players in the world, was right up Taylor's street. He won the first four seasons after its inauguration in 2005 and only Van Gerwen has won it more often.

Grand Slam of Darts – 6: Unless you worship at the shrine of Billy Wright, Stan Cullis and Steve Bull, Wolverhampton is an acquired taste. But Taylor's record there, in a tournament which evolves from a quickfire group phase to knockout ties, was buttressed by the comfort of being able to commute 30 minutes to the Black Country from his Potteries kingdom.

UK Open – 5: The FA Cup of darts, as it is known, brought Taylor regular joy and occasional shock therapy. In 2014, he was knocked out in the third round by factory worker Aden Kirk, ranked No.137 in the world and making his debut appearance on TV.

Given the 135 places between them on the PDC Order of Merit, it was the biggest upset in darts history. Taylor's five wins between 2003-2013 all came in Bolton before the event's move to Minehead.

Nobody has scaled the mountain so often, and left such an eclectic cast in his wake, than the man who was actually nicknamed the 'Crafty Potter' in the early days of his professional career, reflecting his job in the ceramic industry and as a nod to his teacher, 'Crafty Cockney' Bristow.

The 'Crafty Potter' tag had its merits but, for mass appeal, it flickered without ever bursting into flame. It was Sky Sports floor manager Peter Judge, who directed operations off-stage at televised events with regimental efficiency, who came up with 'The Power' as Taylor's moniker at the World Matchplay in 1995.

He had given Judge a lift to the venue and, climbing into the passenger seat, he inadvertently trod on a plastic compact disc case in the footwell. It happened to be 'The Power', a surprise No.1 hit in the UK charts for German Eurodance band Snap. Little did Taylor realise it was about to be adopted as his walk-on song.

Before his first-round tie with Canadian long shot Gary Mawson, as Taylor was being ushered towards the walk-on aisle, Judge told him matter-of-factly: 'Our sound people have lined up that 'Power' song, so from now on you are Phil "The Power" Taylor. Happy? Let's go'.

Taylor didn't have time to protest. Within seconds, he was at the back of the arena, ready to go, unsure how his new theme tune would go down with the punters. He admitted: 'I was thinking, "Bloody hell, what have I done here?" But it was too late to do anything about it. A few seconds later, I was on my way towards the stage.

'Fortunately, Judgey knew what he was doing. He used to be in charge of Chris Eubank's walk-on when he was a super-middleweight boxing champion, and that was always pure theatre in its own right. Eubank used to wind up the crowd with his posing and his strut, and if he was fighting in someone else's back yard all that posturing could upset the natives far more than a darts player's walk-on music, so I was happy to take my chances and put myself in Judgey's hands. "The Power" was a masterstroke. A marketing man's dream.

'Over the years, I asked Robbie Williams several times to write me a catchy new jingle for my walk-on, and every time he's come back with the same answer: "No way – because I'll never be able to top the one you've got already". But for 20 years,

I would go to bed every night with that bloody synthesiser and vocals playing on repeat in my head – and it was still playing when I woke up next morning.

'I had already won three World Championship titles, as plain old Phil Taylor, before I was re-branded 'The Power' by a Sky floor manager. Thanks to that record, it seemed more people called me 'Power' than Phil – there was no escaping it. I watch Premier League nights on the telly now and wonder if some of these players who conduct the crowds singing along to their walk-on music will end up hating their songs.'

On the box, as Taylor is talking, Beau Greaves is making the release of darts seem easier than pinning messages on a noticeboard.

The greatest player of all time was almost envious as the most talented female purveyor of tungsten pegged out the washing with languid proficiency.

'Look at that throw,' says 'The Power' with ministerial approval. 'Effortless. Like a knife through butter. She reminds me of 'Barney' (Raymond van Barneveld) at his best. She's gifted, that kid. The sky's the limit.'

Taylor, who spent a lifetime administering stuffings to outgunned opponents, keeps his arrows in the quiver these days but still knows his sage and onions when he follows tournaments on TV. He hopes Greaves fulfils her potential and will become a contender for distinguished titles and, perhaps, future Premier League casts.

'Beau 'n' Arrow' has a lifetime to reach such a gilded stratosphere, and she would not just be making a huge statement for women's sport if she was admitted to the weekly jamboree. It would be a marketing phenomenon. Conversation with Taylor turns to the ultimate Premier League line-up, an all-time dream team spanning 50 years of the old guard and the 21st century new wave.

The challenge is set: come up with a top 10, from the 1970s to the present day, who would make the Premier League unmissable theatre, combining achievement with personality and maintaining rivalries across borders or through the ages. The only condition, in this exercise of selection and history, is that Taylor himself is included. On any reasonable scale, how could he be excluded?

He scratches his head, draws an imaginary moustache across his top lip with his forefinger and scratches his head again. 'Almost impossible,' he says. 'It's like one of those three-dimensional crossword puzzles. You've never really cracked it. It's not just a question of who you pick – it's who you have to leave out.'

After careful deliberation, Taylor comes up with his Dream Team. Not necessarily in batting order, it's a formidable line-up by any measure, but he accepts it will cause as many arguments as it will solve.

Phil Taylor
Eric Bristow

Michael van Gerwen
Luke Littler
Raymond van Barneveld
John Lowe
Jocky Wilson
Dennis Priestley
Gary Anderson
Adrian Lewis

That's some list. The best pub team in the world. Forty-two World Championship titles between them from 1979 to 2026. Half a century of darts, a golden age, encapsulated in ten names. Taylor admires his draft momentarily, then puffs out his cheeks. 'OK, who's going to tell the players who didn't make the cut? I don't like burning bridges, but I feel like I'm setting fire to Sydney Harbour Bridge, the Golden Gate (in San Francisco), Tower Bridge and that one in Venice (the Rialto Bridge). Some of the people I've left out are multiple World Champions. It feels like pure sacrilege.'

Taylor's selection – four players from the 'old guard' who preceded the Professional Darts Corporation and five from the modern era – is a commendable balancing act, and the first name on his teamsheet is no surprise.

BRISTOW: 'It's flattering when people call me the GOAT, but I've always said Eric was the original superstar of darts and, for me, he will always be the king. He was like a brother to me and I owe him everything. I was absolutely devastated when he passed away suddenly in 2018 because I simply couldn't have achieved what I did without him being a mentor and sponsoring me in the early days. I couldn't afford to go to Rhyl, let alone Canada or Las Vegas to play darts!

'Undoubtedly his biggest influence on me was to install a winning mentality. Like my mum and dad, he was very strict with me, and he didn't want to talk to me unless I'd won an event. I would ring him up and say I'd made the semi-final or lost the final and he'd shout at me, "Only ring me when you've won" and slam the phone down.

'I will always be thankful for the day, in 1988, when he offered to sponsor me as a professional so I could travel the world playing darts.

'It was a big step to take voluntary redundancy from the ceramics factory where I felt comfortable among the toilet roll holders and beer pump handles, but there was no formal contract between us, no legal paperwork. He just told me to pay him back if I won anything.

'We hardly spoke for six months after I beat him, as a 125-1 rank outsider, in my first World Championship final at the Lakeside in 1990, but I had only played the way he taught me – relentless, ruthless, showing no mercy, keeping the pressure on. Deep down, I suspect he was proud of the way I hammered him 6-1 because it reflected well on him as my mentor. I've said before that Eric was like a lion teaching his cub how to hunt. He was the lion king.

'If I lost a game he felt I should have won, I would feel a hand on my shoulder and he would growl in my ear, "Get back on the practice board, you idle so-and-so."

'And if it felt harsh at the time, I never resented him for being a tough taskmaster because it gave me the drive and hunger that I needed. That mentality is his legacy, he started it, made me like it and now the standard will continue to go up because of him. As an only son, I looked up to Eric as the older brother I never had. I still can't believe he's gone, but what a player.

'Everybody knew who Eric was and they still do – the biggest name in the sport. Even when I go about my normal everyday life, down to the shops or out for a walk, I can still hear Eric's voice in my head, telling me to knuckle down and work harder.'

VAN GERWEN: 'When Michael's on song, he's a genius, a magician. And when he's on fire, he doesn't just beat you – he beats you up, he blows you away. That's not a complaint, that's what great champions do.

'When he took over from me as No.1 in the world in 2014, he was just hitting his stride where my race was almost run. Michael says he made me retire, but that's not strictly true: I stepped away because I was getting old and I was knackered from all the travel and late nights. When I called it a day, I was 57 – he was literally half my age.

'He said I was lucky he wasn't born earlier because he'd have been around for a lot more of my career. He reckons I never had him "under control" and I didn't like that. Well, according to our head-to-head stats, we met 59 times in competition with me winning 32 of them and Michael winning 25, with two draws, so you tell me who came out on top.

'Yes, he beat me 7-0 once in the Premier League, but we only met three times at the World Championship – and I won all three, including the final in 2013. And, yes, he hammered me 11-3 in the Premier League play-off final in 2016, but I hammered him 18-9 in the World Matchplay final two years earlier.

'Since the pandemic in 2020, he hasn't won so many big tournaments and I know exactly why he found it harder. He had young children to bring up, for starters. And when you are younger, you don't fear anybody – you went up there, you never thought about it, you were free as a bird and you just did it. I used to stand behind Michael when I was playing against him and think, "How have you just done that?" He was brilliant, out of this world.

'But now he's getting older and he's probably thinking more about it – whether it's changing his darts or tinkering with his throwing action and some of the players have told me, "We don't fear him anymore, Luke Littler and Luke Humphries are calling the shots now." It's a bit like playing at Old Trafford – Manchester United's opponents used to line up in the tunnel and know they were getting beat before a ball was kicked, but it's a different game when the fear factor has gone.

'I had people trying to knock me off my perch for almost 30 years, and Michael was usually at the front of the charge, but nothing lasts forever. What I will say about him is that, for all our battles, the one thing that never left me was my total respect for him. Like I said, the man is a genius.'

LITTLER: 'The only time I've experienced a buzz to compare with the atmosphere when Luke Littler is blowing someone away was when Eric Bristow was at his best. The atmosphere, when Eric walked in the door, was electrifying. He just had that magnetic field around him, and Luke's got that same X factor.

'Not long after he became World Champion the first time, I was walking around the supermarket and at least 20 people came up to me asking, "What do you think of that Luke Littler?" Even the girl on the checkout was talking about him. And then they all ask the same follow-up question: "Do you think he will last?" That's going to be entirely up to him, but if he puts the work in, the hours on the practice board, he's young enough to achieve anything. He's already got a few quid in the bank, so he doesn't have to worry about making ends meet and in any case he's not bothered about money, which is a blessing.

'For a lot of people, once they start earning good money, they want to go out and spend it on flash cars, Rolex watches, flaunting their wealth. Give a young man £1 million and he will find daft ways to spend it, but Luke's just not bothered. When he won £200,000 from his first World Championship, he went out and bought a new Xbox games console – the sort of thing a normal teenager would save up to buy with his pocket money.

'I've seen so many players who start earning big money and it ruins their career. But this lad, he just sits there on his phone. He's quiet as a mouse, he's lovely company to be with, to be honest.

'You do get used to being the man with a target on his back, the man everyone else is trying to bring down to earth. And you have to accept that people will raise their game for you and be talking about you, but that's the best compliment you can have – it's better to have everyone talking about you because if you're not the name on everyone's lips, it means you're yesterday's man and the show has moved on.

'Luke is leading darts into an era where the top players will soon have a lifestyle like tennis professionals – with their own trainers, nutritionists, masseuses and drivers. He will also find that the more he wins, the more it will do his head in when he loses.

'Will he overtake my record of 16 World Championship titles? He could do, he's absolutely fantastic. Would it bother me? Not at all – records are there to be broken, and I've had more publicity since he came on the scene than I ever had when I was winning it. Luke has got age on his side, he's got the ability and he's got a lovely family behind him.

'He is so down to earth, such a nice kid, that if he remembers to live a boring life for the next 20 years – steer clear of nightclubs, booze, fast cars and all the normal vices for a young man – the sky's the limit for him. If he is prepared to make those sacrifices and live like a monk, he could break all sorts of records.'

VAN BARNEVELD: 'When 'Barney' came over to the PDC from the 'other' side, it was the best thing that could have happened to darts at that time. There was a new sheriff in town, a new threat, and he was dangerous.

'In any sport, you need a rivalry – something to make your sap rise, put bums on seats, drive TV ratings through the roof and get the punters talking down the pub. Whether it was Nigel Benn and Chris Eubank, Steve Ovett and Sebastian Coe or Roger Federer and Rafael Nadal, rivalries are box office, and I don't mind a bit of needle in darts if it helps to pay the bills and it doesn't spill over. My rivalry with 'Barney' was the longest-running duel of my professional darts career, and apart from one spat at the 2013 World Championship I would rather forget, it never got in the way of a mutual and lasting respect.

'Our first meeting for big money was the so-called Match of the Century at Wembley Conference Centre in 1999, a one-off contest between the reigning PDC and BDO World Champions, with the £100,000 prize fund being split 60-40 in a match played against the clock – one hour, with the leader taking home the larger share when the countdown reached zero. At the time, I thought it was the biggest win of my career when the clock stopped with me leading 21-10 because of the prestige, and every time I played 'Barney' afterwards there was always a little edge to the occasion.

'According to the record books, in competition I won 61 of our 83 games, including five of our six meetings in major TV finals. The sudden-death World Championship final on New Year's Day in 2007 at the Circus Tavern is the one that stands out because of its dramatic conclusion, and of course I wish it had gone the other way, but two years later I settled the score emphatically.

'Raymond turned that 2009 final at Ally Pally into England v Holland, walking on stage waving the Dutch flag, and although there was a sizeable following from his Barney Army in the crowd that night, it was a massive own goal. The English fans gave him pelters, and I smashed him 7-1 with a 110.94 average, a record for the final.

'From that moment, I never had any hang-ups about facing 'Barney' on the big stage, and away from the oche we became the very best of rivals. He's a big, cuddly, giant teddy bear of a man, but he's one hell of a dart player and he belongs in any Hall of Fame.'

LOWE: 'All of us in the PDC owe John a massive vote of thanks because he saved our original World Championship in 1994. He was one of the 16 players who made the breakaway from the BDO and struck a deal with Sky to show our version of the World Championship.

'But when two players went back to the BDO, Sky warned us that if one more of us pulled out, they would pull the plug – and John was being offered a huge amount of money by one of the BDO's main sponsors to stay on their side of the fault line. If John had followed the money and gone back, that would have been it – Goodnight Vienna. But he insisted that we should stick together.

'I think one of his biggest regrets is that he won the last BDO World Championship in 1993 before the split and he never defended it, but John Lowe's place in history is secure. Like me, he won a World Championship title in three different decades (1979, 1987 and 1993), and in 1984 he hit the first-ever televised nine-darter on TV against Keith Deller, which earned him £102,000 – an incredible amount of money in those days.

'It made him financially secure and changed his life. To put it into context, he revealed his prize money was more than John McEnroe received for winning Wimbledon that year (£100,000) and much more than Seve Ballesteros was handed for winning The Open (£55,000). It put darts on the map. John says he met Seve a few years later and one of the greatest golfers who ever lived recognised him and shook his hand for making history. Famously, after his nine-darter he celebrated by ordering 50 bottles of Champagne at his hotel bar in Slough and drinking the place dry with his friends – I don't blame him.

'Don't ask me why it took until the New Year Honours in 2019 for him to be awarded the MBE, for services to darts and charity, because he had been revered across the sport for 40 years by then. But he's in my Dream Team all day long because he was always such a humble man, a gentleman and a great ambassador for the game.'

WILSON: 'Jocky was my pairs partner for many years and I loved him to bits. We used to have a lot to do with each other, I've got a lot of good memories about him and he's one of those people that when you mention his name, it automatically brings a big smile to your face. He was a great character and I've missed him since the day he passed.

'We both used to appear in the guest slot on *Bullseye*, throwing for charity – if you saw the show, the challenge was to raise a pound for every point with nine darts, but if you hit 301 or more they doubled your score. I'm embarrassed that I appeared on the show every year but I never hit 301, although I discovered later that the board was mounted about four inches too high, which partly explains it – but Jocky had them eating out of the palm of his hand when he scored 305.

'It was great fun doing *Bullseye*, and Jim Bowen was a genial host, although he was sometimes a bag of nerves. In the general knowledge quiz, he would ask the contestants things like, "What is the capital of Paris?" – and they would have to re-shoot that segment of the programme.

'Jocky was even the first darts player to appear on *Top of the Pops* when it was a massive part of our entertainment culture. One night the programme was in full swing, with the studio audience dancing happily to Dexy's Midnight Runners' hit 'Jackie Wilson Said', and in the background, large as life on a mural as requested by the band, was the man himself – the reigning World Darts Champion JOCKY Wilson. I'm not sure everyone understood the joke, and at least one Radio 1 disc jockey thought producers had mixed up a great soul singer with a Scottish darts player, which made it even funnier.

'Dear old Jocky's teeth had all fallen out by the time he was 28 because he loved sweets and he never brushed his gnashers, saying, "My Gran told me the English poison the water." After he won his first world title, it's said he spent £1,200 of his prize money on a set of dentures – but he never took to them, claiming, "I can manage just about anything with my gums." What a character, he was absolute gold dust.'

PRIESTLEY: 'Dennis was my main rival in the 1990s and we often found ourselves contesting the final at major events, including the first PDC World Championship in 1994, but he was such a lovely fella that I simply couldn't find it in my heart to consider him as my enemy.

'We used to go all over the country together in a campervan, sharing twin rooms in hotels or kipping in a lay-by to save a few bob, and to me he will always be nearer a soul-mate than a deadly rival.

'Playing Dennis was hard work because he was steady and methodical, but above all he was just bloody good. When you're playing a good player who is very slow… trust me, it does your brain in. Your mind starts wandering so I tried to make my walk around the back a little bit longer.

'I must admit that, in the beginning, it did put me off. I was trying to figure out the best way to counter it until John Lowe told me to take a bigger walk off, walk a bit further round the back of the oche when you've retrieved your darts from the board and literally put an extra bit of distance between you. That did the trick. Dennis was a very consistent player and if he'd been at his best now, with the boards they manufacture today, he would have been untouchable.

'He will always be in the record books as the first player to win both the British Darts Organisation and Professional Darts Corporation versions of the World Championship, and nobody can ever take that away from him, but more importantly he will always be remembered for being a great man.'

ANDERSON: 'I could always tell when Gary was on it and he was going to give you a hard time. It was the glint in his eyes.

'If Gary Anderson had that look of a spaghetti western gunslinger – that cold expression like a thousand-yard stare – you were in trouble. Some of my best games, and some of the closest, were against Gary, including a World Championship final in 2015 which I lost, and I love him to bits.

'He's one of those people who calls a shovel a shovel, and I love his straight-talking honesty. If he wins a game that doesn't live up to his high standards, he'll say his opponent was rubbish but his rubbish was just a wee bit better.

'I often thought my 2013 Grand Slam semi-final against Adrian Lewis was the greatest game I'd ever been involved in because the scoring was almost off the charts, but the following year I beat Gary 17-15 in a World Matchplay semi-final that squeezed every last drop of nervous tension from my system.

'On his day, Gary was probably the heaviest scorer of the lot, pinning 180s for fun like a postman knocking on your front door. When he won back-to-back World Championships in 2015 and 2016, he was the only player who threatened Michael van Gerwen's long run at No.1 in the world.'

LEWIS: 'Until Luke Littler came along and started winning major tournaments when most kids of his age were still at school, nobody made darts look easier than Aidy. He plays the game at such a pace that it's hard to catch your breath, and his no-look 180 (not even looking at the third dart after releasing it because he's already on his way to retrieve it from the board) is a great party trick.

'I treated him as my own son from the moment his mother, Yvonne, who played at county level for Staffordshire, and his stepfather Steve asked me if I would take Adrian under my wing in the hope I might be a positive influence on an ambitious youngster the way Eric had been such a wonderful taskmaster for me.

'Two World Championship titles later, back-to-back tournaments in 2011 and 2012, they had their answer. He even hit a nine-darter in the final against Gary Anderson, the cheeky beggar. We had the odd falling-out, but when I went through a dip in form, I would sometimes sense this big hulk over my shoulder and a familiar voice would be trying to lift my spirits: "Come on, Phil, you've still got it!" That was a touch of class.

'As a pair, we won the World Cup of Darts four times in five years for England. As well as the patriotic pride of representing your country, it was always a laugh-a-minute with Aidy. Two lads from Stoke-on-Trent, flying the flag, who would have thought it? But as of 2026, we were still the most successful pair in the history of the tournament.'

Taylor's line-up takes some beating, and he is remorseful about some of the names who missed the cut, notably Peter Wright, John Part, Martin Adams, Gerwyn Price, Glen Durrant, Scott Waites, Keith Deller, Michael Smith, Andy Fordham and Luke Humphries. His agonising and prevarication reflects the annual dilemma facing PDC and Sky Sports executives when they have to augment the top four, who qualify for the Premier League by right, with the auxiliaries whose invitations to the Thursday night circus are based on ranking and charisma.

But when the headline acts and supporting cast were decided, the only currency which mattered to 'The Power' was winning. And he had plenty of practice.

It is staggering to think that, his 16 World Championship titles aside, Taylor could easily have won more. Three of the finals he lost went down to a deciding set and, in the case of his sudden-death, white-knuckle ride against Van Barneveld, a decisive leg. But like Frank Sinatra, if he has any regrets, there are only a few – but then again, too few to mention.

'The 'Barney' one I should have won because I was 3-0 and then 5-3 up, and it gave me the kick up the backside I needed,' he says. 'He pulled a fast one on me in the deciding leg when we had to bull-off for the right to throw first (a single dart at bullseye). My dart dipped just below the bull and 'Barney' insisted on leaving it in as a marker, which he was entitled to do at the time, and he landed his shot on top of my dart to win it. Even then, I should have nailed him because he scored only 100 with his first three darts and I hit 180, but somehow I let the advantage slip.

'After John Part beat me 7-6 (in 2003), fans told me it was a classic final because it see-sawed both ways. I should really have won that one, too, but it was very strange – losing was almost a relief. I had gone unbeaten for eight years at the World Championship and there was a danger that people were getting bored of me winning it every time. It needed someone to knock me off my perch so we could all reset.

'My last game as a professional was losing 7-2 to Rob Cross in another final at Ally Pally, but to tell the truth it didn't hurt. I tried my best but he was like me 25 years ago, he was relentless and didn't stop putting me under pressure. It was an old man against a young man, it was a mismatch.

'I think it was the Sky commentator, Stuart Pyke, who asked me once if I ever got sick of winning. Did I ever get sick of winning? Are you having a laugh? Ask Sir Alex Ferguson if he ever grew tired of winning trophies. When Manchester United won the Treble, I don't remember him moaning that they wouldn't have room for the Champions League trophy in the cabinet at Old Trafford. I don't remember Tiger Woods winning his fifth Masters and turning down another Green Jacket because he'd already got four others in the wardrobe.

'Winning isn't a fashion, or a hobby, or something you pick up off the shelves at a supermarket. Winning is a habit – and in professional sport, it's your job. It pays the bills, it puts food on the table and new shoes on your kids' feet. My pal Bob Glenn says winning takes care of everything – and he's right.

'I've seen four decades of dart players, played against nearly all of them, and the best ones at the top of the tree all have succeeded because they are winners. I missed out on playing competitively against the two Lukes (Littler and Humphries). I would have loved to try and beat them. It's a different game now to the one I first played – the boards are better, the wires are more forgiving, the darts are better, the lighting is better – but if I could knock out a good average, let's say 100-plus for starters, and finish well, I reckon I could do it.

'But, look, it's a bit like wondering how much George Best would have been worth in today's transfer market. He used to skip past defenders on heavy pitches wearing things on his feet like a policeman's patrol boots. Just imagine trying to stop him now on those beautiful billiard-table surfaces and lightweight boots like ballet shoes.

'What I did have, and I don't want to blow smoke up my own backside, is a strong mentality. I worked people out, I was a workhorse. Hard work beats talent when talent doesn't work hard, as the saying goes.

'I've seen them come and go over the years – so many talented youngsters who could play like gods, but as soon as they got a sniff of the big time they were out until all hours, drinking and giving it the big 'un.

'I was boring – as soon as I'd won a game, I started preparing for the next one. The only time you saw me out in Blackpool during the World Matchplay was when I had the trophy on the seat next to me. I was lucky that I had a work ethic instilled from an early age, when my mum used to get me out of bed in the morning by throwing buckets of water over me. If I wasn't up with the larks and told her, "Mum, I'm having a day off work today", she would reply "No, you aren't" – and a cold shower from the pail would deliver a wake-up call like no other.

'People used to ask me the secret to winning all those titles, but there was never any great mystery. No magic formula. I practised hard, dedicated myself to improving, sacrificed a lot of family time, missed too much of my kids growing up – and when somebody came along who threatened to knock me off my perch, I practised even harder.

'When the crowds became bigger and noisier, sometimes I would adjust my preparation to suit the occasion. Although I don't like heavy metal rock music, if I knew I was going to be playing at a venue where the crowd was going to be a bit lively, I would practice with loud heavy metal on full blast so I knew my game could cope with the background noise. Instead of trying to shut it out, I just let it wash over me and concentrated on making sure the darts landed where I wanted. I didn't like leaving anything to chance, so when the fans were making a racket, I was ready for it.

'I had moments of luck along the way, but like Gary Player once said of his golf, "The harder I practise, the luckier I get." And you can't put a price on the memories this game has given me.

'If I had to bottle one moment in time so I could live it all over again, I think the two nine-darters in the Premier League final against James Wade in 2010 would be the one. There was an unusual background to that night at Wembley Arena because the play-offs had been postponed for 24 hours after a huge power failure wiped out large parts of the grid across north-west London. When they were rescheduled for the following night, England were playing a World Cup warm-up friendly against Mexico at the national stadium next door and we wondered if anyone would turn up.

'Amazingly, more than 3,000 fans did come to the rearranged date, and I like to think we gave them value for money. Wade was the defending champion, and it took something special to beat him, so I knocked out 174, 180 and 147 – Ronnie O'Sullivan's favourite number – in the second leg and then, with the final locked at 7-7, I found another perfect nine, the first player to hit two perfect legs in the same game.

'I'll always remember walking along the Euston Road, after staying overnight in London, when a bus slowed down to a virtual standstill – even though I wasn't standing at an official bus stop – and the driver leaned out of his cab shouting, "Two nine-darters, Phil! Nice one!". Taxi drivers were tooting their horns and throwing imaginary darts towards me, and everyone who stopped to ask for a picture or autograph said they were watching.

'My biggest regret? For too many years, I always said yes to everything. Appearances, exhibitions, floor tournaments, qualifiers, European Tour competitions, sponsors' evenings, photocalls… I never learned to say "No". But when Barry Hearn was my manager, it was hard to turn down things because his energy and knack for spotting a business opportunity was like the satnav in your car – he always knew best.

'Sometimes I would suggest a new idea, like a range of merchandise, and he would be the one saying no: "I tried that 30 years ago – it didn't work then so it won't work now." But he was a fantastic hustler, one of those people who could pick up the phone, talk for five minutes and when the conversation's finished, he's cut another deal for a patch on your shirt, a watch, a car, shoes, almost anything.

'He was also my biggest supporter if my form dipped. I always believed I had one more major title left in me, whether it was the World Matchplay or a World Championship, because Barry told me so. And Barry was always right – even when he was wrong. Over the years, I did well out of him…and he didn't do badly out of me, either.

'Since Barry got involved in running the show, darts has grown beyond all recognition. The prize money is from another planet. I wish I had been around when there was £1 million on the table for winning a World Championship! But the schedule is so relentless now that I don't think there's room for any more tournaments and players see more of each other than their own families. I'm not saying it's become a single man's game, but it's definitely more difficult if you have a wife and young children.

'It's certainly a different game from the smoke-filled halls we used to play in, which weren't good for your health. I once had tests in hospital where they stuck a camera down my throat and doctors said my vocal cords were enlarged from all the passive smoking.

'I also played in a club where they opened the side doors at the interval and so much smoke came billowing out that a passer-by called 999 because it looked like the place was on fire.'

JOHN PART

BDO World Champion: 1994
PDC World Champion: 2003, 2008

CAN WE have our dart back, please?

The time-honoured petition, when a stray missile flies over the fence between neighbouring properties, is usually reserved for the retrieval of a ball or frisbee.

But John Part's first encounter with a dart, shortly before his fourth birthday as far as he can recall, was an arrow which lodged in his left shoulder as he played catch with his father, Richard, in the back yard of the family home in Toronto's metropolitan sprawl. If the experience was briefly traumatic, happily it did not lead to a sustained tungsten phobia.

By the time he made his mark on darts, the impression Part forged on the oche was like a yeti's footprints in the snow. He became the first non-British marksman to win a World Championship title – on his debut, and only the second unseeded player to do so – in 1994 at the Lakeside with a 6-0 defeat of charismatic crowd favourite Bobby George, who was, in his own words, 'trussed up like a Christmas turkey about to go in the oven' with a back injury constricted by a steel corset. Nine years later, Part ended Phil 'The Power' Taylor's 53-match unbeaten run, spanning nine years and three days, to win the Professional Darts Corporation (originally the World Darts Council) version of the tournament at the Circus Tavern in Purfleet. And when he beat qualifier Kirk Shepherd in the 2008 final at Alexandra Palace, now the spiritual home of the incorrigible fancy dress corps, Part became – and remains – the only player to become a darts World Champion in three different venues: The Lakeside, Circus Tavern and Ally Pally.

As of 2026, he had joined Taylor, Eric Bristow, Raymond van Barneveld, Michael van Gerwen, John Lowe, Martin Adams and Glen Durrant as the only men to win three or more World Championship titles. Only special players present such a formidable curriculum vitae, especially when their careers are almost abbreviated by wayward javelins from next door.

'There was a garden wall, probably not all that tall – maybe four or five feet – between us and the neighbours,' says Part. 'We lived in a townhouse, an end unit, and the guys on the other side of the wall had mounted a dartboard outside. It was a nice day and I was playing catch with a baseball and mitt out the back with my father, when this dart came out of nowhere and embedded itself in my shoulder.

'I don't remember whether it hurt, or my reaction, but I guess it could have turned out a lot worse. A few inches, one way or another, and it might have caught me in the face, in an eye or somewhere sensitive along the spine. I don't remember there being any drama or having any hang-ups about it. Let's just say health and safety standards for young kids with toys were not quite as rigorous as they are today. I don't want to sound too callous, but there was a lot of dangerous stuff in toy stores freely available back then. I don't think kids playing darts in the back yard would have been considered outrageous in the 1960s or 70s. Looking back, I guess I was lucky.'

It was several years later, at a British-themed pub on holiday in Barbados, that Part recalls his earliest fascination with the fine margins and intricate targets of a dartboard, but he was 21 before his parents gave him one as a Christmas present. Barely six years later, he was a World Champion. The proverbial late developer, at first playing the game socially on his transition from high school to university student, was soon a fully-fledged convert.

'I knew of a place where there was a darts shop, called Plum's Emporium, and I became friends with one of the family who ran it. Later we ended up on the same team,' says Part. 'It was one of those places where you could try out different sets and get a feel for the right grip. These days it's pretty common practice, but in those days doing your own market research was only for the real fanatics, but it was fun. Once I had my own board, my own darts and a book called *All About Darts*, written by a couple of ex-pats and detailing some games and practice routines – nothing too deep and with a sense of humour – it put some ideas in my head about how I was going to play the game.'

Remarkably, within six years of owning his first dartboard and the novice's first steps in North America's sketchy but vibrant competitive landscape, Part was making headway at British Darts Organisation ranking events. In collusion with Carl Mercer, he won the WDF World Cup Pairs for Canada in 1993, beating Netherlands double act Van Barneveld and Roland Scholten in the final at the Sahara Hotel in Las Vegas – and it was not a flash in the pan.

Qualifying for the first BDO World Championship since darts' descent into acrimony, in 1994, Part was among the veritable platoon of unsung debutants, dark horses and unknowns with Taylor, Bristow, Lowe, Dennis Priestley and Jocky Wilson among the renegades who were now competing under the 'rebel' WDC banner.

In his book *We Had Some Laughs*, Dan Waddell, son of the celebrated commentary box bard Sid Waddell, compared the tournament with the 1980 Moscow Olympics after the United States boycott or Kerry Packer's rebel circus which filleted Test cricket. It was ripe for a newcomer to make his mark – and at 27, Part seized his chance to fill the void.

'I didn't even start competing in leagues until the fall of 1989, so I guess I was a quick learner,' says Part. 'To beat Raymond and Roland in that pairs' final was a statement in itself. Roland won the singles competition and he was running red-hot at the time. But it left me in good shape for my first trip to England, to play at the World Masters at Earls Court a few weeks later, and by the time the Embassy (World Championship) came round, I had made the acquaintance of the locals, if you like, and I'd had a good look at the field. It wasn't completely alien to me, and going out to the Lakeside was more subdued than the big city. Frimley Green has its virtues, but it wasn't the Wild West.'

For the breakaway movement, it suited the narrative of a diluted competition that an unheralded qualifier should ride into town and abscond with the £32,000 winner's loot. Part only dropped one set in the whole tournament, a feat matched only by Bristow ten years earlier and Taylor in 2001, but he was damned with faint praise as an interloper from North America – hardly an acclaimed hotbed of darts at the time – who flew beneath the radar.

The back-handed compliments were unjust. Like Jan Kodes, the 1973 Wimbledon men's singles champion who capitalised on 13 of the 16 seeds boycotting the strawberry fields of SW19 over the suspension of Nikola Pilić, Part was not just a reserve who got lucky. Kodes won two other tennis Grand Slams, in full-strength fields, and 'Darth Maple' (as he would later be known) was no one-hit wonder, either.

He whitewashed No.2 seed Ronnie Baxter, Paul Lim and Steve McCollum, shipping his only set of the competition against Ronnie Sharp in the semi-finals, before his moment of truth was effectively a walkover against a crocked opponent who could barely stand up straight, let alone maintain the posture required to locate targets the size of a paper clip.

Leaping to celebrate a crucial double in his quarter-final against Kevin Kenny, self-styled 'King of Darts' George fractured a vertebrae in his back as he landed and doctors had advised him to retire hurt.

George, in his book *Still Here!*, writes: 'I was playing well enough to beat anyone before my injury and I think I would have beaten John Part in the final but for the extreme agony I was in. Foolishly, I suppose, I couldn't help but think it was my destiny to go on and lift the trophy at the second time of asking. In 1994, he was an unknown, unheralded player in this country and I know that had I been in good health I'd have beaten him, but it wasn't to be.

'John took his opportunity well, I can't blame him for that. He could only play what was in front of him and couldn't have had an easier night. Sid Waddell, on commentary, said that I looked like the Hunchback of Notre Dame. I was a little disappointed that John didn't at least acknowledge that I was far from being well in his victory speeches.'

While George needed a four-hour operation to repair his broken back, Part had no reason to apologise for his clinical, ruthless whitewash of a pied piper. He says: 'Every time I reached a World Championship final, I was the bad guy. I couldn't even tell you whether the crowd was more against me when I played Bobby George in my first one or Kirk Shepherd in the last.'

Part had yet to adopt his 'Darth Maple' incarnation, walking on stage to the *Imperial March* (Darth Vader's theme in the *Star Wars* movie franchise), but his shirt was already adorned with a black Maple Leaf, a symbol that he was not going to play 'the friendly Canadian who's just going to let you walk over us'. He recalls watching the football World Cup in 1986, Canada's first appearance at the tournament, and each defeat in the group phase feeling like a rite of passage. Unlike his football compatriots, Part was determined never to reach a global showpiece and simply make up the numbers.

Although success initially proved elusive, both on the BDO circuit after his 1994 World Championship coronation and following his transfer to the Professional Darts Corporation in 1997, the turn of the millennium proved the most gilded phase of his career – and a definitive case history for sports psychologists to unpick the hardwire of a champion's supreme willpower.

Taylor, at the peak of his powers, had an aura of invincibility which left many of his opponents beaten before the first dart of any contest. He was a perfectionist who practised longer hours than his rivals and, for a decade, there were no obvious challengers to his majesty.

When Part was demolished in his second World Championship final appearance in 2001, it was not just a procession. Taylor's 7-0 win was a masterclass of annihilation. His 107.46 average and 72 per cent checkout ratio would have been too much for the finest players in any era. He was simply unplayable, and Part collected just three legs, each effectively worth £6,000 towards his £18,000 prize money as runner-up, in the most one-sided final of all time. The pair's next televised meeting, in the quarter-finals of the World Matchplay, offered Part little shelter from another brutal shelling as Taylor romped home 16-4. And their following collision at the World Championship, in the last eight six months later, also proved more one-way traffic than the feared Hanger Lane gyratory.

Taylor's 6-0 win meant he had reeled off 13 sets without reply on the biggest stage against an opponent who was nominally his closest challenger in the world rankings. He didn't just have Part's number; he had the whole telephone directory. To reverse such damaging obliteration in consecutive World Championship encounters would require wholesale rewiring of the brain, let alone a forensic audit of technique.

Part's deconstruction of an empire is one of sport's most incredible turn of events. As a parallel in football, it was perhaps the equal of Crystal Palace losing 9-0 in the League against Liverpool at Anfield in 1989 and somehow beating them 4-3 in an FA Cup semi-final seven months later.

He could have been forgiven for thinking his chance to break Taylor's spell had gone at the 2002 World Matchplay final, where Part led 16-15, only for the magician to pull the proverbial rabbit from his top hat by taking the next three legs to snatch victory. So when they met again in the 2003 World Championship final, privately Part must have felt a sense of apprehension or misgivings about the storm heading his way, but he did not flinch.

'There were places where I would have played Phil and felt comfortable playing against him, such as the Golden Harvest North America Cup where I got to the semi-finals two years running and his aura didn't bother me,' he says. 'He was just a hard player to beat. He was the best player in the world, the best of all time – you don't have to recruit me to hitch my colours to that bandwagon. But it wasn't like you were trying to steal the Holy Grail.'

Give or take Taylor and Van Barneveld's sudden-death epic four years later, Part's 7-6 win in the 2003 final was arguably the most gripping PDC World Championship final of them all. He announced himself in the very first leg of the contest with a 121 checkout on bullseye and raced into a 4-1 lead with the urgency of a man who wanted to rewrite history in a hurry.

The Canadian's effrontery served only to poke the bear, and when Taylor responded by reeling off the next four sets without reply, to most observers the writing wasn't just on the wall: it was trailed in plumes of smoke across the Purfleet night sky. This was the moment when Part summoned the intestinal fortitude of a champion. Fighting back to take the next two sets and move 6-5 ahead, he refused to bow and curtsey in the court of greatness. Even when Taylor took it to a deciding set, Part didn't blink.

When the moment of truth arrived, and he had a match dart on tops to take the title, he grasped the nettle without hesitation. Just as the wayward dart that flew over the fence in the back yard could have changed the course of history, Part's story could have veered off at a less starlit tangent if he had bottled that shot.

'Who knows what would have happened if I'd missed it? Against Phil, you could never be certain you were going to get another chance, especially when you need to win by two clear legs in the deciding set,' admits Part. 'It was a real battle and I had to hold on tight.' He is too modest to say it for himself, so let's spell it out. To beat a deity at a venue where he was virtually untouchable and insulated by nine years of invincibility, when that spear of destiny at tops landed on target, it was the greatest moment of Part's career, a coup he wished he could bottle.

The audacity of his heist has not diminished over the years. 'There were a number of factors that made it special,' he says. 'Phil had won eight straight World Championship titles and, yes, he was seemingly unbeatable. He hadn't just battered me at the Circus Tavern the two previous years, he had battered everybody. Having said that, by 2003 I was ranked No.2 in the world and, on paper, I was his closest challenger. I was the guy to do it.

'Maybe the darts fraternity at large might have put more trust in the likes of Dennis Priestley to be the one who upset the applecart because he had the experience. But, hey, even Dennis was battered so many times by Phil that, in the end, he was indoctrinated into the cult of Taylor. If you ask Dennis now, maybe he would concede he got too close to Phil when the PDC was launched and they shared their prize money. That doesn't mean he was wrong to pursue that avenue, but in the long term I don't think that close association helped Dennis.'

Wayne Mardle, a long-time rival on the oche but now his long-serving colleague in the Sky Sports commentary box, believes Part's mentality set him apart in the pack chasing Taylor, and he has no doubts about Part's place in the darts pantheon.

'I've known John a long time, I played against him for a long time and I've worked with him on the air a long time, so my regard for him is based on almost infinite respect,' says Mardle. 'No offence, but he's never been the sexiest, quickest, most watchable darts player in the world, but he's never been given the credit he deserves as a three-time World Champion.

'You could say the same about Dennis Priestley or even James Wade, who has never won a World Championship but is a multiple winner of TV majors. Have they been given the accolades they deserve? I do believe that unless you're a speedster, or you play in way that changes the game, nobody becomes a headline act, to be fair.

'John has never been a flamboyant darts player – more of a methodical grinder, the ultimate opportunist in the best sense of the word. If you're slightly off the boil, and give him an opportunity, he'll be clinical and make you pay.

'I played against him at the World Championship, the World Matchplay, the Premier League – and I beat him in all of them, by the way, which I still regard as a feather in my cap – and John Part will always be in the top bracket of great players because his achievements speak for themselves.

'Forget that he beat Bobby George in a World Championship final although it wasn't a great contest, forget that he beat Kirk Shepherd in a World Championship final and it wasn't a great contest. Beating Phil Taylor in a World Championship final, at a time when Phil was almost unbeatable, makes him one of the greatest.

'If he hadn't knocked Phil off his perch, even if it was for one night only, there might still have been a little asterisk against his name, a little caveat on his résumé. But there's none of that with John – the man's a darting legend. His knowledge of the game, the way he reads it, his counting, is up there with the very, very best.

'There was no element of his game, not a single one, that was poor. Even if it was one or two per cent off-beam, he was still a difficult man to beat. For me, what set him apart at his peak, and still does, is his mindset. He still loves the game, he still idolises the game, he still wants to play morning, noon and night, he still goes to Q school… he has the mindset of an absolute champion.

'Over the decades when we competed against each other, our levels and head-to-head record were fairly similar – but I couldn't match Party's mindset. I simply didn't have that mental strength about me. If you put us in a room with a dartboard, I could play well, he could play poorly and he could still beat me because he would find a way, and that's what makes him special: champions find a way.

'Don't ever lose sight of the magnitude of John beating Phil in that 2003 final at the Circus Tavern. Let's remind ourselves that in the two previous years, he had been wiped out 7-0 in the final, winning only three legs in the entire match, and 12 months later he was whitewashed 6-0 in the quarter-finals.

'To hold your nerve in a deciding set, and unseat the greatest player who ever stepped up to the oche, that's not just a turnaround in luck or form. That's a sea change in mentality, a belief that another clean sweep simply isn't gong to happen again. It's the mindset of a natural born winner: "I'm better than that, you can't do that to me this time." What a turnaround, what a performance.

'I still get quite emotional about it, and I've told John many times, when I think of him beating Phil that year and the way he took out 77 to seal it: big 19, big 18, a single dart at tops bang in the middle. Fancy having a single dart to win the World

Championship, lay all those demons, and you absolutely nail it. I remember him clasping his own hands, and congratulating himself, because there was nobody else there supporting him. You used to get the odd coachload of punters coming round the M25 for a night out in Purfleet, but you didn't see any buses coming in from Ontario or day trippers all the way from Canada.

'To all intents, he was a man alone – and he played a brilliant hand in one of the best finals we've ever seen. What a moment that was, and I've told John I often wish I'd been there for him, just to give him a big old cuddle. I didn't realise it would mean that much to me.

'Anyone who thinks John Part is not one of the greatest players ever to play the game doesn't understand darts.'

Although he enjoyed several televised wins against Taylor along the way, the five years after his crowning glory in 2003 would be tinted by regrets as much as rewards for Part. He fell at the first hurdle in his defence of the World Championship in a surprise defeat by Mark Dudbridge, and although he was part of the inaugural Premier League cast, his form collapsed in the second half of the campaign.

By the time the PDC circus had moved its big top to Alexandra Palace in 2008, Part had not reached the competition's quarter-finals since his epic triumph in the final, so it was a considerable shock when he conquered the hilltop fortress.

His path to glory was cleared, to some extent, by defending champion Van Barneveld's third-round exit at the hands of Kevin 'The Artist' Painter and, even more surprisingly, Taylor's failure to reach the PDC World Championship final for the first time since the nascent tournament 14 years earlier.

If Taylor's quarter-final defeat by Mardle was largely unexpected, the big story was 1,000-1 rank outsider Shepherd's rise to prominence, out of nowhere, in a classic rags-to-riches fairytale. As a sheet metal worker in a Ramsgate factory, Shepherd earned just £5.25-an-hour making nuts, bolts and screws until his giddy slalom through the main draw at Ally Pally took out Terry Jenkins, Peter Manley and Mardle. But within four years of becoming the youngest finalist at 21, until Luke Littler shredded the record books, Shepherd was down to his last brass tacks. By his own admission, his life 'went a bit doo-lally' in a tailspin of drinking and gambling, and Shepherd's £50,000 payday as runner-up became a cautionary tale for every player chasing the rainbow as he found himself slipping down the world rankings and struggling to keep his Tour card.

Speaking, with admirable candour, to the *Daily Mirror* in 2023, he admitted, 'It was a fantastic run, one of the greatest weeks of my life. What kept me going was being the underdog – I was riding the wave, I went up on that stage fearless and relaxed because I had nothing to lose, and I didn't want it to end. But I went from being a normal lad working in a factory to back-page headlines and a nice big pay cheque. After that, the devil came for me. I went a bit doo-lally and got carried away by it all.

'I thought everything was going to fall on a plate for me and it was the start of a new beginning, a bright new dawn, but I stopped putting in the effort. I got lazy. From earning £50,000 as runner-up at the World Championship in 2008 and having some wealth, four years later I was living on my own in a flea-ridden one-bed flat.

'I went through a crazy phase because I had suddenly come into all this fame and I didn't know how to deal with it. I'd gone from nowhere to a big final, without reaching the last 16 or quarter-finals of other competitions along the way, and I had nothing to fall back on by way of experience.

'Much as I hate to admit it, I was gambling and turning to drink. I had no manager to straighten me out and I went off the rails. In hindsight, reaching that final at Ally Pally was too much, too soon. It was my first-ever success at a major tournament and, in hindsight, I wasn't ready for it.'

In an era where 100-plus averages are the accepted norm for World Champions, it is intriguing to note that Shepherd's highest average in the tournament was a modest 89.70 – and in his 7-2 defeat in the final, it slipped to just 85.10 – not that it diminishes the magnitude of Part's triple crown.

He says, 'I don't know where it figures among my achievements, but I was always proud that I won a World

Championship in my 20s, my 30s and my 40s. I was trying like hell to win another one in my 50s, but it didn't happen. I was even tempted to try going down the WDF route (the rebranded Lakeside version after the collapse of the British Darts Organisation), but I had too much going on elsewhere. You always think you can do it, but as you get older sometimes the darts have other ideas.

'I still know all the guys, I respect them and understand what they are going through, and it's certainly a big advantage if you're not fazed by it. But no matter how old you may be, you still get nervous. I've watched the 2008 final a couple of times recently, because it happened to be on TV in the background at the venues where I was working, and although I went 4-0 up and never felt like I was going to lose, it was a reminder that those early sets were all very close. I didn't run away with them, I did a really good job to win them and it could have been a lot different.

'It took me back to 1994 and Bobby George – injured or not, he had darts to win the first two sets. What if he had taken those chances? I know, from experience, that if you're winning, this game's a whole lot easier. You get an adrenaline rush and you find your way through. I can pat myself on the back for the job I did in 2008, it wasn't easy but I held it together. Kirk's average in that final wasn't much different from all the games he'd won earlier in the tournament, so his form didn't tail off. Mine was just good enough to get the job done.

'There are only four of us who have won both BDO and PDC versions of the title. I like the ones where you are first to achieve something because you never lose that – they can never take it away from you – and I was the first non-UK player to win both, which is probably a shallow viewpoint but it's true. A lot of people think 'Barney' was the first, but that's not the case. He's gone on to win a lot more things that I couldn't, like the Premier League, Grand Slam and UK Open. Above my pay grade, for sure, but for two versions of the World Championship I got there first.'

For Mardle, in particular, Part's completion of the full set – Lakeside, Circus Tavern, Ally Pally – in 2008 felt like a case of missing the boat. Historically, the man who knocked out Taylor would go on to become World Champion, but 'Hawaii 501' (Mardle's nickname, based on his lurid, kaleidoscopic aloha shirts) didn't just miss the boat: he let a giant ocean liner cruise up the Thames without laying a foot on the gangplank.

He never won a World Championship title – and would never again be presented with such an opportunity. Mardle says: 'If I remember it correctly, after I beat Phil in the quarter-finals Dave Clark (the Sky Sports anchorman) interviewed me on stage and said, "Wayne Mardle, World Champion – how does that sound?" He obviously meant that the biggest obstacle, if you like, and the heavy favourite was now out of the running and I must have fancied my chances. I told him, "Hang on, let's not get ahead of ourselves here! There are more hurdles to clear."

'After being beaten in my four previous World Championship semi-finals, I knew only too well what could go wrong and I went into my next game against Kirk Shepherd not even thinking about being in the final. Unfortunately, on the night it went wrong for me again – my attitude was amateurish and I thought I just needed to stand up, keep breathing and I'd be all right. It comes back to mentality, and John was never going to come a cropper in that final.

'In essence, that tournament highlighted the difference between me and Party: John saw the opportunity and took it, I had the same opportunity and thought I'd muck around with it. I rolled the dice and left myself open to jeopardy, but John didn't leave anything to chance. He got the job done.

'Sportingly, after he'd won it, John told me, "I don't think I'd have beaten you in the final, Wayne" and that made it even worse that I'd passed up the opportunity. I suspect he only said it to make me feel better, which speaks volumes for the man's class. I've never been envious of someone else's success or been too hung up on what might have been. I've never had a chance to win the World Championship because I've never been in the final. Do I ever think about 2008 as the one that got away? No – if anything, my mind goes back to New Year's Day in 2006, when I was 5-4 up against Phil in the semi-final and lost 6-5. But if you present John with that kind of opening, he takes it.

'You can probably count on one hand the opportunities he hasn't taken – and that is the champ in Party.'

Just as Part's defence of his first PDC title proved short-lived, he suffered ignominy when he returned to Ally Pally wearing the crown – and it was dislodged, in straight sets, in the first round by Bill Davis. As of 2026, Part was the last reigning champion to be knocked out at the first hurdle, but he insists it was not a bolt from the blue.

'The thing with Bill was that he was an American and we had played against each other so many times on the circuit in the States and Canada,' says Part. 'From memory I had only lost to him once, but on the day it just didn't happen for me. I hit a lot of 180s but couldn't hit a double when I needed one. I was far more shocked when I lost against Mark Dudbridge the first time I was a defending World Champion because I really felt like I was the best player in the room. But after working so hard to win the first World Championship at Ally Pally – there you go, another 'first' you can't take away from me – it was sad to see it go in about half an hour.'

Although he has never laid down his darts and retired from competition – in his 60th year, Part was still trying to retrieve his PDC Tour Card at the January bunfight known as Q school – his main day job now is in the Sky Sports commentary box. As a three-time World Champion, Part's expertise on the airwaves is unrivalled and when he talks, we are well-advised to listen.

'I try to throw tips out there all the time. Always have. You never stop learning how to play this game,' he says. 'I was the first commentator who was a player, at least certainly at that level. Sid (Waddell) was still at the BBC when he called my first World Championship in 1994, and in those days we didn't have all the stats stored on computers – we used index cards, fairly basic stuff like results, sets and tournament records. What we have now is amazing, but as far as insight goes, I've always tried to convey the player's perspective to the viewer.

'Most commentators have always had a pretty good idea of what's going on, and the "spotters" backstage who predict where the next dart is going are real assets to television coverage, but I suppose my value was based on the experience of someone who's been there. Instead of second guessing what's going on in a player's head, deep down you want to know. As a player, I was quite good at reading my opponent's body language and using that to my advantage if possible.

'But these days, even the guys who've never played darts have a phenomenal understanding of players' mentality and what they are trying to achieve. That aspect of commentary has really changed and developed.'

Mardle, whose vocal contortions have brought so much enjoyment to viewers – notably when Michael Smith landed a perfect nine-dart leg in the 2023 World Championship final, and he shrieked, 'That is the most amazing leg of darts you have ever seen in your life. I can't spake! I can't spake!' – can only admire Part's avuncular delivery.

'Believe it or not, he's not very serious: in the commentary box, I'm the serious one,' he claims. 'I like to be as professional as I can be, which means doing my homework and being studious off-camera, but John is a great ad-libber. He reacts to what's happening and he brings the multiple World Champion's mentality to live broadcasts. His expertise comes from the mindset of someone who's been there, seen it and done it – three times, in three different venues, over 15 years – and he has this vast reservoir of knowledge from a lifetime in the game.

'If I've got John next to me in the commentary box or the studio, I would never say, "As a World Champion, you would feel like this" or assume I know how it feels to wear the crown. I'll just say, "John, how does it feel?"

'And John's response will be all the things a viewer could want: educated, thoughtful, eloquent. Just a loveable human being.'

Part's mood was darker when, in 2012, he was omitted from a gallery of champions at Alexandra Palace. While there were giant murals of other champions staring down from the arena's walls, Part's face was missing… and he was not amused. Michael van Gerwen, who had yet to triumph at Ally Pally, was there, but Part and Dennis Priestley – both multiple World Champions – were not.

Speaking after his first-round win over Joe Cullen, Part said: 'It sounds pretty vain now, but when you are in the middle of the match and you are looking around, there has always been every champion on the wall here previously. When you were the first guy to have won it in this venue and you are not there, it is pretty conspicuous. I had to fight hard not think about it and get on with my business. It is not nice and, I deserve better. Who wouldn't take it personally? How many double champions are there here? I should be up there with those other guys.'

On a lighter note, his win at the 2006 Las Vegas Desert Classic – Part's only other title in a PDC Premier competition – was a triumph of application over wardrobe malfunction.

In a sartorial emergency backstage, he had to borrow Van Barneveld's trousers before dispatching Ronnie Baxter in the first round before a reunion with Barney's slacks in the final. When the $15,000 top prize was up for grabs, it was Part who wore the trousers, so to speak, with a 6-3 victory against the Dutch master.

The tale of second-hand slacks was recycled the night he was inducted into the PDC Hall of Fame in 2017. 'Barney and I met in the final, and I defeated the very trousers that got me started in the tournament,' he laughed.

Part was never a player who could be knocked out of his strides for long. When he's not on the oche or enlightening TV audiences with his articulate, insightful commentary as he clocks up around 150,000 air miles a year commuting between

Canada and the United Kingdom, you'll find a connoisseur of Westerns who knows his Billy the Kid from his Wyatt Earp.

Those outlaws didn't mess about. They could take out rival gunslingers with a single shot. That's all it needed for John Part to break Taylor's spell back win 2003 with that golden arrow at tops. And thank goodness that single dart which flew over the garden wall was the beginning of his story, not the end of 'Darth Maple'.

RAYMOND VAN BARNEVELD

BDO World Champion: 1998, 1999, 2003, 2005
PDC World Champion: 2007

HAPPY EVER afters are rarely delivered to order in sport, but when the sunset beckons Raymond van Barneveld, history will remember him as the real king of Holland.

No disrespect to the House of Orange-Nassau, where King Willem-Alexander has reigned since 2013 as sovereign monarch, nor to Michael van Gerwen, whose version of heavy metal tungsten turned him into the world No 1 in darts' solar system for seven years.

But when 'Barney' joined Phil Taylor and Eric Bristow as the sport's only five-time World Champions, he planted the Dutch standard on the oche in the same way that Rinus Michels was godfather of Total Football, where the beautiful game transcended cynicism and expediency, in the 1970s.

After conquering the Lakeside four times under the British Darts Organisation banner between 1998 and 2005, Van Barneveld exported his fluid, unhurried throwing action to the

Professional Darts Corporation. If his PDC career was defined by a dramatic, sudden-death eclipse of Taylor in a desolate sporting winter elsewhere, spawning a rivalry for the ages, his exhilarating double-header against Van Gerwen in 2016 and 2017 provided two of the greatest World Championship matches ever played at Alexandra Palace.

The Barney Army, an ever-present rolling maul of cheerleaders offering vocal support wherever he played, required no membership card and no formal allegiance. Others have since claimed to be the people's champion, but if popularity was a currency, Van Barneveld – once an unsung postman in The Hague – cornered the market.

By his own admission, the journey contained potholes which, at his lowest ebb, left him grappling with depression. Thankfully, the love of his second wife Julia, and a more contented outlook on his life's work, has restored happiness to a pioneer whose success turned the Netherlands into a powerhouse of world darts.

On the approach to his 60th birthday, as he continued to compete on the PDC circuit, he was unpacking boxes after moving house to Milton Keynes in between exhibition appointments and Pro Tour events at calling points along the M6. The only inconvenience was having to get out of his left-hand drive car to pay motorway tolls.

'I still spend a lot of time travelling to play darts, which is not a bad thing, but when you are living out of a suitcase it becomes a chore to fit your whole life into a 23kg baggage allowance to travel by air,' he says.

'I can't afford to live in London – there are so many extras like the congestion charge and tolls to cross the river – and Milton Keynes is in a good position to reach most venues within a couple of hours.

'When you are nearly 60 years of age, you have to be kind to yourself. We all know what I can do with darts in my hand, but it's not happening all the time now and I can take some of the stress out of my life, so that's why I decided to move to England. Travel-wise, it's much better for me. Of course I still have my family back in Holland, and I will still visit them often, but I will get more rest over here.

'It's coming up to 20 years since I won my last World Championship title, and if people had told me in 2007 that I wouldn't win another one, I would have thought they were kidding me. When you are struggling a bit, as I have been lately, everyone is focused on you and looking for reasons. It's like being in the jungle when there are wounded animals and everyone is after them. You feel hunted, and I don't need that.

'One day, the time will come when you decide "This is enough" – but I'll never give up, and maybe a fresh start will help.'

The memory of that sudden-death final on New Year's Day in 2007 still burns bright, even if Van Barneveld did not realise that celebrity was lurking in the shadows of a Purfleet nightspot.

'I wasn't aware of the Circus Tavern being a lap-dancing club,' he says. 'But I remember it being hot, with a low ceiling, and only about 900 spectators in the main arena. I survived match darts against Colin Lloyd in the second round – after that I played a great competition and never dropped another set until the final, but I was lucky to be there in the first place.

'When I joined the PDC in 2006, it was impossible to shoot all the way up the rankings in your first 12 months – and when the World Championship came round, with only the top 32 players qualifying, I was ranked No.33 so I was destined to miss out.

'But a Belgian player, Erik Clarys, worked in a warehouse and he fell off a ladder, breaking his elbow in five places and dislocating the joint, so he couldn't compete – I was called up into the automatic 32 qualifiers as the first reserve, or next cab off the rank as I believe you say in English. Erik was about No.26 in the rankings at the time and he never played professional darts again. His misfortune was my biggest stroke of luck.'

Erik 'The Sheriff' attempted a comeback throwing left-handed, after 11 operations failed to restore full use of his right arm, but was unable to reach a competitive standard. Van Barneveld, who had beaten Clarys in a World Championship quarter-final at the Lakeside four years earlier, spectacularly made the most of his reprieve.

'Before the final, my manager insisted on me practising 13 sets of match play, morning and afternoon, in case it went the distance,' says Van Barneveld. 'I protested that it didn't make sense – if I won seven sets, I win the match, so why take it further? But he was insistent – to beat Phil Taylor, I might need the stamina to go 13 sets and he didn't care if I won 13-0 on the practice board, I had to be prepared to go all the way.

'It didn't look like going all the way when I was 3-0 down. Phil had won nine out of the first ten legs and my head was gone when we went to the break. I wasn't there at all. But that's where the small venue, and the compact stage, worked to my advantage. You could hear every comment, and as I approached the stage before the restart I heard my manager calling, "Do you want to go back to being a postman?"

'That was the wake-up call I needed. Darts can be a demanding profession, but I was in no hurry to go back to getting up at 4am, the early mornings delivering mail in the rain and the fog and the cold. To be fair, that comment was like an electric shock. After that, Phil never got away from me.'

When the finalists could not be separated, and the title came down to a sudden-death leg, Barney pulled a masterstroke. Throwing for the bull to determine who would throw first in the deciding leg, Taylor's arrow slipped fractionally south into the 25 bed – and Van Barneveld insisted on leaving his dart there as a marker. The Dutchman duly stacked a perfect missile in the bullseye, yet his advantage appeared to be short-lived.

'The Power' opened with his tenth 180 of the contest, but once Barney had replied with his 21st, the momentum shifted. With Taylor waiting on 90, Van Barneveld nailed tops to clinch his fifth World Championship, and his celebration with arms spreadeagled remains the signature image of his career. Think of Tim Robbins busting out of Shawshank by crawling through a sewage pipe, and reaching fresh water when his escape was complete, and you get the picture.

What a moment for Barney. In defeat, Taylor may have lost his aura of invincibility, but darts had soared into the realm of ratings big-hitters on television. In a threadbare winter for connoisseurs of sport, England were getting wiped out on their Ashes tour of Australia, a showjumper had won BBC Sports Personality of the Year from a desperately thin shortlist and Premier League football had become a tedious squabble between the usual suspects. More than any single match, Taylor and Barney's thriller was a reference point in darts history. In the modern era, it was the night when lines on all the major graphs – public interest, prize money, TV coverage – started climbing sharply.

At 39, Van Barneveld had not only climbed his Everest but conquered the north face. For all the hysteria generated by Luke Littler's feats almost two decades later, this was a watershed moment for the sport.

'Around that time I was doing a lot of Zen meditation, about 20 minutes twice a day,' says Barney. 'It was so relaxing, so good for my inner temperament. I was so focused that if you had dropped a bomb right next to me, I wouldn't have heard it.

'Phil complained that I had been allowed to leave his dart in the board when we threw for the bull in that sudden-death leg,' says Barney. 'He obviously had a point because the PDC changed the rules afterwards. But after winning 13 World Championships and being almost unbeatable for so long, maybe he was used to having everything his own way – and I don't mean that in a disrespectful way.

'It was good for darts that someone had come along to challenge him. For years afterwards, at every tournament and especially at the World Championship, Taylor and Van Barneveld was the match-up everyone wanted to see. But the tournament moved to a bigger venue at Ally Pally, and for some reason the move worked out better for Phil than for me.

'I still won majors like the Premier League, the Grand Slam and UK Open, and on my day I was still a match for anyone, but suddenly at the World Championship – which had been so good to me at the BDO and the PDC – I didn't have as much joy.

'To beat Phil in that last leg, when it was all or nothing, meant so much to me as a person. I had beaten him in the UK Open and drawn with him in the Premier League, so I knew I could reach his level, but it kind of validated my career. He was one of my heroes, I was always following Phil back in my years on the BDO, where I had won four world titles, and I remember the day I cracked and decided it was time to join the PDC.

'I had reached another final at the Lakeside, it was all set up for me to equal Eric Bristow's record of five World Championship titles and Eric was there, but it never happened. Jelle Klaasen beat me 7-5, and during his celebration the fans were chanting, "Barney, Barney, who the f*** is Barney?" I thought, "Right, let's show them who you are, Ray."

'It was one of the best steps of my life. There were a couple of players in the PDC I didn't really like that much, and there were times when I wondered if I really belonged there. I needed to adjust to all the noise of the walk-on, and during my first year I changed my darts to use a set costing the equivalent of £1 from a store in the Netherlands when I wasn't happy with my form. When I hit my first nine-darter on TV (in the 2006 Premier League), I didn't celebrate it and people slagged me off. I was only trying to stay focused – if you lose concentration because you're leaping all over the stage, it can cost you a lot of money. I prefer to celebrate when the job is done, not when it's still in progress.'

Nobody in their right mind could have denied Barney his celebration when that famous double top landed and he turfed Taylor off his throne. At every level, he felt vindicated.

'Phil always was, and always will be, the greatest darts player on the planet, but that sudden-death leg changed my life,' he says. 'I was so happy to be the best player in the world that night. It made me walk so tall.'

When Barney and Taylor's collision course at the 2009 PDC World Championship brought their paths converging again, inevitably, in the final, it was the showdown fans wanted. 'The Power' had gone almost three years without wearing the crown – a lifetime by his lofty standards – and fans settled in, expecting another long night like their Circus Tavern epic.

As he now concedes, Van Barneveld made a big mistake before the first ripple of tungsten through the north London air. He marched on stage wrapped in a Dutch flag, brandishing it in front of the mainly British crowd, who responded with a symphony of boos.

It was music to the ears of Taylor, waiting at the end of the runway for his walk-on, because he was convinced it would turn a 50-50 contest between the world's two best players into England v Holland. Barney soon discovered that the crowd's dissent was the highest form of patriotism. 'The Power' unleashed a devastating barrage of arrows, and nobody could have lived with his three-dart average of 110.94.

'Phil was 100 per cent right. I made a miscalculation with the flag there and it backfired on me,' says Van Barneveld. 'I'm a proud Dutchman, I had won the title two years earlier by beating Phil and I wanted to show I was ready for him again.

But the fact is he beat me 7-1, everyone was singing "There's only one Phil Taylor, walking in a Taylor wonderland," and you want to go back to your mum, with your thumb in your mouth, hoping she'll make it better.

'I was asked by my manager, "What on earth were you doing?" We soon found out it was the stupidest thing I could have done, but strangely I averaged 101 on the night, which was more than I did at the Circus Tavern two years earlier. And of the eight sets, five of them were 3-2 in legs, so it's not as if I played terrible. But in every newspaper the following day, it said I had been thrashed 7-1, and that's the bottom line.

'Sometimes the margin between winning and losing can be very small, but for me the difference was in my reception when I got home. After winning in 2007, there must have been a thousand people waiting for me outside my residence – TV and radio crews, Press guys, photographers, neighbours… it was chaos. A beautiful but slightly mad chaos.

'This time, when I got home, the street was empty. Nobody there. Zero. I've always thought that if you don't win a tournament, second place is just the first step for all the guys who didn't win. Yes, you earn some prize money, but second doesn't mean anything. Second is nowhere. The runner-up is the first loser. I went to the football World Cup Final in Johannesburg (in 2010), and in my dreams I can still see Arjen Robben with a big chance to score, and it looks like he's going to be the hero… but Holland lost. Same as 1974 and 1978. Close, but not the glory.

'I was invited on to a sports TV panel show hosted by a famous presenter and I was sitting at a table with a couple of footballers and a Formula 1 driver. The presenter said, "Ray, you are so hard on yourself, but losing a final is OK – you can still be proud of yourself, you are fantastic." I replied that, yes, I was a five-times champion, but then I asked, "How many times have I lost in a World Championship final, then?"

'He was like, "Well, er…" He didn't know it was my third loss in the final because everybody only talks about the winners. It's like those two very different homecoming welcomes in my street – 1,000 people the first time, nobody the next. I could have been the World Champion eight times if I'd won those three other finals, but it's easy to look the other way and pretend they didn't happen.

'You know, it's harder to win the Premier League than a World Championship because you are facing the best players in the world every week. You can't have a lucky draw – it's full-on every week. At the worlds, if someone takes out one of the big guns, it can clear a path to the final.'

They say life begins at 40, and for Van Barneveld the advent of double top on the birthday charts seemed to offer a plethora of horizons for him to conquer. His celebrity brought him unexpected bonuses, like having tulips named after him and a photo opportunity flying an F16 fighter jet.

Success, however, proved a fickle companion. In no particular order, but of roughly equal distress, he would soon find himself staring down the demons of diabetes, blackmail, depression, armed robbery and divorce.

In between the dispiriting intermissions, there were plenty of good times to keep the Barney Army in good voice, including back-to-back UK Open titles, the first nine-darter at a PDC World Championship (against Klaasen in 2009), followed by another against Brendan Dolan the following year, four World Cup of Darts pairs titles and winning the Premier League in 2014 – which proved to be his last major individual title at 47 years old.

As the first World Champion from the Netherlands, and the first from continental Europe's mainland, he was proud to be a 'pioneer' in his homeland, but Van Barneveld admits his life turned into a 'bumpy road' with few shock absorbers to cushion the blows.

For long-term effects, being diagnosed with type two diabetes in 2009 was the most damaging on his career. On holiday in Spain that year, he awoke every morning with pins and needles in both arms, and tests revealed his blood sugar level was four times beyond permissible limits. Although he did not need to inject insulin, fatigue began to impact his performances on the oche. Sometimes he felt so tired that the prospect of another 13-set marathon in a World Championship final was simply unthinkable. Physically, he would not be able to cope.

At face value his last match of 2009, against Kevin Painter at Alexandra Palace, might have looked like a routine 4-1 win. For Barney, however, it was a frightening taste of that bumpy road ahead when he blew the chance of a whitewash, lost the fourth set as fatigue set in suddenly like a blanket of fog at night on the motorway, and at one stage he was so shattered it was an effort to retrieve his darts from the board.

Only a handful of sugar tablets, a guzzle of apple juice backstage during the break and the remnants of muscle memory, guiding the darts to roughly the right areas in a thankless fifth set, carried him over the line. It was a frightening experience, and although it did not curtail his competitive nature, it preyed on his mind.

'You try hard in everything, whether it's a ProTour competition or a major, but when you are suffering from diabetes and it kicks in, you are dealing with an opponent you don't fully understand,' says Van Barneveld.

'The fact is, over the last eight or maybe ten years, I couldn't do it anymore – not at the same level – and that's pretty hard for me to take. Too many times you don't find the answers but you question everything about your game, and the questions are always the same. What am I doing wrong? Is it the diabetes? Is all the travel to the ProTours taking too much out of me?

'When you travel to places like Wigan and Barnsley, you get knocked out in the early rounds and you go back to the hotel to stare at the four walls, it can be soul-destroying. You feel flat, you feel lonely, and you have not even covered your air fare or expenses.

'Since (being diagnosed with) diabetes, I had problems with my eyesight. In darts, your hands, arms and eyes are the tools of your trade, but if you cannot focus sharply on small targets, it's an extra handicap.'

Losing weight, in the fight to reverse type two diabetes, brought RVB some results on the bathroom scales – but little joy. He lost around 30kg (four-and-a-half stone) in five years but admitted: 'I probably look better, but I don't feel better.'

A narrow 6-5 defeat by Australian Simon Whitlock in the 2010 PDC World Championship semi-finals did not lighten Barney's mood, and during the Premier League he went six weeks without a win, missing out on the play-offs amid the dark shenanigans of a bizarre blackmail plot.

He told the *Daily Mirror*: "I was in Belfast when I started receiving a lot of crank calls because somebody had posted my cell phone number on the internet. At first they were just silly nuisance calls, but suddenly they became more sinister. One said he was going to hack into my computer, download child porn and destroy my reputation… and then came the blackmail.

'This guy told me, "Come to Rotterdam Zoo and pay 10,000 euros or we will post a sex tape of you and another woman on the internet." At first I ignored the calls, because no such tape could possibly exist, but they would not go away and they were very threatening.

'There were text messages saying, "We know where your children go to school" or "We saw your wife out shopping today" and their information was accurate. I was terrified they would kill my family. On another occasion, I was away playing darts and my wife was unsettled by a car parked outside our home. They began calling her to put pressure on her. When the threats are aimed at your wife and family, that is when you get scared, and I had to go to the police.

'Fortunately the police took it very seriously and they told me this guy had been calling me from a pre-paid cell phone. They managed to trace him and make an arrest. I have no idea why I was singled out as a target for this blackmail.'

At a time of personal crisis, Van Barneveld found out who his friends were on the circuit – and depressingly, few came forward to offer him support. Compatriots Vincent van der Voort and Co Stompe were sympathetic, but the only other player to stick up for him was Taylor, who even took him in as a house guest for a few days.

'That spoke volumes for the man,' says Van Barneveld. 'I can't speak highly enough of him as a player and a host. I can't remember if we even practised together during that time; if we did, it must have been about nine darts.'

A shock first round defeat by bricklayer James Richardson, ranked a lowly No.85 in the order of merit, at the 2012

World Championship did little for Van Barneveld's morale. He collected only four legs in one of the tournament's greatest upsets.

Raging against the fading light of youth, Barney reached another three World Championship semi-finals in five years, arguably playing the best darts of his life in the process, but the closer he came to rekindling the golden days of winning the title, the deeper anguish would tear at his soul when he fell just short.

The first of those three close calls with glory culminated in a momentary falling-out with Taylor in an explosive post-script to an enthralling match in 2013.

Trailing 5-1, Barney fought back to take the next three sets and Taylor was visibly relieved to stagger over the line before the pair were involved in an angry confrontation. 'The Power' took offence when Van Barneveld pulled him back after their handshake, apparently to try and give him a man-hug in a spirit of sportsmanship, but it descended into an unsightly tug-of-war and both players were escorted off stage by security staff. Barney later insisted he was only trying to congratulate Taylor, who briefly threatened to walk away from the sport after reviewing his conduct before he apologised 24 hours later.

Van Barneveld's next dangerous liaison with the Sid Waddell Trophy came in the 2016 tournament, where his collision with fellow Dutchman Van Gerwen in the last 16 was a thunderous contest, Barney edging it 4-3 against the odds – MVG had come to Ally Pally as holder of no fewer than seven major titles in 2015, having reached the final in the other two. It was always going to take something special to stop Van Gerwen, and Barney procured it in one of the most spellbinding games in the PDC's greatest hits compilation.

'I was convinced it was going to be my year,' says Barney. 'In the next round I was 3-0 down against Michael Smith and came back to beat him. I thought the stars were arranged in the sky for me, but Adrian Lewis beat me in the semi-finals. The following year, I beat Adrian and Phil before facing Michael again in the semis. I averaged 109 and played out of my skin but still lost 6-2… what can you do?

'To play so well and lose those three semi-finals was very hard to take. It's great that people remember those games and still talk about them as classics, but in the end I lost them. Since then, I have never looked at averages anymore – what is the point? You walk backstage and no one is interested in the guy who lost. I was there so many times, and I was hard on myself. Maybe too hard.'

Van Barneveld tried everything to find the so-called marginal gains that mark the frontier between triumph and torment. He tried wearing glasses on stage at the European Championship in 2014 but ditched them before turning to a bizarre face-palm ritual to boost his eyesight.

He swore by a routine known as the Bates Method – where he rubbed his hands together, placed the warm palms over his eyes and the heat from his hands gave him extra optical energy.

It sounded a bit Hands Christian Andersen, but at first it seemed to work. If his dabble in alternative medicine sounded more Bates Motel than Bates Method, there was no disputing Van Barneveld's accuracy when he sustained a 125.25 average in the third set of his 3-0 whitewash of Rowby-John Rodriguez at Ally Pally, including 167 and 170 checkouts – numbers to make your eyes pop out.

But in the land of the blind, the one-eyed man is king, and the fad was short-lived. Speaking in December 2014, Barney explained: 'Last year my manager, Ben de Kok, thought my eyesight was getting bad and, although I won the Premier League and the World Cup of Darts this year, I noticed a difference. When I was getting back to the hotel after playing or practising, I could not read the lines of tickertape and the scores at the bottom of the TV screen.

'So I started wearing glasses at the European Championship and it went well, but I was 9-7 up against Michael van Gerwen and lost 10-9. Then I lost to Keegan Brown at the Grand Slam, so I decided I didn't want to rely on glasses to the extent that I can't play darts without them. I went on YouTube and found something about palming called the Bates Method. If you rub your hands together and make them very warm and then cover your eyes for ten minutes, the warm hands improve your eyesight.

'I'm doing it twice a day, morning and night. I've known about this method for two years but I've been too lazy to do anything about it until now. I think darts affects your eyesight because we play so many matches every week under bright TV lights. The tension of playing and practising is virtually non-stop.'

If Van Barneveld's experiment with face-palming was faintly ridiculed back home in the Netherlands, there was only shock and revulsion at the ordeal of his ex-wife, Silvia, when three armed robbers raided the couple's home in 2018 and held a loaded gun to her head.

Barney accepts his marriage was already under strain because of his exhaustive schedule of travel, tournaments and exhibitions, but the terrifying incident proved a tipping point. Wracked with guilt that he was away playing at an exhibition tournament in Barnsley at the time his home in The Hague was violated by intruders, he admitted to *The Sun*: 'I let my wife down by not being there for her, which is stressful.

'She didn't want to live in the house anymore because she was frightened. She wanted an apartment. She was scared. We had to live separately. You have to deal with that.' The couple divorced in 2019.

Another defeat by Van Gerwen, in the 2018 World Championship quarter-finals, was offset to some extent by the compatriots retaining the Netherlands' title at the World Cup of Darts, but Van Barneveld could sense the magic was becoming harder to mine, and his lowest point was yet to come.

In the 2020 edition two years later, having announced his intention to retire after the tournament, he crashed out in the first round against American outsider Darin Young and the crestfallen former champion left Alexandra Palace lamenting: 'I'll hate myself every day.'

He relinquished his PDC Tour Card and quit professional darts two weeks later, but did a U-turn later in the year when the COVID-19 pandemic kiboshed his plan to go full-time on the exhibition circuit. To his enormous credit, Barney did not seek any short-cuts to regain his place on the PDC roster, nor did he attempt to ask for favours as one of the sport's most decorated players of all time. He joined the annual bunfight at Q School where, typically, there are around 30 Tour Cards to be won each year from entries running into many hundreds in both the UK and European competitions – and he made the cut.

'I was convinced I'd have a good run in the 2020 World Championship, even though the whole year had been poor,' he says. 'When I was beaten by Darin it felt like the floor was gone under my feet. I thought: "Wow, this isn't happening." I gave a stupid interview to Sky Sports. I was devastated. This was my only and last chance ever. I couldn't forgive myself.

'I'm the worst loser in this darts world. I don't want to play one or two rounds and then go home again. I'm not a person like that. I'd rather retire and sit home and watch the darts, do exhibitions. I'm a winner. I want to lift trophies. Going out in the first or second rounds – those moments are devastating and it kills me inside.

'I'm still one of only three players who have won five or more World Championships. The others are Phil Taylor and Eric Bristow. I'm proud of that. Later that month I stayed with my girlfriend Julia in London. I was really depressed at Christmas as well. Never happy. Julia helped me through it. On January 1, I said to myself: "Ray, this needs to stop. You still have a fantastic life, you've had a fantastic career, a lovely new girlfriend, you have kids and family – now we'll stop this. We'll show them the new, better Ray."

'When Phil reached the final in 2018, where he got beat by Rob Cross, he had a chance to say thank you and go out at the top. I wanted to do the same, and a lot of players were telling me I was too young to retire, but I was suffering from depression and my whole life was collapsing.

'It wasn't the happiest part of my life – I was going through a divorce, people were talking negatively about me in the press and I was struggling.

'I had my reasons for retiring – there were troubles in my head and I wasn't winning anymore. And if you know you're good but it just isn't working out, it becomes harder and harder. I wasn't a nice man to be around anymore. I was depressed and thought it would be a good idea to just give up.

I thought I could do exhibitions and it would be better to live without the stress of winning and losing. But I couldn't do anything because of Coronavirus. There were no exhibitions. I wasn't earning any money.

'So I was left thinking: what happens now? The PDC somehow managed to keep staging major tournaments and maintained the prize money during lockdown, which was an amazing thing to do, and I decided to go for it.

'I managed to qualify for the 2022 World Championship, which was a strange time with all the Covid screening and controls. Players were being forced to withdraw if they tested positive, and the day after I lost to Rob Cross in the second round I tested positive on Christmas Eve. Happy Christmas, Ray – two red lines.'

Out of darkness must come light, and Julia Evans, an avid darts fan who worked at Transport for London, didn't just turn out to be a ray of sunshine in his life. She transformed Barney's outlook, made him happy again, and in 2023 she became his wife.

Albert Einstein once claimed, 'A table, a chair, a bowl of fruit and a violin: what else does a man need to be happy?' Well, how about Cupid's arrow? When it found Van Barneveld again, on the north side of 50 years old, it landed bullseye in his heart.

'It was time that the sun shone on me,' he says. 'We started talking on Instagram. Julia was a big darts fan and

I first met her at an exhibition in Southampton. Phil Taylor and Simon Whitlock were there as well and it was a fun night. We stayed in touch and at first it was a long-distance relationship.

'Since then we grew close and she has brought so much happiness to my life. She is my rock, my soulmate, and I can't believe how lucky I am.

'When I rushed into retirement, I stayed at her place because she was still working for TfL, but after (Covid) restrictions were lifted, we made a decision to live in Holland. It was a big step for her, with a new language and culture, but she fitted in perfectly. People tell me, "Ray, you are different now" – and I think it's true, maybe I'm more laid-back. Previously I was always so focused on darts that I had no time for others. Now I can be myself.'

On a weekend trip to Paris, Barney went down on one knee and proposed in front of the Eiffel Tower in February 2022, and the couple tied the knot the following year in Cyprus. In 2026, they moved to Milton Keynes – no fanfares, no hue and cry. In the land of concrete cows, Van Barneveld is seen but not herd. He is happy to blend into the spiritual home of the roundabout.

Darts has been good to Van Barneveld since he received a dartboard as a present on his 17th birthday, which turned a keen interest into a passion, if not an obsession. But the reverse is also true: he has been a rare gift to darts. No other player commands such swathes of public adulation that turns whole congregations into regiments of the Barney Army.

He has some reservations about the modern game, from the masonic draws at ProTour events to squeaking chairs at the Milton Keynes arena where 128 hopefuls sign on for Players Championship competitions at 11am and by 7pm it's down to last man standing, but his PDC career has straddled an extraordinary growth in the sport.

When battles are fought out on stage, and crowds flock to watch the best marksmen since Private Daniel Jackson, the sniper in the bell tower in the epic war movie *Saving Private Ryan*, few can transform an auditorium like Van Barneveld when the Barney Army foot soldiers convene and his 'Eye of the Tiger' anthem unites them in a call to arms. Nobody does it better.

'Of course, the prize money is good, and the top players are making serious money now,' he says. 'But even if you are making a few thousand pounds every month, half that money goes to paying for your flights and hotels, paying your manager, paying for your food and drink. If you're not winning anything, there's no profit. You're doing it all for nothing. That's the reality.

'And the world is a much angrier place now. It's not easy to escape the anger, especially on social media. The pen is mightier than the sword, and as a sportsman you can't hit back if someone posts something terrible about your wife or children. If you dare to respond, you are accused of being unprofessional, so you have to take it on the chin and that's the hardest part. It kills you inside.

'People are gambling on darts matches now and if you play a bad game and lose, suddenly you get tagged on social media by some punk saying, "You cost me £20 tonight, I backed you to win, why did you play like crap?" We shouldn't have to put up with that kind of rubbish, and some of it feels sinister.

'After losing to James Wade in the Premier League once, there was a knock on my hotel door quite late at night and this voice calls out, "Room service." Without opening the door, I replied that I hadn't ordered any room service and suddenly the guy turns aggressive: "You cost me money, blah, blah, blah." Someone downstairs at the reception desk must have given him my room number, and I didn't feel safe.

'What if I had opened the door? He might come for me with a knife, I might have been fighting for my life. These things are happening and players need to be aware. But in my opinion it starts with social media and betting.'

When Barney speaks, we should listen. Raymond van Barneveld wasn't just on the launch pad when darts enjoyed lift-off with that sudden-death final on New Year's Day in 2007. He provided the rocket fuel, spacesuits and lunar module when a sport reached for the stars.

He was the postman who delivered five World Championship titles in ten years, the pioneer who brought Total Darts to the Netherlands, the man who turned the first Premier League night in Rotterdam into an orange procession.

One of Van Barneveld's secret passions in life is his collection of more than 1,500 Marvel figurines. Little did he realise that, by lifting darts from oblivion to the front line of a nation's sporting compass, he was the original marvel.

All rise for the king of Holland.

ADRIAN LEWIS

PDC World Champion: 2011, 2012

HIS 'JACKPOT' nickname is one of sport's most colourful and autobiographical monikers, but he should really be known as Adrian 'Two Jackpots' Lewis after a remarkable double on the one-armed bandits in Las Vegas.

Lewis landed the $72,000 top prize (around £45,000 at the contemporary exchange rate) on a slot machine during a night out on The Strip when he was playing at the Las Vegas Desert Classic in 2005 – but he was not allowed to claim his winnings under Nevada state laws because he was under 21 at the time.

Remarkably, on a subsequent visit to Sin City with his wife Sarah – who was then his fiancée – six years later, he took her back to the spot where he became the unluckiest gambler in town... and she scooped the $21,000 jackpot.

In the spiritual home of Elvis-style wedding chapels, Lewis is still all shook up when he recounts his extraordinary reversal of fortune. The Lord giveth and the Lord taketh away, but not usually in torrents of dimes and quarters from machines which usually offer only short-cuts to broken dreams and destitution.

If he's told the tale of his hard-luck story a thousand times before, the sequel is less well-known.

'I was only about five months short of my 21st birthday,' he says of his near-miss with life-changing riches. 'I could have bought a house in Stoke with £45,000 at the time but rules are rules,' he says, reflecting ruefully on his forfeit. 'And at least I've made up for it since.

'I was out with an Irish lad called Steve Byrne – he was on the blackjack table and I was on the roulette, and we were doing OK. We'd won something like $1,000 between us when he switched to blackjack and I went over to try my luck on the slots.

'Normally, if you put me on the penny slot machines in an amusement arcade all day, they would take my last copper off me without any joy. I'd never won anything apart from a teddy bear on one of the grabbers at the seaside, so I didn't have any expectations of cleaning up in Vegas, of all places. Usually there's only one winner, and it's not the punter, is it?

'Anyway, I had no joy on my first three or four spins, but then all the lights on this machine just flashed, saying I'd won the big jackpot, and it started raining money.

'The Desert Classic, which was being staged at the MGM Grand, was a relatively new tournament and I think it was worth about £15,000 to the winner – all of a sudden this slot machine was telling me I had won three times as much.'

If something seems too good to be true, there is usually a catch – and for Lewis, the punchline was cruel.

'I knew you needed ID to claim the jackpot, and of course your passport gives the game away how old you are,' says Lewis. 'While the machine was making a lot of noise, Steve has got his chips, come over to me and I tried to make out it was my mate who'd won it, but they came back and warned me it had all been captured on CCTV. Then it started getting a bit hairy, with questions about what I was doing here and asking if I had been drinking any alcohol – in Nevada, you have to be 21 to buy or drink beer – and it sunk in pretty quick. I wasn't going to be walking out of that casino as a rich man.'

All of a sudden, Lewis realised he was being watched. In Martin Scorsese's brilliant crime movie *Casino*, Robert De Niro's lead character Ace Rothstein captures the culture perfectly and Lewis could readily identify with the scene where De Niro says: 'In Vegas, everybody's gotta watch everybody else. Since the players are looking to beat the casino, the dealers are watching the players. The box men are watching the dealers. The floor men are watching the box men. The pit bosses are watching the floor men. The shift bosses are watching the pit bosses. The casino manager is watching the shift bosses. I'm watching the casino manager. And the eye-in-the-sky is watching us all.'

With jackpot winners required to submit ID and fill in a form for tax purposes, Lewis was forced to accept his giant windfall wouldn't be going home with him. On the oche, he lost in the first round of the Las Vegas tournament, 2-0 against Kevin Painter in a best-of-three sets contest, and for the remainder of his trip he felt like a punter under surveillance. 'It threw me a bit,' he admits. 'Every casino I walked into, I had security approaching me, saying "Make sure you stay on the red carpet, sir." In other words, behave yourself. But to miss out on forty-five grand... yeah, I was gutted.'

Payback for the jackpot that got away was six years in the making, and Lewis was already a World Champion when it happened, but it was still a sweet moment when he took Sarah to Vegas and providence played a kinder hand.

'We were getting married not long after, and she was not impressed that I had lost probably $15,000 gambling. She hates gambling, and I don't like it anymore,' he says. 'But I took her on a trip down Memory Lane, to the same part of The Strip where I had won all that money but wasn't allowed to claim it, just to show her where my 'Jackpot' nickname was born.

'It wasn't exactly the exact same machine, and it might not even have been the exact same establishment, but history sort of repeated itself. She won $21,000 (about £13,250 at the exchange rate), and I couldn't believe it. Sarah made sure it went towards the wedding, but there was a twist.

'When we got back home and went to the Post Office to convert the money back into pounds sterling, they said some of the notes were counterfeit money. Fortunately, we had kept the receipt from the casino to prove we had won such a substantial amount of money, and they honoured the transaction. I didn't even know what they meant by counterfeit money at first – one dollar bill looked much the same as any other to me – but you wonder what might have happened if we hadn't kept that receipt.

'So, I'm not the real 'Jackpot' in our household – Sarah's the one who actually came home from Vegas with the money. When people tell me I hit the jackpot by marrying her, they're not wrong.'

When Lewis won the 2011 Professional Darts Corporation World Championship, he became the first player to do so without having won the BDO version at the Lakeside previously. In fact, he competed in only one professional tournament under the BDO banner, the 2003 World Masters, before joining the PDC without ever qualifying for the Frimley Green showpiece.

His passage to the 2011 final was relatively uneventful – until he planted a kiss on Prince Harry while celebrating his semi-final win over Mark Webster and feared the royal protection cops were about to pull a gun on him.

The King's younger son had enjoyed a night at the arrows with some mates from the Army after being smuggled into Ally Pally in a hush-hush operation, and in his excitement at reaching his first World Championship final, Lewis admitted he breached royal protocols.

He told *The Sun*: 'I'd just come off stage when Prince Harry came up to me and put his arms around me. As I normally do, as people have seen me do loads of times, I kiss people. On this occasion, it was Prince Harry. Then the shock hit me. Oh my God, I've just kissed Prince Harry. There was security looking at me and I'm thinking, "Oh s***, here we go..." Luckily it didn't escalate.'

Lewis decorated his 7-5 win against Gary Anderson in the final, to become champion at the age of 25, with a nine-darter in the opening set. It was the first perfect leg in a World Championship final, and his barrage of 20 maximum 180s was indicative of a man in the form of his life.

Only Jelle Klaasen (aged 21 in 2006), Eric Bristow (22 in 1980), his then-manager Keith Deller (23 in 1983) and Webster (24 in 2008) had been younger darts World Champions, all of them at the Lakeside.

'I did feel in my water that I was going to do it,' says Lewis. 'I had beaten Phil Taylor in the semi-finals at the World Grand Prix three months earlier and I remember thinking that if I could beat him over a long format, I could beat anyone. As soon as I got past Tony Eccles in the first round, I thought it was going to go my way.

'I had fancied my chances of hitting a nine-darter all through the tournament and, in a way, I was disappointed that I had to wait until the final to make it happen. But if you're going to produce something that's never been done before, you might as well save it for the biggest stage, and the biggest occasion, of the darts calendar. Everyone talks themselves up about hitting nine-darters on the practice board – it's much better to do it on stage, where it really matters.'

Lewis had been billed as Taylor's protege in the build-up to the tournament, and it is true that they had been long-time practice partners. Although 'The Power' was a tough taskmaster, refusing to let Lewis win their practice matches to build his resilience, he had also been generous with advice on board management and preparation.

'Jackpot', however, felt the connection had been over-egged in the media, and following Lewis's triumph in the final, Taylor was listening in as the new champion announced: 'A nine-darter in the final has never been done before, not even by Phil, so making that bit of history is big for me. It's time to stop calling me Phil's protege – all I've ever done is to practice with him, but I used to practice with my dad and nobody calls me his apprentice.

'How much of my success is down to Phil? He passed on a few tips, like going to bed early and telling me a few things I should be doing as a professional, but I had qualified for three (major) tournaments on the circuit before I even met him. For years I have lived with this thing about being his understudy, but since I beat him at the World Grand Prix he has not played as well as he can. I think that defeat hurt him more than any other because he had not lost on TV for ages. We had a bit of a falling-out at the Grand Prix, but that was something and nothing. Every now and then we have a bit of a bitch-fight – and I'm the biggest bitch!'

Taylor, who had invited Lewis to his house as an 18-year-old to practise after learning of him winning the British Teenage Open in 2003, immediately recognised the natural throw in a building site worker who used to beat his colleagues at darts during weekend debriefings in the pub.

Their practice match format was usually simple – first to 18 legs – but Lewis claimed he never won because if Taylor was losing, he would suddenly remember he had an urgent appointment to keep. It was his way of keeping Lewis hungry, but he was concerned that ability alone would not be enough to turn latent promise into major titles. 'Even when you're naturally talented, like a Paul Gascoigne or a George Best, you still have to put the effort in,' Taylor later observed.

Lewis, however, was determined to be his own man. His PDC World Championship debut in 2006 at the Circus Tavern had ended in a tetchy quarter-final defeat by Peter Manley. At one point Lewis hit a 'blind' 180, turning to face Manley while the third dart was still in the air, and walked off stage when his opponent appeared to mutter something while 'Jackpot' was throwing. Lewis lost the match 5-3, but had laid down a marker that he would not be messed around.

That perhaps explains Lewis's bullish mood, and his attempts to distance himself from Taylor's tutelage, after winning the World Championship title.

'I think I had got under his skin a little bit when I beat him at the Grand Prix, where he didn't like some of my antics on stage and I ended up getting a fine for conducting the crowd against him,' he says. 'It was only a slap on the wrist, really, but he didn't like it. And he didn't speak to me for a few weeks after turning up to watch the final at Ally Pally, but let's have it right. Phil was a great influence on my career. I just think the first time I beat him on TV was a bit of a back-handed compliment. It was my way of saying, "You taught me well." But, of course, I love him to bits.'

Taylor and Lewis would form a dream team for England at the World Cup of Darts, winning the tournament four times in five years and encouraging each other like a pair of brothers. Their sudden-death leg to pip Australia in the 2012 final, where all four players missed match darts before Lewis pinned double five to deny Simon Whitlock and Paul Nicholson the glory, was gut-wrenching drama of the highest order.

By then, Lewis was a two-time World Champion after sealing back-to-back titles with a 7-3 win against fellow Potteries marksman Andy Hamilton, but the real drama of his second coronation came in the semi-finals, where the turbulence was by no means restricted to 'Jackpot' overturning a 5-1 deficit to beat James Wade 6-5.

In a dramatic late-night thriller, with Alexandra Palace still full when the last dart landed at 12.48am and the last trains long since departed, play was suspended for 25 minutes after both players complained of a draught blowing across the stage and sending their darts off target.

Wade was 2-0 up and Lewis, distracted by the conditions and a partisan crowd backing 'The Machine' to reach his first final, was grateful for the delay. His form did not improve immediately upon the resumption, however, and he survived a match dart, which slipped agonisingly wide of double 18, before the momentum turned inexorably in his favour.

Lewis's complaints about the draught seemed to carry more weight than Wade's mild protests, and the Aldershot southpaw returned to the stage, to practise alone, long before the defending champion reappeared.

After their prickly Premier League meeting ten months earlier, Wade had poked the hornets' nest by claiming: 'I keep hearing everything about Adrian and how good he is, but if I'm playing my best game, he's not good enough to tie my laces.'

And after his best chance of reaching a World Championship final was gone with the wind, Wade admitted he had been 'too nice' by agreeing to suspend the match when he was clearly on top and conceded: 'I should have dug my heels in harder.'

Had Wade's match dart found its target, he would have taken out a 121 finish and completed a 6-1 rout, but Lewis made the most of his reprieve, picking off a 98 checkout – and he never looked back. By the time he took the chequered flag with a stunning 161 finale, Wade's resistance had melted away into weary resignation.

'I had changed my darts manufacturer earlier in the year and the people at Target, my new suppliers, were brilliant – but I'd been struggling to find the right ones,' says Lewis. 'It's important to have confidence in the arrows in your hand, otherwise it's pointless throwing them. It's even more difficult when you get gusts of wind blowing them off-course and very early in the contest I was saying to Wadey, "Can you feel it? My darts are wobbling all over the shop." Trust me, it wasn't just a breeze drifting across the stage – it was nearer a gale-force wind.

'James mentioned it to referee Bruce Spendley and he confirmed it (was a problem). When we came off, the PDC tried to check all the air vents and doors, and backstage I was having a go at tournament director Tommy Cox, asking how this could be happening in a World Championship semi-final – and Tommy, bless his soul, said it wasn't him blowing air across the stage. It was probably accentuated by both me and Wadey having lightweight darts, 20 or 22 grams, not the heavy 32-gram spears some lads use today.

'Once we got back on, my game didn't improve straight away, but after he'd missed that dart for the match and I'd taken out 98, I remember thinking, "You're back in it now –

make him pay." I got on a roll, and although he was only three legs away from the final I didn't really give him a sniff once I'd got it back to 5-2. I won ten legs in a row.

'I said afterwards that it was the best win of my career, and I certainly can't recall coming from further back to win a game. Once I found my range, I was unstoppable. Wadey might think now that he was too nice and should have dug his heels in, but once the seed of doubt was there in his mind, I could tell it was getting to him.

'He can put his foot down as much as he wants, but the angles are the same and the targets are the same. What I will say is that James is the best player never to have won the World Championship – he's only a couple of years older than me and he might still pull one out of the fire, but as I speak only Phil and Michael have won more majors than him and, to me, he will always be classed as the best finisher in the world.

'Under pressure, his clutch finishing has always been up there with any of the greats. I've got so much respect for him.'

PDC boss Barry Hearn, who was tuning into the ill wind on TV at home, made light of the interruption, saying: 'I would not have been surprised if Michael Fish the weatherman had appeared on stage to inform us of a hurricane. I was in touch with our men backstage and they did a great job to check that every air-conditioning unit was turned off, every door was shut and to get the match restarted.

'There is a theory that the atmosphere generated by 3,000 fans and the heat of the TV lights caused turbulence in the micro-climate of a hot arena, but we've never known anything like it before. In the absence of a more plausible explanation, I'm going to jump on the bandwagon and blame it on our old friend global warming.'

For Lewis and Wade, their late night's work was far from over once the decisive bullseye had landed. As they filed backstage, exhausted, UK Anti-Doping drug testers were lying in wait. After playing 11 sets under the punishing TV stage lights, and perspiring prodigiously in the heat, calls of nature can prove a long waiting game – and for Lewis, drinking too much water on stage during the marathon contest to stay hydrated was now a problem. To comply with testing requirements, urine samples have to be a certain strength; solutions diluted by too much water are not acceptable.

'It's not a glamorous part of the job,' he says. 'Standing in a cubicle with your trousers down, trying to pee into a specimen bottle in front of a stranger with a clipboard isn't much fun. Especially when it's the middle of the night and you want to hit the sack.

'For ages, Wadey and I were sat opposite each other, not saying a word. I mean, what do you say to a bloke you've just beaten 6-5 from 5-1 down? "Hard luck about that double 18, mate" doesn't really cut it at two o'clock in the morning, does it? I felt sorry for him. He's just lost a World Championship semi-final and I didn't know what to say. We just wanted to get out of there.'

Darts continues to be derided, in some quarters, as a pub game, but Lewis has little time for such metropolitan sneering.

'If it's not a "proper" sport, how come we are held to the same drug-testing rules as Usain Bolt and Olympic athletes? If they find something in our system which shouldn't be there, we're in hot water,' he protests. 'I've always said darts should be in the Olympics – it's more of a sport than some of the games they play now. Archery is in the Olympics, isn't it? That's basically the same as darts – shooting at a target, except it's further away. I've never seen anyone from Stoke doing archery, but I know a lot of people who play darts. Down the years we have faced a lot of prejudice about darts being a pub game, but one thing we have got now is genuine global appeal.'

As New Year's Day dragged into the small hours of January 2, Lewis still hadn't fulfilled the demands of UKAD's official at Alexandra Palace. He had to be back at the venue in 12 hours for the final, and he hadn't even been to bed yet.

'Apparently your wee has to have a tinge of colour to it, and not just be transparent, but after drinking water on stage to try and stay hydrated, what do they expect? After a couple of failed attempts, it got to about 5am and they said, "Have you tried eating a biscuit? That might help." By this point I was starving and I said, "Biscuits? Why didn't you tell me in the first place, about four hours ago?!"

'I can't even remember what time it was when I made it back to the hotel, but when I slumped in through the door, Jason Thame (then Wade's manager) was having his breakfast. He must have thought I'd been out clubbing or something and asked, "Where are you going?" I looked at him wearily and said, "I've only just got in!" To go out and beat Andy (Hamilton) in the final a few hours later wasn't a bad effort.'

Consecutive world titles, plus his runner-up cheque in the 2011 Premier League, was worth the thick end of half a million pounds in prize money for Lewis, but affluence was not all it seemed.

Once he had treated himself to a £50,000 Jaguar, there was not a lot left in the kitty after the taxman had claimed his share of the earnings. With prize money going through the roof in the Luke Littler era, Lewis feels there needs to be a greater accent on players setting aside part of their earnings for the proverbial rainy day.

Lewis says: 'The PDC have done a great job in lifting prize money to astronomical levels, and the PDPA (Professional Darts Players Association, effectively the players' trade union) have programmes for wellbeing and financial advice. But I do think the game needs to do more to make sure players don't get caught out by a whopping bill from the taxman. There's not enough education on that side of it. If you win the World Championship, great – you're a rich man overnight. But not as rich as you think.

'I was lucky – when the tax people came after me, I could afford to pay my bill. But in recent years we've seen top players like Mervyn King and Rob Cross have run-ins over tax, and they are good lads. Maybe we need to spell it out more – if you win some prize money, put 40 per cent of it aside. If you work in a factory or an office, tax gets taken off your wages, on your payslip, right? But if someone hands you £200,000 for winning a darts tournament, nobody gives part of it straight to the taxman. You have to do that yourself. I found out the hard way.'

Lewis has always met the slings and arrows of life head-on. In April 2023, he took the brave decision to step away from darts because his wife was receiving treatment for a chronic kidney condition and, with his form 'going nowhere' in the rankings, he was in danger of falling out of love with the sport.

'The thing with darts is, you have to be in a happy place,' he told the *Guardian*. 'When you're up, everything's free, everything's flowing. Don't think, just throw. Just get up there, get into a rhythm, bash-bash-bash. You don't feel like you've got a burden on yourself.'

When self-doubt crept in, and the enjoyment was draining like a slow puncture, he realised something had to give. 'I was leaving the house, not enjoying it,' he said. 'Even when I was winning, I wasn't enjoying it. I was basically just going through the motions. Like a ghost. Winning, losing, I wasn't fussed. My ability had never been in question. But my mindset, that was my big bugbear. I found it hard to get myself up for games, even if was against Michael or Phil.'

The decision to walk away was a big call, and led to endless speculation about whether he had retired, but his answer was always the same: he was just on a break and he would be back when his mind was right. By mid-2026, he was four stones lighter, enjoying the odd window of meditation at the end of a fishing rod, and the cycle of hospital trips and school runs had settled Lewis into a pattern of contented family life.

He would watch football on the box and contemplate the sliding-doors moment when his dreams of becoming a professional footballer bit the dust as a teenager. At 6ft 3in in his boots, he wanted to be England goalkeeper – and had the physique to fulfil his ambition – until his football prospects were ended by a fight at a bus stop.

The scar on the back of his right hand is still there from the wintry night in the Potteries, back in 2001, when Lewis sprang to the defence of a friend who was set upon by a yob with an Alsatian. The damage to his throwing hand did not stop Lewis from becoming a darts World Champion and, by his own admission, turning his life into 'an episode of the *Jeremy Kyle Show*' – but it was the punchline which changed his life.

Lewis told the *Daily Mirror*: 'Coming from Stoke, I wanted to be the next Gordon Banks and, to be fair, I was a promising goalkeeper as a teenager. Seriously, I wasn't bad. I was on the books as a schoolboy at Crewe Alexandra and Dean

Greygoose, the goalkeeping coach, was going to give me a trial with the first-team squad, even though I was only 16, when I seriously injured my hand.

'Along with a mate, I was at a bus stop in Newcastle-under-Lyme around eight o'clock one night when this guy came along with an Alsatian. My mate asked, "Does your dog bite?" – and all of a sudden this fella turned nasty. I don't know if he was drunk, drugged-up or just a plain chav, but he started punching my pal in the face for no reason.

'Mates are supposed to look after each other, right? So I grabbed this bloke and hit him back once, in the face, and caught my knuckle on one of his teeth. It broke a bone on the back of my hand and then the wound became infected. It turned the back of my hand black in a crescent moon shape, and I needed an operation to clear it up.

'Obviously I'm not proud of hitting anyone, and I don't want to glorify what I did, but I wasn't the aggressor. I'm still in touch with the mate who was set upon, but we never speak about what happened. It stopped me playing football because it took a long time to heal properly and a keeper is about as much use as a chocolate teapot if he can't use one of his hands.

'I played a few games for Newcastle Town reserves later, but I could already throw a dart at that age. On Friday afternoons, after finishing work in the building trade, I would have a chuck with the lads, and I suddenly thought, "Hey, you're half-decent at this."

"By now my aim was to join the Parachute Regiment – you know, still an action man at heart – but I didn't pursue it very far. Then my mum entered me for the British Teenage Open, and I won it. I only dropped a couple of legs in the whole tournament. So from then on, it was full steam ahead with the darts – and I've never had many regrets about missing out on a career in professional football.

'They are both mentally demanding, but darts players don't have to run six or seven miles a day and our lifestyle isn't as strict. Some footballers seem to get carried away with money, but my only extravagance is the Jaguar I bought after winning the World Championship. But my driver, Craig, gets to drive it more than me.

'I like to think I won't change as a person, even if I go on to win 20 World Championships. I will still be just a working-class lad from the Potteries, the same daft old me.'

In some ways, Lewis is glad the door closed on him becoming a goalkeeper before it could open. Since the days of Banks sprawling to keep out Pelé's header at the 1970 World Cup, when all the geometry suggested it was impossible, a keeper's role has changed from simply stopping shots to a feeble pretence of playing sweeper.

He hates the modern fad of goal-kicks being a five-yard sideways tap to a centre-back, who taps it back when opposition strikers bear down on the six-yard box and instigate a sense of panic, which spreads to the supporters.

'Give me diving around in icy puddles to that rubbish any day,' he scoffs. 'What do they call it – playing out from the back? I know what I'd call it, and you wouldn't be able to print it in your book. Football used to be a simple game, like darts. Now it's been taken over by coaches who think we all want to watch a goalkeeper standing with one foot on the ball, pretending he can pass it like a quarterback. But there's a reason why you play in goal – it's because you're better with your hands than your feet.

'It drives you mad. At Stoke City, as soon as the people in charge decided they wanted more sophisticated football, we got relegated.'

The *Jeremy Kyle Show* reference pertained to a choppy spell in his private life and a stormy night at the Premier League in Glasgow, where he ran the gauntlet of a thirsty Caledonian gathering of the clans and he drew the short straw – playing the 'Flying Scotsman' himself, Gary Anderson, whom he had just beaten in the World Championship final.

Lewis was pelted with coins and cigarette lighters, doused in lager during the walk-on and endured the kind of hospitality once reserved for Eric Bristow when he ventured north of the border to play Jocky Wilson.

'After I beat him at Ally Pally, Gary said something like, "Wait till he comes up on to my turf" and the crowd took it too far,' says 'Jackpot'. 'Maybe they should have put us on first, not last, when the crowd hadn't had so much to drink. It didn't help that PSV Eindhoven had just knocked Rangers out of Europe that night, so some of them were in a bad mood already, but it was a bit wild.

'A few coins whacked us a few times, but fortunately I was carrying a fair amount of podge back then so they bounced off me, but they could have hit Gary or the officials as well. At one point I said if one more effing coin hits me, I'm walking off. I beat Gary 8-3, but it was my worst experience in the Premier League by far. He beat me in the play-off final a couple of months later, though.'

Guiding Lewis through the rapids at the time was his former manager Deller, an ex-World Champion who stunned Bristow with a 138 checkout in the final set to win the BDO world title in 1983. His insight into the making of a champion is compelling.

'I took on Ade when he was No.6 in the world and his mother asked me to manage him,' says Deller. 'There was no questioning his talent – that was already there in abundance – but I told him, "You are going to have to change a few things if you want to reach the top."

'Some of them were only minor, but often it's only the rough edges that make the difference between champions and contenders. For instance, he used to almost run down the walkway like a contestant from the audience on *The Price Is Right* (a hit ITV game show hosted by Bruce Forsyth in the 1990s) and I told him to slow down because he was sending out the wrong message to his opponent. Instead of looking them in the eye, and showing he meant business, he was this bundle of energy. He was also too easy-going and chatty in the practice room. I wanted him to change his attitude and be more ruthless.

'He would pitch up three hours before a tournament and sit in the practice room chatting away to other players. He would say he was only talking to his mates but I said to him, "If they all had big families and asked if they could come and stay with you for a month, would you let them all move in with you?" When he said no, of course not, I replied, "In that case, they aren't your mates, are they?"

'Concentration was a natural weakness and it needed fine-tuning, so even if I was working for Sky Sports (as a spotter in the production truck), I would come into the players' room 45 minutes before he was due on stage and tell him, "Right, I don't want you talking to anyone" and I used to set him targets: ten throws to score 100-plus with each set, then with 20 minutes to go it was 301 with eight darts, then 201 with five darts – and you knew he was on it when he hit them for fun.

'On the night of his first World Championship final against Gary Anderson, I walked in at 6.40pm and told Ade to hit five 170 checkouts to sharpen his mind. He went treble 20, treble 20, bull; treble 20, treble 20, bull; treble 20, treble 20, bull. Bang, bang, bang, just like that. I said he would hit a nine-darter in the final and guess what? He produced one in the opening set. Gary was sitting there watching and he probably wanted to talk, but I said "You are not going anywhere near him – normally in the practice room he's your mate, but tonight he's the guy who wants to take £200,000 off you. Have a beer with him later if you want, but there are no friends here until the show's over. Right now, he's the enemy."

'Adrian Lewis is one of the most naturally gifted players ever to throw a dart, and although he could have gone on to win two or three more world titles, for me he's still in the top ten of all time.

'If you put together his ability with Phil Taylor's mentality – that tunnel vision that turned Phil into a serial winner – you'd have one hell of a player on your hands, but Ade always had a short fuse and he was easily distracted.

'That's not to say he couldn't play. For two or three years, he was awesome. We all knew he was a great talent but we had to toughen him up mentally to get the best out of him. It's no good being mates with everyone in the practice room if they are going to pick your pocket on stage.'

From his vantage point on the outside, during his extended break from the professional circuit, Lewis admired the expansion of darts as an industry and how the rewards had increased in a mushroom cloud of proliferation.

He says the proportion of women and children, many of them in replica tops in homage to their favourite players, who attend exhibition nights is 'brilliant to see'. But he observes pointedly: 'Have the standards gone up that much? I'm not sure about that – it's more about the depth. There are so many players out there who can average 105. If you put together a top ten to play in the Premier League, the next batch of ten would be almost as strong.'

In an age of plentiful prize money, hitting the jackpot on a one-armed bandit in Las Vegas would be more like topping up your pension than a start-up fund. Strictly for over-21s, of course.

A legend departs: Dennis Priestley is applauded off by opponent Paul Nicholson after his 4-2 defeat in the third round at Alexandra Palace in the 2009 PDC World Championship
(Photo: Lawrence Lustig/PDC)

'The Power' and the glory: Phil Taylor celebrates his crushing 7-1 win against Raymond van Barneveld in the 2009 PDC World Championship final (Photo: Lawrence Lustig/PDC)

Words of wisdom: John Part won world titles at three different venues in his 20s, 30s and 40s – now he's a hugely respected TV commentator and pundit on Sky Sports (Photo: Taylor Lanning/PDC)

Sudden death: Raymond van Barneveld has just beaten Phil Taylor in the 2007 final at the Circus Tavern – next stop for the PDC World Championship is Alexandra Palace (Photo: Lawrence Lustig/PDC)

Pleased as punch: Adrian Lewis won back-to-back world titles in 2011 and 2012 after a hard-luck story in Las Vegas generated his 'Jackpot' nickname (Photo: Lawrence Lustig/PDC)

Green machine: Michael van Gerwen's top was a symbol of sporting greatness, like an All Blacks rugby shirt or the leader's Yellow Jersey on the Tour de France (Photo: Taylor Lanning/PDC)

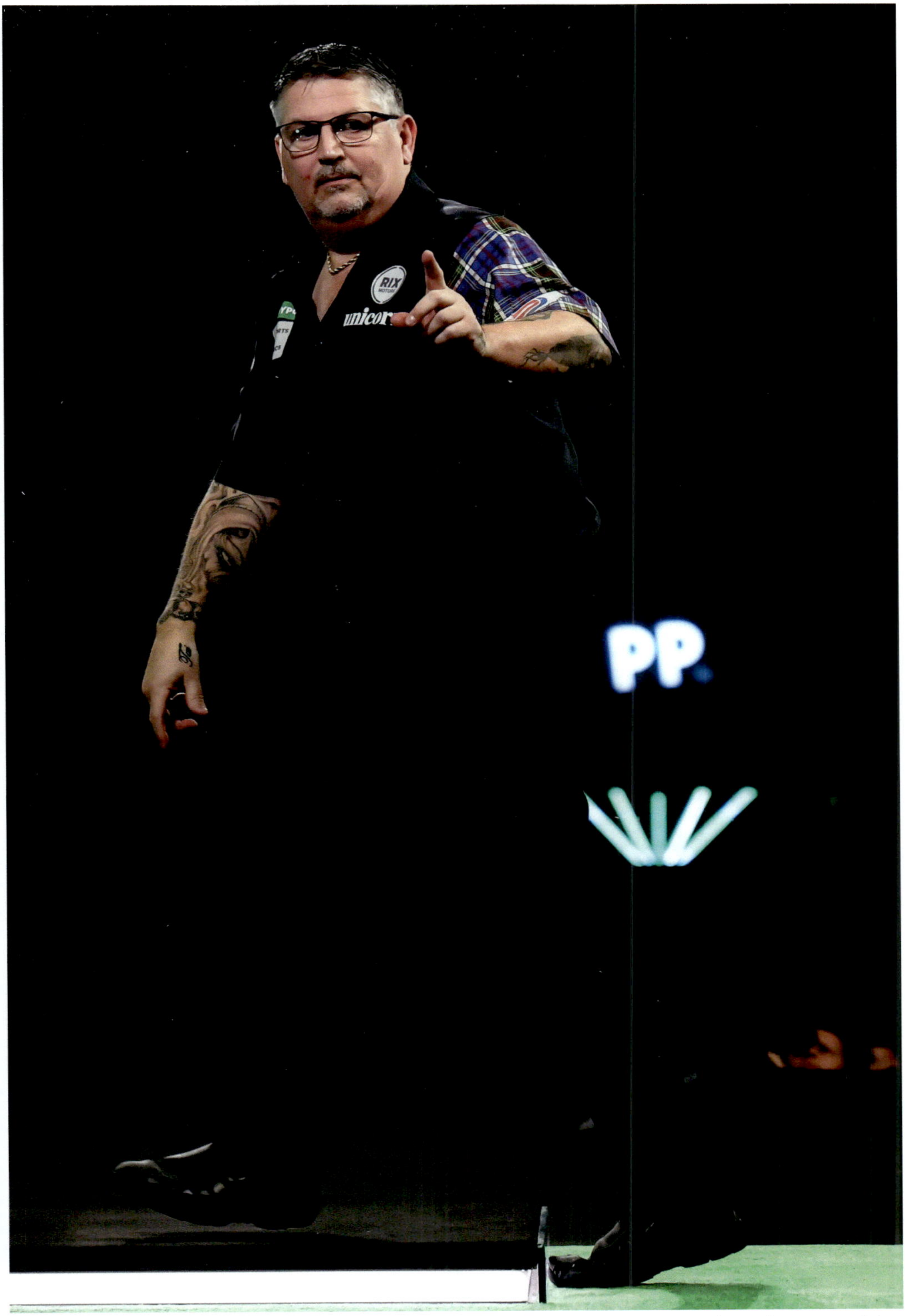

A different kettle of fish: Gary Anderson owns private fishing lakes in Somerset where the carp weigh up to 25lbs, but his biggest catch was the PDC World Championship trophy – twice
(Photo: Taylor Lanning/PDC)

Fuse a clever boy, then? Rob Cross was an electrician before his shock 2018 World Championship triumph and (below) with PDC president Barry Hearn

Snake charmer: Peter Wright is overcome with emotion after pinning double 10 to win his first World Championship title in 2020, beating Michael van Gerwen in the final
(Photo: Taylor Lanning/PDC)

The sky's the limit: Gerwyn Price glances towards the heavens, in memory of his late mother, following his triumph behind closed doors at Ally Pally in 2021 (Photo: Taylor Lanning/PDC)

Sweet dreams: Michael Smith takes the Sid Waddell Trophy to bed after becoming PDC World Champion in 2023 (Photo: Taylor Lanning/PDC)

The shower and the glory: It's raining tickertape as Luke Humphries celebrates beating Luke Littler in the 2024 final – the most-watched darts match in Sky Sports history (Photo: Taylor Lanning/PDC)

Who do you think you are kidding, Mr Littler? Luke 'The Nuke' Littler was a two-time World Champion at 18 and reached another final at 16 – one of sport's greatest teenage achievers Photo: Taylor Lanning/PDC)

Stick it in the family album: 'Bully Boy' Michael Smith rushes to embrace his family in the crowd after his world title success (top); and Luke Littler is joined on stage by father Anthony (right), mum Lisa (left) and brother Leon, for a snap with the trophy (Photos: Taylor Lanning/PDC)

Sealed with a kiss: Peter 'Snakebite' Wright and wife Jo, his manager and hair stylist, after his second world title in three years in 2022 (top); and Luke Humphries' father, Mark, gets up close and personal with double eight after his son's winning dart hit the spot in 2024 (Photos: Taylor Lanning/PDC)

Eyes on the prize: Phil Taylor is a study of concentration (Photo: Lawrence Lustig/PDC)

Stardust: Peter Wright, in full 'Snakebite' regalia, and 16-times World Champion Phil Taylor shake on it (Photo: Lawrence Lustig/PDC)

MICHAEL VAN GERWEN

PDC World Champion: 2014, 2017, 2019

PULL UP a bar stool, top up your glass and let's put our house in order.

The greatest darts player of all time is Phil Taylor, right? Numerically, his 16 World Championship titles and 87 majors are unlikely ever to be surpassed.

And to date, the most talented darts player of all time is surely Luke Littler – agreed? To win two PDC World Championships by the age of 18, and reach another final at 16, is not just precocious talent running riot: it's outrageous flair, an unprecedented affirmation of youth.

But for 2,559 days, from New Year's Day in 2014 to 3 January 2021, when Michael van Gerwen enjoyed an unbroken run as No.1 in the Professional Darts Corporation Order of Merit, he was unstoppable, unplayable.

He doesn't blow his own trumpet where a whole brass band is available to deliver the fanfares and Van Gerwen admits he may not be the GOAT, but he is arguably the BOAT (Best

Of All Time) because peak MVG would have been unbeatable in any era.

From the moment he unseated reigning champion Taylor in the play-off final to win his first Premier League title in 2013, until his third World Championship conquest six years later at Alexandra Palace, Van Gerwen was the Dutchman dubbed 'Clog Almighty'. In a competitive sense, he brutalised opponents with heavy scoring and his quickfire delivery never gave them a moment's respite. Few players, if any, could live with him.

For all Taylor's precision, for all Littler's nerveless adolescence, nobody ran amok on a dartboard like Van Gerwen. And he wasn't just the most destructive player on the planet – he was the most intimidating. It was almost as if the sight of his semi-fluorescent green shirt melted his challengers' resistance.

Think of the All Blacks performing the Haka before unleashing battering ram Jonah Lomu on a rampage down the wing. Think of Tiger Woods on the first tee before the final round of The Masters, always in a blood-red shirt, a tradition often described as his 'Sunday Red' because his mother, Kutilda, believed it was his 'power colour'. Think of the Tour de France champion's fabled maillot jaune (Yellow Jersey), sport's ultimate statement of power and endurance. For the best part of a decade, Van Gerwen's lime-green top intimidated opponents halfway towards submission before a dart was thrown. In the Netherlands, his dress code was almost as famous as the national football team's sacrosanct orange strip.

In 2025, he switched to a predominantly black shirt with Shrek-green trim, but the psychology of his 'Green Machine' persona was never lost on MVG.

'I don't think opponents are intimidated by me now,' he admits. 'But sometimes when they arrived on stage and saw my green shirt waiting for them, mentally they were one leg behind already.

'The green shirt will always be part of me, part of my story. Everyone knows me for the colour of my shirt. Sometimes I would walk down the street and strangers would walk past me before turning back and saying, "Sorry, I didn't recognise you without your darts shirt." I didn't set out to wear green – it's not even my favourite colour. I prefer blue, but early on in my career, I wore a green shirt and it felt comfortable, so I decided to stick with it.

'Of course, maybe it's different when my shirt is black, but they are still playing the same opponent. I know people are waiting for me, and I know I always have a target on my back, but I enjoy winning. If you asked any of the top players who they wanted to avoid meeting in a big tournament, who is the biggest problem for them, they would have said it's me. And if they didn't, they were lying.

'They know I'm here to win. I'm not a happy to be a runner-up when the other guy walks away with a trophy and you get one half the size. I'm a winner, simple as that. I always believed I would become a World Champion, for as long as I can remember. I always believed I could do it. That's what champions do – they believe in themselves.

'It didn't happen as soon as I would have liked. In my first final against Phil (in 2013), I was 2-0 ahead then 4-2 up, and I missed darts to make it 5-2, the same as Luke (Littler) in his first World Championship final.'

Taylor went on to win 7-4, claiming the last of his 16 World Championship titles at the age of 52, but the disappointment only hardened Van Gerwen's conviction that his accession to the throne had only been postponed, not terminated.

'It's hard when you lose a big final, but it makes you humble,' he says. 'Maybe you have to go through something like that to learn how to be a great champion afterwards. You learn to be hungry, you learn how to be ruthless. If you have the chance to win, you must take it. Always an important lesson. That's hard to do, trying to become a winner. You first need to know what it's like to lose before you can win something, and maybe it's the same in life as well.

'The way I look at it is that Phil is the greatest of all time – but I am the best of all time. It's not possible to become the greatest ever because I cannot win 16 world titles, but at my best, yeah, I think my level is hard to reach.'

Once he had his first major title in the bag, Van Gerwen's absolute domination of the PDC circuit was as easy to forecast as blizzards in the Antarctic or sandstorms in the Sahara. We knew the changing of the guard was coming, but the manner in which Taylor was bundled from his sentry post was mind-boggling in its abruptness.

On a stunningly prophetic night in Liverpool, just 37 days after he had beaten Peter Wright 7-4 to lift his maiden World Championship title at the age of 24 – then the youngest player to wear the PDC crown – Van Gerwen began his defence of the Premier League with a merciless 7-0 demolition of Taylor. 'The Power' had just returned from a three-week detox camp at a Portuguese spa resort, shedding three stone on an all-juice diet backed up by ten miles of walking a day. Although Taylor looked trim, the break briefly appeared to diminish the 'snap' in his throw, and where he seemed to be lobbing cocktail sticks into a headwind, Van Gerwen was ramming his darts into the target like spears from Rorke's Drift.

Taylor suffered the only whitewash of his Premier League career, and MVG recalls: 'I was also the first one to beat Phil 3-0 in sets. I was only 17 at the time.' Van Gerwen, who decorated that feat at the 2007 Masters of Darts in the Netherlands by clinching victory with a 164 checkout on bullseye, adds: 'But that was only the beginning.'

In his debut season among the Premier League elite, Van Gerwen became the first player other than Taylor to finish top of the table, ending his eight-year reign at the summit. He won the tournament five times, and reached the play-off final twice, in his first seven years on the Thursday night carousel. The following year, 2014, he won four TV majors including the blue riband event at Alexandra Palace; in 2015, the harvest was seven premier events; in 2016 he hoovered up nine of the big prizes. Only a stupendous third-round defeat by compatriot Raymond van Barneveld in the third round at Ally Pally denied him a clean sweep of all the individual premier events on TV in a 12-month cycle.

And his astonishing 123.40 average against Michael Smith in the Premier League, a record on TV, was early rocket fuel in his remarkable 45-match winning streak in the majors. Van Gerwen was indomitable, apparently impregnable, and in a single calendar year his domination of the PDC circuit yielded 25 titles and £1.5 million prize money in 2016, winning 91 per cent of all his competitive matches.

Inevitably, his imperious form spilled over into a second World Championship triumph in the opening bars of 2017 – or, as the *Daily Mirror* put it, after Hogmanay came Clogmanay.

Like all great champions, Van Gerwen never took his success for granted. He would often reflect on the fallow years when his rich promise was in danger of withering on the vine after switching to the PDC from the British Darts Organisation roster in 2007. 'Of course I can remember, I had too many [difficult times]. I had moments where I was better than 90 per cent of the field, but I also lost to 90 per cent of the field,' he told Sky Sports. 'You need to ask, "What am I doing wrong? Where can I improve? What can I do to change things around?" I also had a couple of years like a beginner because I wasn't confident and I couldn't win a tournament. But you need to try and change that around. You need your opponents to look up to you, not the other way around. If you look up to someone, you fear them.

'Of course it's nice when people from other walks of life recognise what you do. Ronnie O'Sullivan, what he said about me in one interview was fantastic. He called me the greatest sportsman on earth, and that's a big compliment. He's probably the most dominant snooker player, and the best of all time. He can hit a 147 with his right or left hand. But if you only listen to the praise, it doesn't make you a better player. You have to listen to the criticism as well, and I am my own biggest critic. Talent doesn't disappear or go away overnight, but it's not enough on its own. If you want success, you have to fight for it. You must work for it.'

As if to underline his mutual appreciation of sporting celebrity from another orbit, pride of place in Van Gerwen's office at home in Vlijmen is a signed portrait of Roger Federer, the tennis player he regards as the greatest of all time even if Novak Djokovic and Rafael Nadal, statistically, have won more Grand Slam tournaments. At his best, the Fed Express was incomparable for style and grace; even when his backhand misfired, and the Swiss master became Basel Faulty, there was a poetic quality to his skills.

With the greatest respect, nobody would compare Federer's elegance with Van Gerwen's gurning, chest-beating, fist-pumping or roars of celebration when he lands a big double, but they shared a key facet of success: at the peak of their powers, they were untouchable.

In isolation, a mere chronology of MVG's 2,559-day reign as world No.1 only scratches the surface of greatness. It included an astonishing sequence of winning 28 consecutive last-leg deciders – on a heads-or-tails basis, professors and anoraks of mathematics reckon the odds of that happening are one in 250 million. But after he landed his first PDC major title at the 2012 World Grand Prix, beating Mervyn King 6-4 in the final (having trailed 4-1), greatness visited him quickly.

The following month, he reached the Grand Slam of Darts final, where it took Van Barneveld's rage against the fading light of youth to deny him – MVG only lost 16-14, but he was never ahead in the contest – before progressing to his first World Championship final six weeks later, when Taylor scaled his Everest for the last time. It would be their only meeting in an Ally Pally final as the contortions of fate, and Taylor confronting the sunset, kept them apart on the biggest stage thereafter.

Even as runner-up, Van Gerwen had still managed to provide the tournament's stand-out moment – 17 consecutive perfect arrows in his semi-final win against James Wade, following a nine-darter by narrowly missing double 12 for back-to-back perfect legs. It would have blown the roof off Ally Pally if that last dart had found its target, but to unfurl such nerveless bravado in a World Championship semi-final was simply extraordinary.

Soon enough, Van Gerwen's timeline would be littered with finals and trophy lifts. There is not a single PDC Premier event he has not won at least twice – not bad for a player who was still working two days a week as a tiler when he was 18. By the time his winning streak was at full tilt, every week seemed to bring him a night on the tiles in a different sense.

In the early days of his rise to prominence, apocryphal tales appeared that he had tiled Dutch football legend Dennis Bergkamp's bathroom. There was, in reality, only a grain of truth to the story – if you count pollen seeds transferred on the wind as grains of truth.

'I did the tiling at a house across the road from Bergkamp,' he says. 'Sure, it was a very posh area and we had to make sure we did a really good job on it. You don't want to mess up when you are working for a legend like Bergkamp, but I was never working at his actual house. It belonged to somebody else. When I was fitting those tiles, I never thought I would be a millionaire by the time I was 24, but it proved that if you work hard and do well at the major tournaments, you can make a good living out of being a professional darts player. I don't think I would have been this rich if I had worked as a tiler until I was 70.'

As his star continued to rise, Van Gerwen's appearance was likened, by one writer in the *Guardian*, to 'a bulldog kissing a wasp'. In the upholstered sewers of social media, flattery was in short supply again when others compared him with animated ogre Shrek or Uncle Fester from the *Addams Family*.

The bulldog analogy strikes a chord with him because it was, he reveals, an early contender for his stage nickname. 'When I started playing competitions, my first nickname was 'The Bulldog' before I became 'Mighty Mike'. I found out someone else was already called 'The Bulldog', so I had to find another one. When I was younger, I had a scooter and my cousin called me Mighty Mouse after the cartoon character. He said, "Why don't you change it to 'Mighty Mike?'" I thought, "That's quite good, so 'The Bulldog' had to go." From then on, it was 'Mighty Mike', 100 per cent.'

From the night he found the antidote to 'Snakebite' Wright's venom to land his first World Championship, Mighty Mike went from strength to strength. Van Gerwen had trailed Gary Anderson 3-1 in the third round, but he summoned a fightback to win 4-3, a result which still rankled with the 'Flying Scotsman' more than a decade later. He saw off former BDO Lakeside champion Mark Webster 5-3, whitewashed an out-of-sorts Adrian Lewis 6-0 in the semi-finals and his triumph in the final lifted him to No.1 on the PDC ladder.

Although 'Barney' denied his countryman in the Premier League play-off final and Taylor, recovering his form after his juice-fuelled detox, averaged an impressive 107.27 to claim his 15th World Matchplay crown, and seventh on the bounce, at Van Gerwen's expense in Blackpool, MVG's career was gaining irresistible momentum. Among the PDC's constellation of talents, he was the shooting star. And those seven years at the top of the charts, a longer run at No.1 than Band Aid, was the proof.

Professional Darts Corporation president Barry Hearn, who orchestrated the sport's explosion from a peripheral curiosity to a ratings winner drawing bigger audiences on Sky Sports than any other programmes bar Premier League football, watched Van Gerwen's rise to seize Taylor's throne.

Hearn always contended that it was too easy for dystopian critics to sneer at darts, and the challenge had been to package it as a legitimate, mainstream sport while the punters were having a party and TV viewers were transfixed by easy-to-follow drama. What he needed, to verify his product, was sporting excellence and characters with whom the paying spectator could identify. Eric Bristow's 'Crafty Cockney' charm wasn't to everyone's taste, but he caught your attention – and Taylor's gift for raising the bar for almost 30 years was vital for the credibility of darts until Van Gerwen announced himself in 50 shades of green.

In his autobiography *My Life*, Hearn wrote: 'In the end, however good you are, the pack will close in on you. It happened to Steve Davis, to Stephen Hendry (in snooker) and, in the end, to Phil. Michael and a host of other great players were hunting him down and putting in the hours that Phil used to put in.

'Suddenly there was a new kid on the block – Van Gerwen. He struggled for a while and was only ranked 38th in the world at the start of the 2012 season. By the end of 2013, he had started winning events and from that point he never really looked back. Michael is living proof that if you have the ability, you can achieve your dreams. He is one of the darts players capable of annual earnings in excess of £2 million.'

When Van Gerwen hit that record televised three-darts average of 123.40, Hearn observed that Bristow used to win BDO World Championships with averages in the high 80s. He said: 'That is a testament to the improvement in standards at the top, thanks largely to the great flag-bearer, Phil Taylor and, more recently, to the likes of Van Gerwen.'

Should MVG have won more World Championship titles? Yes – between 2013 and 2025, he lost more finals (against Taylor, Peter Wright, Michael Smith and Luke Littler) than he won, and either side of the COVID-19 pandemic he explored some exotic ways to get knocked out at Alexandra Palace, some of them beyond his control and others beyond belief.

In 2016, Van Gerwen lost a pulsating third round contest 4-3 against Van Barneveld despite posting a 105.78 average – then the highest losing average in PDC World Championship history – although the roles were reversed in the semi-finals

12 months later, when 'Barney' posted a formidable 109.34 and still lost 6-2 in another double-Dutch classic.

Then, when the Covid plague bared its teeth in a deadly second wave in December 2020, much of mainland Europe threatened to close its borders with Britain by severing rail and road links through the Channel Tunnel. Van Gerwen, who had only just returned home to spend Christmas with his family in Holland after safely negotiating his second-round booby-trap against Ryan Murray, had to turn round two hours later and race back to the Channel ports to beat the blockade. His dash to catch Le Shuttle before the shutters came down was initially rewarded with a comfortable whitewash of Ricky Evans and a memorable white-knuckle ride against Joe Cullen, who missed two match darts at bullseye, before he walked headlong into the most inspired night of Dave Chisnall's career.

Out of nowhere, 'Chizzy' – who had never won a TV major – procured an incredible 5-0 wipeout of the hot favourite in the quarter-finals with a 107.34 average. No disrespect, but it wasn't just the proverbial rabbit from a hat: Chisnall's outrageous heist was like concealing the entire population of *Watership Down* inside his trousers. It was a sensational upset.

PDC bosses had advised overseas players to remain in London over Christmas to avoid being caught out by Covid travel restrictions, but Van Gerwen could not have envisaged his screeching U-turn, nor the firestorm of Chizzy's arrows heading his way – and providence was unkind to him again at Ally Pally the following year.

In line with tournament rules, the 'Green Machine' withdrew from his third-round tie against Chris Dobey after a lateral flow test returned the dreaded two red bars, confirming he had tested positive for COVID-19. Fellow Dutchman Vincent van der Voort and Chisnall were also forced to abandon their crusades after contracting the virus, while 'Barney' – who had lost 3-1 to Rob Cross in the second round – reported developing a fever and shortness of breath after the match, although he felt fine during the contest. Sure enough, he tested positive and spent Christmas in self-isolation in London.

Van der Voort and another Dutch player had joined Van Gerwen for a festive meal on Christmas Eve, with two of them reporting positive tests and forced to isolate in their hotel. Asked what went through his mind when he saw his positive test result, MVG shrugged: 'I wasn't really sick or anything. Nothing whatsoever. Everything goes through your mind, I am not going to lie, but I decided to withdraw myself, simple.

'I was more annoyed because I was playing well and I knew I had a chance to win it. That's what hurts. I made a decision, I did it with a clear mind and you need to stand behind your decision.'

As if Van Gerwen had not already invented enough ways not to win a World Championship when he was the pundits' choice and bookmakers' likely lad, his bull-in-a-china-shop charge to the 2023 final against 'Bully Boy' Smith looked destined to end in triumph, only for him to become the best supporting actor in the greatest leg of darts ever played.

Leading 1-0 and with the second set in the balance at 1-1, Van Gerwen speared eight perfect darts into the board before the decisive double 12 for a ninth escaped, by the width of a toothpick, the wrong side of the wire. Incredulously, ridiculously, Smith then stepped up to complete his own nine-darter, and the audacity of his opportunism inspired a 7-4 win, his first world title following earlier defeats in the final by Wright and Van Gerwen.

But enough of a great champion's dignity in the face of hard-luck stories. Van Gerwen's career is defined by success, not counting the cost of adversity. His journey from the 13-year-old who parked his dreams as a robust footballer and began to throw darts, with conspicuous accuracy, to one of the Netherlands' most decorated sportsmen is littered far more by trophy-lifts and triumph than disappointments.

One of his finest moments was his third World Matchplay title in 2022. Just six weeks after undergoing surgery on the wrist of his throwing arm to treat carpal tunnel syndrome, a common neurological condition caused by compression of a median nerve leading to numbness and a tingling sensation in the thumb and first three fingers, he beat Gerwyn Price 18-14 in the final. He had gone into the tournament wondering if his throwing action would be compromised irrevocably by the operation.

'I wasn't 100 per cent ready, so I can't really complain about the way it turned out,' he says. 'Tournaments like the World Matchplay are more suitable if you are recovering from an injury because you play one night and then get a day off. If you play the ProTour, you play so many games across so many hours in a single day, and I wouldn't have been ready for that. It's why I went on holiday to prepare – I know, from my practice, that when I played a lot it started to get itchy. It was a big risk for me to play, of course, but I didn't have a choice, I had to get the surgery done or I could have been left with permanent wrist damage – and as a darts player, you don't want to cause that for yourself.'

If the mid-2020s were lean years by his lofty standards, Van Gerwen's biggest 'win' was to come through 18 months of gruelling dental surgery to re-align his teeth. Three operations to remedy a troublesome overbite, which involved doctors breaking both jaws, extraction of teeth, wearing braces and daily painkillers are enough to make your eyes water just listening to his explanation of the process. Living through it, and still being able to focus on targets the size of an insect, sounds almost superhuman when he goes into the gory detail and the effects on his bite, breathing and even his sleep.

Speaking in 2024, he said: 'They are going to break and re-set my upper and lower jaw. My upper jaw they are going to take out six millimetres forward, and my lower jaw they are going to put back just three millimetres. I have a big underbite, a penny bowl, as they call it. That bothers me a lot. With eating, your teeth also wear down and you snore more because of it.

'Even a slice of ham, I cannot even bite properly. Things like a steak or a crispy baguette are out of the question. And because my upper jaw is too small also you get less oxygen through your nose. That creates headaches, less sleep, things like that. You have to plan things, especially with my schedule. I can still eat, but you bite wrongly. You don't eat how you should eat. It's the same as the year before with my carpal tunnel syndrome. It (the surgery) had to happen. There are no other options. For me, it's not really a big thing.

'Anyone who's ever had root canal treatment at the dentist, and knows what that feels like, I can tell you that this is a little boy compared to what I went through. Given everything that's happened, sometimes I do underestimate that. I think to myself, "Why am I so hard on myself all the time?" But that's the way I am.'

If smiling, or grimacing, through the pain of physical hardship became a recurring mark of Van Gerwen's steel, a trait which earned him colossal respect beyond the practice room, his winning mentality never wavered.

From the moment he discovered rocket thrust on the gearbox, the trail he blazed was littered with preposterous numbers.

In a Championship League whitewash of Steve Beaton in 2012, he averaged 121.86; in the same year, he ended a 15-

game losing streak against Taylor at the Grand Slam of Darts with a 108.38 going rate, a performance he described at the time as the best of his career; in his next match, against Scott Waites, he nailed two 170 'big fish' checkouts, and the huge numbers kept coming. At full throttle, MVG's scoring power was not just on another level: he was bringing a Ferrari to the starting grid where others were rolling up in a Nissan Micra.

That 109.59 average to whitewash Taylor 7-0 in just 13 minutes for his opening statement of the 2014 Premier League was not a flash in the pan. It was the shape of things to come. In the European Championship, he averaged 111 over 15 legs in his quarter-final win against Dave Chisnall, and the bar kept rising:

114.05 – his 2017 semi-final takedown of Van Barneveld was the highest average in World Championship history.

115.19 – Over a comparatively short distance (a 5-2 win in the group phase), Van Gerwen's performance against Joe Cullen at the Grand Slam in 2021 was a tournament record.

118.52 – Another competition record, this time with Ross Smith on the receiving end at the 2023 Players Championship finals. MVG would go on to lose 11-9 in the final against Luke Humphries, but only after seasoning the pot with a nine-darter.

123.40 – His televised record average against Michael Smith in the 2016 Premier League, shattering the 118.66 set by Taylor six years earlier, was from another solar system. Fun fact: Van Gerwen missed three shots at double 18 for a median in excess of 133. 'This is ridiculous, absolutely ridiculous,' stammered Sky Sports commentator Wayne Mardle. 'We expect players to reel off two, three, four (exceptional) legs, but this is incredible – the finest darts we've witnessed anywhere… the greatest darts ever seen. This is like breaking the 100 metres world record by two seconds.'

Van Gerwen's pre-eminence, on the night he secured his second World Championship title at Alexandra Palace in 2017, earned him a personal accolade from Dutch Prime Minister Mark Rutte – more recently secretary general of NATO – in the aftermath of his 7-3 win in the final against Gary Anderson. Midway through his post-match media conference, MVG took a congratulatory call from Mr Rutte.

After the conversation, Van Gerwen revealed: 'He asked me if I could have imagined, ten years ago, sitting here having won my second world title. Did I vote for him? No – but he's still a very nice man.'

A politician hitching himself to a champion's bandwagon was not the only person to interrupt the great man's memorable night. As Van Gerwen prepared an ill-starred attempt to take out 115 for the title, a spectator emerged from the crowd, clambered on to the stage and tried to lift the Sid Waddell Trophy from its plinth on the stage before being bundled away by security. Clog Almighty went on to lose that ninth set, delaying his tickertape shower and his clean sweep of TV titles. 'Even after winning 25 tournaments in 2016, it would have been my worst nightmare to leave here empty-handed,' he admitted. 'I have fought so hard for this and now I have a full set of the major trophies, but this is the one that matters most of all.'

A known internet prankster from a group responsible for previous stunts, including pitch invasions at Tottenham Hotspur football matches and an unscheduled stage appearance at ITV's X *Factor* singing competition, was soon unmasked as the social inadequate who desecrated Van Gerwen's big moment. It's a good job the interloper did not attempt his tedious antics on the night when Prince Harry made an appearance at Ally Pally in 2011. Royal protection squads would not have stood on ceremony and waited to find out the prankster's next move before intervening.

A late-night chat with the Prime Minister was by no means the end of Van Gerwen's cabaret. The following month, in February 2017, he became only the second player in history (after Phil Taylor at the Premier League play-off final in 2010) to hit two nine-dart finishes in the same match. The World Champion completed twin perfect legs in his 6-2 win against Ryan Murray in a Coral UK Open third-round qualifier in Wigan – after surviving two match darts to scrape through the previous round 6-5 against Adam Hunt.

A rugby league town famous for its Wigan Pier – which was, in fact, a coal-loading wharf, not a seaside promenade – is among the PDC's unglamorous venues for floor tournaments, but Van Gerwen was now making hay at every opportunity as well as being feted back home in Holland.

'I know people are waiting for me, I know I am now the one with a target on my back, but I enjoy winning and I am enjoying being World Champion again,' he said. 'I was taken on a lap of honour around the PSV Eindhoven ground, which was something special because things like that don't normally happen to someone like me. They even baked me a special MVG cake. It looked a bit ugly, but it tasted good.'

The year 2017 would also serve as a punctuation mark in Van Gerwen's life when he became a father for the first time and daughter Zoe was born. A son, Mike, would follow two years later. There was no obvious decline in his hunger, in a fierce competitor's appetite for winning titles and prize money, and a third World Championship garland in 2019 suggested the fire burned as brightly as ever. But turning the corner into parenthood was nonetheless a significant marker buoy as he navigated the rapids of work/life balance.

In a revealing interview with Donald McRae in the *Guardian*, in December 2025, MVG hinted at a sea change in attitude which, at face value, may have tamed the all-conquering beast's ferocious winning mentality – and no self-respecting father would think any less of him for it.

Speaking after going through divorce, following 17 years with his ex-wife Daphne, and witnessing the devastating ravages of cancer on his father, Henri, he said: 'It has made me understand what's most important in life. It has to be family. Of course, I love darts but I love my kids much more. Before, when I didn't have kids, it was easier. Darts was always my number one. Then, when I had kids, darts was not my number one anymore. You have to try to balance things a little better.'

Taylor held the previous record for the longest run as world No.1, but as McRae pointed out, the lengthiest of his eight stints at the summit was still more than 500 days shorter than Van Gerwen's epic seven-year reign. Taylor was so driven that, by his own admission, he didn't often allow family commitments to curtail his insatiable hunger for success.

'I spoke with Phil about it and he fell out (with his family) sometimes because he always put darts as No.1,' said Van Gerwen. 'I think if you now ask Phil, "Would you do it differently?" he might say yes. My priorities changed 100 per cent, straight away. I think it should. It would be weird if that wasn't the situation.'

Did fatherhood remove that ruthless edge from Van Gerwen's game? On a sporting level, it's a legitimate question. Between 2020-25 he won nine premier PDC titles – by no means a slouch, and more than any other player over the same period. But during the previous six-year window, from 2014-19, he had carried off 37 major trophies.

'Maybe, I don't know,' he says. 'It did change my mindset. Darts was not the most important thing in my life anymore, and if that's the reason I didn't win so often as before, then I accept it. I have no reason to apologise for it. I'm still capable of winning more tournaments, I haven't gone away yet. I'm not going to retire yet, not for a few years.

'And I feel I will always be involved in darts because it's all I've known in my adult life. One day I will decide when I'm going to play and where I'm going to play instead of other people deciding for me and I don't have to follow the whole tour. I'm not sure I see myself becoming a coach or a consultant because I'm a different thinker and it wouldn't be fair on the other person if I was telling them what to do. But I wouldn't go back to tiling bathrooms, that's for sure.'

For a man who has lived out adolescence, adulthood, parenthood and sporting greatness largely in the public eye, Van Gerwen is a remarkably equanimous fellow. He has never sought to blame others for his defeats or shortcomings as a player – not that there have been many of them – and when he glances in the rear-view mirror, there are few regrets.

'Why count your regrets if you can count your blessings? As a darts player, I have won everything there is to be won,' he says. 'For sure, I could have won more World Championships – the year I lost against Rob Cross in the semi-final, I missed six match darts and I was sick about that one because I had been playing really well. And the first final, against Phil, I should have won that one as well, but looking back doesn't change anything and looking too far into the future often doesn't help.

'I'm one of those people who always waits to see what comes in my path – you never know what's around the corner, but you end up on the same path, know what I mean? When things have gone wrong, or not gone according to plan, you can't go round blaming other people. You must always start by looking at yourself. Life is not a sprint, it's a marathon, so let me enjoy it doing what I do best, and I'm not asking for anything more.

'If I lost a bit of form during my problem with carpal tunnel syndrome or the surgery on my jaw, I'm not going to cry about it – why would you? Some people might blame the pain or bad feelings, but not me.

'When I was winning, I was doing what I love the most – playing darts at the highest level, and what gives you the most confidence at that level is winning. I have never looked at my accomplishments and said, "Look at me, I did this, I did that" because you are only as good as your last dart. If I play good, that's who I am.

'But I can't lie, sometimes I can be a miserable b******. People don't understand how painful it is when you lose. We all hate losing. When you are standing on a stage with a runner-up trophy, it means you have just lost – and if you don't mind losing, you can't be a great sportsman. I'm not a good actor – I'm sick when I lose.'

In 2018, Van Gerwen was presented with a medal, on behalf of King Willem-Alexander, as a Knight of the Order of Orange-Nassau, the Dutch equivalent of the MBE, the youngest to receive the award. A multiple World Champion by royal appointment.

Back on the bar stools, however, we are probably no closer to settling any arguments definitively. Where peak Taylor beat everyone in his path, and Littler simply dazzled all-comers with his precocity, peak Van Gerwen destroyed them.

What remains beyond dispute, however, is that when Michael van Gerwen marched on stage to his 'Seven Nation Army' anthem, in that radioactive-green top radiating conviction, he conveyed an unrivalled sense of invincibility. He is one of the all-time greats, unquestionably, and his loudest cheerleaders would argue he is the most accomplished purveyor of tungsten bar none.

When his race is run, it won't just feel like the curtain falling on greatness. It will be the end of an aura.

GARY ANDERSON

PDC World Champion: 2015, 2016

GARY ANDERSON belongs to a select club who have hit a nine-dart leg, a hole-in-one on the golf course and a century break at snooker.

But apart from landing the winning dart, and the satisfaction of being a two-time World Champion, now his greatest joy is the sanctuary of two words which often define escapism: Gone fishing.

Anderson owns an idyllic anglers' retreat in rural Somerset, where the big fish is not a 170 checkout but a 25lb carp, but his crowning glory at Alexandra Palace almost turned into a fisherman's hard-luck story of the prize catch that got away.

Thud – treble 20. Thud – another perfect arrow in the treble 20 lipstick. Then, unbelievably, a crash of tungsten, like a bag of spanners falling out of the loft, as his third dart dislodged the first two and they landed in a pile on the floor. 'No score,' called referee Russ Bray in his unmistakably gravel tone.

Anderson retrieved his ammunition scattered on the deck with the look of an aggrieved angler whose catch of the day had escaped as he prepared to pouch it in his landing net.

That was his fate in a World Championship final, with a gripping contest against the legendary Phil Taylor locked at 4-4, when a textbook 180 turned to diddly-squat through an outrageous stroke of ill fortune which would have broken lesser men – especially when 'The Power' stepped up to open with a maximum 180 of his own.

Anderson, however, refused to be consumed by self-pity. Summoning all his 'Bravedart' resistance, he landed the Big One – a maiden World Championship title – in a thrilling final set. Never mind carp, perch or pike, the 'Flying Scotsman' managed to reel in the biggest beast in the lagoon.

He enjoyed it so much that when he returned to Alexandra Palace 12 months later, Anderson was a different kettle of fish to the rest of the field again.

In truth, he has never chased celebrity and would happily run a mile from it, but for the former grate builder who used to get up at 4am to work on fireplaces in Edinburgh for a princely £250-a-week, all rods lead to his fishery these days.

Anderson still considers himself as a 'pub player' as much as a back-to-back World Champion who lifted the Sid Waddell Trophy in 2015 and 2016. When he reached the semi-finals at the age of 55, he was closer to the summit than any player beyond his half-century bar Taylor, who was 57 when he bowed out in his 21st final.

If longevity is the key to respect, Anderson cracked the code eons ago. But he believes his enduring standards with darts in hand have been sustained by his parallel universe as owner and gamekeeper at the Lands End Fishery, which has turned him into a full-time conservationist and rekindled a boyhood love of angling.

From TV stars to sporting distinction, fishing has always been a preferred church for those seeking to switch off the foghorns and impositions of everyday life. Comedians Bob Mortimer and Paul Whitehouse scored a life-affirming hit with a TV series exploring Britain's inland waterways, while the likes of Eric Clapton and Lord Ian Botham are passionate fly fishermen.

And when footballer Paul Gascoigne was hyper in-between games at Euro 96, team-mate David Seaman was instructed by manager Terry Venables to take him fishing to harness his nervous energy. The England goalkeeper's tales from the riverbank include Gazza throwing himself into the water trying to cast his line into the next county and, after helping him clamber out of the water, finding him fast asleep and wet through on the jetty after taking a sleeping pill.

For Anderson, the glorious solitude of one man and his rod is a rare luxury, but he is never happier than sharing his thoughts with nature.

'I would be perfectly happy to be a recluse,' he says. 'I do like the quiet life, and the lakes are like a doctor's prescription: peace and quiet, no traffic, just me and the wildlife. That's what made me buy the place – and the wildlife doesn't answer you back.

'In all, there are four lakes and the whole estate covers about 14 acres. We're open from 8am to 8pm and a day licence costs £10. The odd person moans about paying a tenner to fish for a day, but what else can you do for 12 hours that costs less than a pound an hour? You can't even park your car in most town centres for that. A round of golf, a night at the theatre, going to the football? They will all set you back way more than a tenner.

'If you get a bite, there are some big beasts lurking in the water. I think the biggest catch so far is a 24lb carp, but we're starting to re-stock with more different species and going down the route of smaller fish, so your daily catch may not weigh as much but there's more of them.

'So, yes, I like the quiet life. When I'm out and about, I'll often have a hat on with the peak pulled down over my eyes, so nobody knows who I am. Although I don't get much time to do much fishing myself because maintenance of the lakes is a full-time job in its own right, darts is the last thing on my mind if I'm casting a line into the water and staring into the distance.

'In fact, I hardly think about darts at all when I'm at home, full stop. I don't have time to practise because there's always something on site that needs doing, whether it's strimming the hedgerows, felling trees, checking the water or maintaining paths.

'The only time I really think about darts now is when I walk into a venue, switch into competitive mode and get my game head on. It's been my life for the last 30 years, and I'll be forever grateful for what it's done for me, but I've found something else to think about now. Some of the people closest to me think it's helped to extend my darts career because it's given my mind another avenue to explore, and they may well be right.

'Gone fishing? I leave that to the anglers who come down here. I just try and keep the place ticking over. When I'm running the lakes, I'm not a World Champion – I'm just a ranger, and I like it that way. Being famous, or infamous, whatever you call it, I prefer to stay away from all that and keep in the shadows, to be honest. Stay in the background.

'If I'm not away playing darts, I'm there trying to keep the site in order. When the branches grow and the leaves fall, there's raking and scraping and cutting back to be done. It's a lot of work, but in winter I've learned the hard way not to touch a chainsaw until January.'

When Anderson acquired his corner of fishermen's paradise just months before Covid brought Europe to a standstill, his darts career had been hampered by two years of back problems. Approaching his 50th birthday, there was a sense that he may have crested the hill after reaching three consecutive finals at the World Championship but bowing out to Taylor in the quarter-finals in 2018 and taking only seven legs off Michael van Gerwen in a one-sided semi-final 12 months later.

He was forced to withdraw from the 2019 Premier League through injury, missing the tournament for the first time since 2010, and Anderson, growing weary of living out of a suitcase, began to cut back on his appearances at European Tour events. But a specialist cured his spinal issues, he joined forces with Peter Wright to win the World Cup of Darts for Scotland and his enthusiasm for tungsten combat soon returned.

'I enjoyed the time off. In fact, being at home so much could have destroyed me,' he admits. 'Getting my interest back in playing again was the hardest part. I was always classed as a bit of a lazy player by some because I never really needed to put in the hours that others do, but I was starting to get asked every year if I was going to retire and there was no way I was going to give it up too soon. You're a long time retired.

'People kept telling me it must be a great life on the road as a dart player and, yes, it's great because of what you can make from it as a living. But if you've got a family, it's hard if you're never there. It's a Catch 22 – if you want the lifestyle, you've got to be away winning the prize money and that can cause friction back home if there's no hot water or the electrics are on the blink. And if you're out on the road, living out of a suitcase for weeks and months on end, it's hard going. You miss your family, you miss your kids and it's tough. The top boys now are away for 250 days a year, I don't know how they do it.

'When Covid came round, I'd just bought the lakes, which wasn't great timing and there was a lot to do to get the site in shape. But once the restrictions were lifted, we were just about ready to open and it's been a big part of my life ever since.

'Now, if I go to a tournament and get knocked out, it's nae bother – I get to go home to the family and the lakes. And if I go deep, it's a win-win situation: I go home with a few quid in the bank. I still like playing darts, but if you want to be up there you have to commit 100 per cent to it.

'There are days when I turn up in an empty room (for ProTour events) and wonder what I'm doing, but the fire's still there when I'm on stage. I can't be bothered until my foot lands on that top step and all of a sudden you feel the energy's back. Even if you get knocked out of the first round at a big tournament, it's still a payday and there's another one to aim for in a few weeks. Back in the day at the BDO, if you were on your way home after the first round, you didn't make enough to buy a bag of chips.'

Anderson's renewed love affair with rod, reel, line and bait was down to him sharing accommodation at Ribby Hall, near Preston, with fellow darts player Ian White during the World Matchplay. The holiday village has its own private fishing lake and White, a keen angler, soon reeled in a kindred spirit.

'Yes, it's all Whitey's fault,' laughs Anderson. 'Nah, to be fair I used to fish when I was younger – on the fly rods. Salmon and trout were my thing, but when darts came along, fishing took a back seat for thirty-odd years, probably even longer. When we stayed at Ribby Hall for the Matchplay, I used to share a bungalow with Ian. Like I said, I hadn't fished for years but one morning, when neither of us was playing at the Winter Gardens later that day, he says, "Oh, there's a couple of lakes here, do you fancy a lazy day by the pond?" We ended up doing a bit of fishing, I really enjoyed it and the next year we did the same again.

'We stayed at the same place, had a couple of days fishing, I really got the taste for it, and next thing you know I ended up buying a fishing rig. That's how it all started. I just like being out in the fresh air. Phil Taylor used to own a place at Ribby Hall and base himself up there during the Matchplay. It's obviously got some therapeutic qualities for darts players – he won it 16 times.'

Once his love of rod and reel was rekindled, Anderson set his heart on owning his own fishing empire – and he didn't have to look very far from his West Country base to find it. Set on the edge of the Somerset Levels, midway between the coast at Burnham-on-Sea and the Wookey Hole caves, Lands End Fishery was more than just Anderson's playground. It was the key to longevity at the top end of the Professional Darts Corporation rankings.

Maintenance of the grounds does, however, come with inherent risks. Anderson blamed his shock early exit from the 2025 World Championship, a second-round whitewash at the hands of Jeffrey de Graaf, on a shoulder injury caused by tree-felling, and the lumberjack promised to lay down his chainsaw after an unfortunate case of trunk and disorderly estate management.

Neither the 3-0 scoreline nor his mediocre 92.51 average did Anderson justice – or pull up any trees – at Alexandra Palace, a venue where, as of 2026, only Van Gerwen has won more matches since the tournament moved to N22 in 2007.

'There's always a hell of a lot of work to do at the lakes and when the leaves come down, that's the time we've got to do it,' he told the *Daily Star*, *The Sun* and *Daily Mirror*. 'My buddy helps me out now and again and he goes, "Do not touch a chainsaw until after the Worlds." But I'm saying to him, "We need it done before March." What happened last year? I was trying to cut through a trunk, but I was on my tiptoes with a chainsaw in one hand, stretching above me.

'I knew there was a problem because when we went to London, in the practice room I'm about to throw a dart, and I could not reach the bullseye. That's about as high as I could get the dart to go. I thought, "I'm in trouble here" and I was right. Now I just get on with it – keep the mouth shut and get on with it.'

Anderson never harboured any dreams of being a darts player, let alone becoming the world No.1 as Scotland's greatest conquering 'Bravedart' since Jocky Wilson. As a teenager, he was a summer holiday hustler on the pool table until it put a strain on his pocket money and he fell into the ranks of tungsten marksmen almost by accident.

'The family often stayed in a caravan park on our holidays and I used to play a lot of pool, but when the cost of a game of pool rose from 50p to a quid, which was a lot of money back then, things started to get a bit tight,' he says. 'If you played half a dozen games, it left a big hole in your pocket. There was a set of darts lying around and my mate said, "Come on, let's have a game."

'He had to explain the rules, but with my first nine darts I hit 140, 180 and 140. You can call it beginner's luck or whatever, but his dad came up and asked, "How long have you been playing darts?" I replied, "About 30 seconds" and he signed me up to play darts for his pub team a fortnight later. I didn't even know what I was doing. Didn't have a clue.'

Anderson started using beer mats for target practice, aiming for the 'O' in a brand's messaging, the size of a fingernail, and hitting it for fun. Then he started leaving the doors of his dartboard cabinet ajar, leaving a crack just wide enough for him to hit the treble 20 bed, tops and bullseye down the centre of the board. His sure-fire aim was not manufactured – like the angles of steering balls into the corner pockets on a pool table, accuracy just came naturally, and he has remained faithful to his throw ever since.

Mechanically, it hasn't changed in almost 40 years, apart from a minor adjustment since he began wearing glasses, lowering the point of release so the flights don't catch the frame, but he found it easier than pushing a light switch.

'Making the darts go where I wanted was not a problem,' he says. 'Counting was my biggest embarrassment – and it still is today.'

Growing up, Anderson's only memory of darts was his father cheering on Wilson when the last king of Scotland was playing on TV and Keith Deller shocking Eric Bristow in the 1983 final with his famous 138 checkout.

That beginner's luck soon translated itself into tidy profit on the pub circuit – £500 for winning a tournament on Friday nights, £1,000 a tournament on Saturday nights – a handsome payback on his £2 entry fees, and he was blissfully unaware that the opponents he was beating were county players or internationals on his 'fun night out with the boys'.

Players in the East Berwickshire League, where Anderson cut his teeth on the oche, remember him putting a flight in his glass so none of his pals would drink his pint, an idiosyncrasy which continued with the on-stage water throughout his professional career, but darts wasn't the only game where he excelled.

He's hit a hole in one playing golf on a nine-hole course at Portobello, a coastal suburb of Edinburgh, and his highest break in snooker is 113.

'The golf course is all gone now,' he laments. 'They have built a school there in the park. One of my claims to fame buried in concrete. To be fair, I didn't see it drop – I spent ages looking for the ball and eventually found it in the hole. I knew it was on target from the moment I hit my tee shot, but I didn't know it would be that close.

'And I used to play snooker years ago, but since I developed a large belly, I can't bend over the table. I've got a wee table at home now, which my son Tai plays on. I hit a few centuries back in the day, but I always liked pool. It's a smaller table, easier to get around.'

Anderson's success in the Professional Darts Corporation ranks is at odds with his record in the British Darts Organisation set-up, where he struggled to make an impact at the Lakeside World Championship.

Whether it was the more genteel atmosphere, the relaxed environment of the players' lounge backstage or the dark horses in the field, his performance timeline at Frimley Green was dreadful. Apart from reaching the semi-finals in 2003, and being knocked out two years running by Raymond van Barneveld, some of his vanquishers were barely household names in their own households: Stefan Nagy, Albertino Essers and Fabian Roosenbrand should not have been able to live with

Anderson's scoring power. It was only when he crossed the floor to the PDC that the 'Flying Scotsman' worked up a real head of steam on the big stage.

'I don't know what it was about the Lakeside that didn't agree with me because I lost in the first round five times in eight years at the BDO World Championship,' he says. 'The crowds were always respectful but for whatever reason, I couldn't play on that stage. That was the biggest platform for BDO players, but I never produced my best darts there. Win or lose, every year I used to throw my darts in the lake. Jocky (Wilson) did the same – there will be a few sets of darts in that pond, I can tell you. It became a ritual.

'I probably joined the PDC a year or two later than when I should have made the move. My first major tournament was at the Grand Slam in 2007 when I was still at the BDO – and I got absolute dog's abuse. I went from quiet crowds applauding you at the Lakeside to this verbal rampage, and you know what? I actually liked it. For some reason, I preferred it.'

Anderson's cameo appearance in a Premier League meeting at Cardiff in 2009 was a sign of things to come, beating three-time World Champion John Part 7-4 with a sparkling 107.40 average.

'Wayne Mardle had pulled out with mumps and I was called up as a guest replacement,' he recalls. 'I remember going to the arena with Mark Webster for a look around before they had put out all the table seating on the floor and the stage was still being built, and it was just massive. I thought, "Oh my god, what is this?" I had been used to playing in small halls, so when you find yourself somewhere like that for the first time it blows your mind. Now darts is played all around the world in huge arenas and we're treated like rock stars. If you'd told me 15 years ago that this is where darts was heading, I wouldn't have believed you.'

Initially, Anderson's decision to jump ship was a source of friction. He complained the BDO used to 'promise the world and nothing would change' and, when he finally made the switch, it wasn't universally accepted with good grace.

'A few people stopped talking to me, but if that's how you want to carry on, so be it,' he told referee Huw Ware's *Tops and Tales* podcast. 'But I wanted to go, see what it was like and I wish I had done it sooner.'

Initially, Anderson's reluctance to move to the PDC was fuelled by inane whispering campaigns along the lines of 'You don't want to go over there because they don't pay you.' But in his two Grand Slam campaigns as a BDO player, he had reached the semi-finals on both occasions and he was convinced he could earn a decent crust on the other side of the divide.

'That's why I still love the Grand Slam to this day,' he says. 'My first semi-final was against Phil Taylor and it was a good game, a tight game (13-11), and that's what pushed the buttons for me. It's still my favourite tournament, even though I got dog's abuse that first time. I made the final one year, where

Phil gave me a right battering, and I had only brought enough clothes to last me three or four days because I was playing so poorly. I had to wander into town and buy some new clobber to last me the full week.'

More of Anderson's rise to a hall-of-fame orbit shortly. Before he announced himself as a champion in waiting at the PDC, however, he became a starmaker.

At the suggestion of his manager, Tommy Gilmour, he was assigned to scour the ranks of promising young players and, for the want of a better description, sign them up. Potential is easy to spot in an identity parade of ambitious apprentices, but world-class potential is not so obvious to the uneducated eye.

'Tommy said we needed to get a couple of younger players on the team so I said I'd do a bit of scouting at a junior event and see what we could find,' says Anderson. 'Then I was at an event one day, watching all the darts going in, and my head was scrambled watching all the 180s being scored. I thought, "My god, how do you pick a needle from this haystack?" There were so many to choose from. In the end I pointed at one big lad and decided, "Right, I'm going to have a word with him." It was Michael Smith, and I walked away with two names in the book – Adam Hunt was the other one.

'They were just kids back then. Tommy and the management team looked after them, I was just the babysitter. That's why I've got all the grey hairs now – from looking after Smithy all those years. Nah, but seriously, it was a very proud moment when he went on to win the World title because I'd been saying for years he was going to win it. We had parted company, in terms of management, by then, but he had all the talent in the world and I was only surprised he didn't have it wrapped up earlier than that. It was written in stone that he was going to win the World Championship sooner or later.

'Back then, we all knew how good Michael could be, and he was only going to get better, but how did I know he was World Championship material? I liked the way he went about the game – no fuss, throw your darts, collect them from the board, get out of the way.

'What else are you looking for? Temperament, for a start. I've always said you have to learn how to lose before you learn to win. When I watch kids, I want to see how they react, and sometimes their attitude sucks if they are getting beat, with chairs getting kicked all over the house and all sorts.

'Yes, you want to win, but if that's the game you want to play, forget it. If you're not hitting 180s and 140s all the time, that's no excuse to turn the furniture over. It's the same with football – some of the carry-on you see from kids who are copying the adults they see on the telly is embarrassing. Everyone wants to be the greatest player on the planet, but for someone to win a game of darts there has to be a loser. Just enjoy the game, and if you want to scream at the four walls, wait until you get home so nobody else can see your frustration. It's not rocket science.

'I've had my say in the past on players resorting to gamesmanship or dirty tricks, whatever you want to call them, but I know where the line is. People used to moan at Justin Pipe because he took so long to release his darts, but that's the way he plays and good luck to him. He didn't stand around, after his third dart hit the board, admiring the shot to slow you down. He collects his darts and he's on his way.'

Although it was a puerile episode, straight from the Billy Bunter tuck shop of schoolboy giggles, one of the most memorable spats from Anderson's close encounters with 'dirty' tricks was a row at the 2018 Grand Slam, where he finished runner-up to Gerwyn Price in a bad-tempered final.

Price and Anderson brushed shoulders, with the 'Flying Scotsman' earning a formal warning from the Darts Regulation Authority for shoving his opponent in a split-second of retaliation. Price, whose exuberant celebrations had rattled his opponent, was heavily fined. It must be said that Anderson's conduct on the oche down the years has otherwise been exemplary. If he takes a dim view of opponents 'snarking and sniffing' as cheap gamesmanship, he is on the right side of rectitude.

In that regard, Anderson is a role model for young players: a fierce competitor who leaves theatrics and melodramatic artifice at the door.

'If I had to give youngsters starting out one piece of advice now, above all it would be this: Don't get cocky,' he says. 'Keep a level head on your shoulders. If you start giving it the big 'un, I've always said you know what dart players are like – they are like a pack of wolves. If you upset them, they will soon gang up on you.'

There was no arrogant strut, no histrionics, about Anderson's game, but his switch to the PDC in 2009 somehow conveyed the message that he meant business. He ditched his original 'Dreamboy' moniker in favour of 'The Flying Scotsman' nickname, after first checking with Jocky Wilson that he was free to adopt it. Fortified by winning the International Darts League and World Darts Trophy back-to-back in 2007, he was ready to broaden his horizons.

They were significant milestones because the fields included top-ranking players from both the BDO and PDC. His victories in the two events included wins against four past and future World Champions – Mark Webster, Part, Adrian Lewis and Taylor.

'Let's get it right – Phil is the greatest player of all time and you have to respect the man for what he did,' says Anderson. 'But he didn't have it all his own way against me. The very first time I played Phil, in a pub, I beat him. I beat him in the final of the World Darts Trophy in Holland – and I beat him well. Not long after I remember beating him again in Ireland, at the Citywest Hotel in Dublin, where there was a big practice area. As I was warning up, I could sense Phil looking across and keeping his eye on me. When I was practising on the outer ring, he wanders past and says, "Don't miss, Gary." That was his way of letting you know he rated you, and the respect was mutual.'

As Anderson's star continued to rise, he won the Premier League in 2011 and the Players Championship Finals three years later, but the big one – World Championship glory at Alexandra Palace – looked a distant prospect. Shooting star Michael van Gerwen usurped Taylor's place at No.1 in the rankings and his form was beginning to look forbidding if not unstoppable.

If anyone was going to apply the brakes on the MVG juggernaut, Anderson's heavy scoring and steely nerve under pressure looked the best bet, but in a thunderous third-round duel at the 2014 World Championship he missed the boat, letting a 3-1 lead slip as Mighty Mike fought back to win 4-3.

'I was raging afterwards,' admits Anderson. 'Absolutely steaming. I was playing well, I'd got him where I wanted him and lost the momentum. Honestly, I was absolutely fuming. I don't normally get nasty when I lose, but that did my head right in. I said to the other half, "That ain't happening again." The following year our paths crossed once more, this time in the semi-finals. Although I was in front and he came back again, I wasn't going to let it slip. I was like a dog with a bone.'

Anderson's progress to his second final – Lewis had prevailed in the first – set him against Taylor, another momentous test of mind over matter.

'The Power' was favourite to win a 17th World Championship title, and the odds tilted further in his favour in that extraordinary incident when Anderson's darts landed on the deck in an unseemly pile. Taylor had just missed darts to go 5-3 up when Anderson suffered his unspeakable misfortune: no score, and nothing he could do about it.

Among the chattering classes, there were suggestions that Taylor should have responded by wasting his first three darts as an act of sportsmanship, but he was not obliged to play Mary Poppins with a £250,000 payday at stake and Anderson did not expect any charity.

'No two ways about it, I was really narked,' he admits. 'I can remember Phil looking at me and saying, "What the hell just happened there?" Then, with his next three darts, he hits 180 and I'm thinking, "You little so-and-so – but it lit the fire. What happened wasn't Phil's fault, but when I get fired up, it makes me a better player. You don't want to play me when I'm in a bad mood or narked about something. I actually won that leg, and in some ways it was a turning point.'

Anderson surged into a 6-4 lead, only for 'The Power' to rally and force a deciding set, but Taylor's 55 missed attempts at doubles ultimately proved his undoing. He became the first player to average in excess of 100 in the tournament but still miss out on the title.

'To win my first World Championship was special, to hold my nerve in a deciding set and win it 7-6 made it even better...

but it meant more to me that I had to do it against the great Phil Taylor,' says Anderson.

'We had fall-outs, we banged heads now and again, but playing Phil on that stage... that was his domain, wasn't it? I was the underdog, and I liked being underdog because there was no pressure. I just went in there thinking, "Don't make an arse of yourself, stick with him and see what happens." You deserve to be champion if you have to beat Michael in the semis and Phil in the final.

'The way I tell people about the World Championship – it's not about winning it, it's about qualifying and earning the right to be on that stage. It's every dart player's dream to play at Ally Pally. Once you are there, you have done well. Even if you lose in the first round, it's worth a few quid and you can say you have played on that stage.

'People tell me I always raise my game at Ally Pally, but if the World Championship doesn't bring out the best in you, where are you going to make a name for yourself? I've been playing darts for 30-odd years now and I still get the jibbers driving up that hill.

'Before that tournament in 2015, I went to watch them build the stage and set up the arena. It's an incredibly complex jigsaw puzzle and those boys have got it down to a fine art. You would never believe how much work goes into building that stage – there are miles and miles of cables, and it's such an expert operation.

'I like seeing how things are made, and when I spent a day watching the stage go up at Ally Pally I felt like I was there from start to finish, from the first rigging to the last dart of the tournament.

'I don't watch much television these days – I cannae be bothered with soap operas or comedies that aren't funny, and it's depressing to watch the news, but I was watching a documentary about Japanese craftsmen making clay pots and I was hooked.

'Watching things grow, seeing how things are made from scratch, that's more like it.'

After watching the stage under construction ahead of the 2015 World Championship, Anderson resolved to own it when defending his title – and he was as good as his word.

Dropping only two sets on his march to the final, he looked every inch the man to beat. Andy Boulton (3-0), Daryl Gurney (4-1), Vincent van der Voort (4-0), James Wade (5-1) and Jelle Klaasen (6-0) had offered little resistance, with Klaasen's surprise win over Taylor in the quarter-finals trashing the Hollywood script of Anderson and 'The Power' staging a re-run of their epic final in the last four.

A nine-darter and 107.32 average proved much too good for Klaasen in the semi-finals, and although Adrian Lewis peppered the lipstick with 19 maximum 180s in the final, Anderson's 170 finish broke his spirited challenge and a 7-5 win clinched back-to-back titles.

He would go on to reach a third consecutive final in 2017 and put up an almighty fight before Van Gerwen loosened his grip on the Sid Waddell Trophy in a game featuring a record 42 maximums. Up to 2026, apart from Anderson, in the PDC era only Taylor, Dennis Priestley and Luke Littler have reached three World Championship finals on the spin. At the age of 55, Anderson then reached his eighth semi-final at Ally Pally, knocking out Van Gerwen along the way, before rising Dutch star Gian van Veen prevailed in a high-class shoot-out.

With 56 wins, from 2010–26, on the stage he liked to watch under construction, only MVG stood above him in terms of matches won at Alexandra Palace. It is an accurate barometer of Anderson's standing in the game. He is unquestionably in the top ten players ever to throw a dart, and quite possibly in the top six.

'I used to panic if I missed the first darts at a double. My head was gone,' he says. 'I've lost a lot of games because of missed doubles. If it was first to five and I went 3-0 down, I used to give up and think, why bother? But now, if I go 3-0 down, my mindset is to think I can still win 5-3. You get older and wiser, and when I turn up to play now, there's no pressure. What is scary is all these youngsters coming over the hill – the boy Littler is a fantastic player, but there are plenty more where he came from.

'What you have to remember about Luke is that he's walked into a room full of people two or three times his age.

When a teenager mixes with Michael Smith and Michael van Gerwen, who are in their mid-30s, James Wade in his 40s, me in my 50s, what's he going to talk to us about? Apart from darts, what have we got in common?

'Van Gerwen was scarily good when he was 14 or 15, but Luke is just as good if not a wee bit better. Look after him.'

An hour in Anderson's company is affirmation of the important things in life. Give him a fishing rod, a coffee machine, a dartboard and his family – not necessarily in that order – and there's a desert island waiting for him to check in.

The champion who found peace of mind at his anglers' retreat, and probably extended his career on the oche by ten years or more as a result, is the reel deal. Gone fishing, indeed.

ROB CROSS

PDC World Champion: 2018

HE WAS the electrician who didn't get his wires crossed and became a darts World Champion at the first attempt.

And if his feat was enshrined as a Hollywood movie, it would belong in the *Star Wars* franchise: The Ampere Strikes Back.

Rob Cross was a 125-1 long shot before his first arrow hit the board at Alexandra Palace in the 25th PDC World Championship. By the time he had shocked reigning champion Michael van Gerwen in the semis, and sent tungsten royalty Phil Taylor into retirement through a blaze of anti-climax in a surprisingly one-sided final, Cross would never need to fix another fuse box as his day job on the beat in Sussex.

He used to get up at 4.30am in Hastings, where kings have been unseated by hails of arrows since 1066, and drive to London to install plug sockets and wires in embassies for a living. And Cross could not have caused a bigger shock on the power grid than his brutal demolition of 16-time champion Taylor.

The champion nicknamed 'Voltage' missed the birth of his daughter Maddison to chase ranking points at a floor tournament in Barnsley on the countdown to glory at Ally Pally. At least the World Championship novice wasn't eeh bah glum when he completed a stunning triumph as Van Gerwen blinked first in a final-set decider before Taylor's legend was dismantled before a nation's disbelieving eyes.

In many respects, Cross is a poster boy for Professional Darts Corporation president Barry Hearn's sales pitch that darts, more than any other sport, can transform the lives of ordinary working people, from any postcode or background, simply by lobbing a few spears at a wagon wheel and in 2018 Cross added his name to the most famous residents of Electric Avenue.

Sport and showbiz have offered sanctuary to a remarkable cast of A-listers who started out as sparkies. Cross was virtually an unknown before he joined the lights on the dashboard, and he has not always relished the celebrity which came with his life-changing feat on New Year's Day in 2018.

A life without fame, as broadcaster and writer Clive James once observed, can be a good life, but fame without a life is no life at all.

Elvis Presley was a trainee electrician before, as he surmised, he 'got wired the wrong way round somewhere along the line' and snake hips proved more lucrative than a junction box. George Harrison admitted he was a 'terrible' apprentice wire technician who regularly blew things up inadvertently before he settled in as the quiet one in The Beatles. Rowan Atkinson, comedy legend Mr Bean himself, graduated from Queen's College at Oxford University with a master's degree in electrical engineering.

And former England footballer Stuart Pearce used to advertise his alter-ego in self-employment as an electrician on the pages of Nottingham Forest's matchday programme. Pearce recalls the day he was lined up in the Wembley tunnel before an England international and, surveying the rows of faces, a brutal truth dawned: 'I realised I was the only electrician there.'

Cross didn't have to repair any irons, toasters, vacuum cleaners or other domestic appliances to announce himself in the darts elite. By his own admission, he did pile on five stone in weight in the months after his World title, but if success was unkind to his waistline at first, at least it never went to his head.

'I wouldn't be at peace with myself if I didn't win another World title. I'm not one of those people who thinks once is enough,' he says. 'If you can't be the best player in the world then what's the point? If I had a chance to become No.1 in the world but I settled for No.2 it wouldn't be good enough. I want to be the best.

'Yes, I've won a World Championship and other big ones like the World Matchplay and the European Championship, and when I look back, of course I can take satisfaction from knowing I've won the most important prize out of everything.

'But looking at it now, what I've done is nowhere near enough. Luke Littler's reached three finals in a row (2024–26), and he beat me on the way to two of them. Everyone says he's great, and rightly so, and the first time he demolished me in the semis, fair enough, but two years later in the fourth round I missed a dart at tops to get back to three sets all and he went on to win 4-2. Now I have to live with wondering what might have happened if I'd taken that chance.

'No disrespect to anyone else, but I was probably the only one who flustered him in that tournament. For some reason, 90 per cent of the time I play well when I turn up at Alexandra Palace and I adore the place. I know my game is there, and I don't worry about my ability or the bottle because when you come back from 4-0 down in the quarter-finals to beat Chris Dobey 5-4 as I did (on New Year's Day in 2024), you know you can handle the pressure.

'You've got to have bags of bottle to win that World title, and I don't feel like it's ever left me. I'm still there at the party. I just need to get the stars to align.

'I can understand it when some people say they have won the biggest thing there is to win in their profession, and it can never be taken away from them, but I'm not counting down the days to retirement. I've got years left as a darts player and I don't want to spend them coasting. Some people think they have completed the course when they win it once, but life doesn't work like that – at least, mine doesn't work like that!

'If you don't work hard enough, you aren't going to stay at the top, or at the same level, because there will always be people who come along and work even harder. You ain't going to stay there just because of your name.'

When Cross landed the World title, he resisted the temptation to lavish his life-changing wealth on the stereotypical, material trappings of affluence. Instead, his biggest indulgence was a JCB digger.

'Darts is a very different sport now compared to what it was a few years ago and the impact my success has had on my family has been incredible,' said Cross, speaking to *the Irish Independent* in 2019.

'I have been able to buy a house with a swimming pool and everything we do now is completely transformed compared to what it was like when I was an electrician. We have had a few nice breaks away that we might not have been able to go on before, and we moved into a new house that is probably a bit bigger than I would have been dreaming about a couple of years earlier.

'Buying a house with seven-and-a-half acres of land and a swimming pool wasn't really on my agenda when in my old job, and while I haven't spent too much money on cars or any other expensive gadgets, I did treat myself to a JCB digger. There was a lot of lifting we needed to do at the new house and I didn't want to injure myself, so I thought it was a wise investment to buy a JCB! It was cheaper than hiring it every week so why not.

'Hopefully my story shows that if you work hard, you can get what you want in this world. I remember saying to my mum, when I was about 14 or 15, that I wanted to be a professional darts player. She gave me a funny look at the time.'

Cross later moved to a handsome plot in Lincolnshire, where the skyline is populated not only by birds of a feather but the Red Arrows aerobatic team, based at RAF Waddington, and when the darts leave his hand in optimum rhythm, BAE T1 Hawk jets travelling at 645mph are not the only things travelling through the air in perfect collaboration.

'It probably took me 18 months to get settled in there,' he says. 'It's a different pace of life from down south, a bit slower. I still like to have that sense of purpose where I get up every morning and practise – I guess it goes back to the days of having a job where you have to go out to work.

'It's a different world from sitting at home not wanting to practise, but now I've got my routines and, like I said, I'm trying to be that best version of me. I'm a big fan of routines, it feels like they hold me together. Without them, I'd be sitting on the garden fence, wondering which side I was going to fall.'

His Lincolnshire estate gave Cross another project to focus his mind away from the oche. 'Darts has given me a life I could never dream of, but what made me the person I am is using my hands,' he says. 'I find it most satisfying when you start something from scratch and you can see the end result and you feel like you've achieved something.

'Sometimes I find it hard to process darts if it's not going well and there are times when I do miss using my hands, but I can only be grateful to darts. Another person out there would bite my arm off to lead the lifestyle I've enjoyed.

'I still try to do a bit of electrician's work every now and then, just to keep my hand in, and I'm going to do some concreting for a mate. If it doesn't sound glamorous, it will help to flex a few muscles and make sure I don't burn out mentally. I've also started going to the gym when I can – it's not easy when you are travelling and you're getting in from somewhere at two o'clock in the morning, but it's made me feel better.

'My life is more complicated than it used to be so I'm trying to rationalise it. I've started counselling this year and I actually quite enjoy it. I do an hour a week but the time flies by and it feels like I'm only in there for ten minutes.

'When I first walked in, I just wanted a normal life – just Rob Cross, not the dart player – to try and conquer a few demons and bad habits. But after two weeks, he sat me down and said, "Rob, darts is a massive part of your life and we need to sort that as well. We can sort your life out, but if you're spending 85 per cent of it travelling and only 15 per cent of the time is your own, darts is more or less the driving force."

'To be fair, I feel so much better. It's like the old saying – that a problem shared is a problem solved. In 2025, I had a bad year and I make no bones about it: I had no love for it, no interest in it, no enthusiasm and it felt like all the effort wasn't worth it. With hindsight, missing out on the Premier League in 2026 was a blessing in disguise because I didn't deserve it and it's given me more time to myself. I never thought that throwing darts was the problem – it was the bloke throwing them who was making life complicated.

'It's not going to be a quick fix, there's no magic wand, but it's really helped me. In the past I've always bottled-up stuff, and tried to deal with any problems myself, and I was probably a bit too old-fashioned around other people – not much of a talker. You tend to look at mental health as a taboo, but that's not the case these days. You have to be the best version of yourself that you can be, and I'm glad I've implemented the support I needed.

'I never really wanted to go there, or make it public, but I went from nothing in my first year (on the circuit) to the centre of attention, and I had never been the centre of attention before in my life – not at school, socially, on nights out, none of that. But at the same time, when my turn came and I was in the spotlight, I didn't really like it, either.

'To be put on that pedestal, if you're not ready for it, is a bit intimidating. Luke Littler, Luke Humphries, Van Gerwen, they are fantastic at handling it, they wear it so well. I didn't seem to be cut from the same cloth, do you know what I mean?'

Whatever the cloth Cross was wearing when he qualified for his first PDC World Championship, if he arrived in rags, he left in ermine robes.

He was not a no-hoper, in the sense that he had already announced himself as a force on the floor in ProTour events and reached a major final at the 2017 European Championship. But Rob Cross was not a name on the lips of any pundits or expert talking heads before the first jug of lager had been swilled in the Ally Pally party zone.

'I was the new kid on the block,' he says. 'I'd only won my PDC Tour Card and turned professional the year before so, yeah, in a way I suppose I came out of nowhere.

'Don't get me wrong, I knew I could play – I won my first PDC ranking title a week after being knocked out of the UK Open by Peter Wright, who went on to win it, and I won another three Players Championship gigs that year as well as reaching the European Championship final.

'After starting from scratch, I went from a bloke who'd done nothing to having a good year and qualifying for all the major ranking events. In that regard, I'd worked up a bit of wind in my sails by the time I got to the World Championship. But I was learning on the job, and the more I learned, the better I was getting. Everything was going great, life was grand and you start to blossom, even though no one else seems to notice.

'Van Gerwen was amazing that year. He was unbelievable, he really was. He stopped me in four of those majors, although some of them were close. But I always practised in the set play format – best of five – because in every set there's always a pivotal moment where a contest can turn. If you play best of 21 legs and you're 7-0 down, the game has run away from you and you're packing your bags. With set play, you have to be a bit sharper. One break can make all the difference.

'People talk about turning points and, sure, my semi-final that year could have gone the other way. But for me, the turning point was against Michael Smith in the second round. I banged in a load of 180s at crucial times to match his heavy scoring, and I found a way to win 4-3 when it was in the balance right up to the winning dart. It was a belting game and I remember thinking, "Hang on, you're on to something here."

'Ally Pally isn't the biggest capacity venue by any stretch, but it's so loud. At most places, you're on stage and the crowd is behind you, but at the World Championship it feels like you're surrounded or being ambushed. Some people shrink in that atmosphere, but others get off on it. I loved it.

'I'm one of the lucky ones who finds the noise helpful. The louder it is, the more comfortable I feel and the easier it is. In other aspects of life, I'm a bit different and maybe a little bit awkward with certain situations. If we played in a quiet room, I'd struggle because I could hear myself think. When there's all the noise swirling around, you have to play more on instinct, which suits me fine.

'By the time I faced Van Gerwen in the semi-finals, I was ready for him. Mano-a-mano, me and him, let's have it. He had stopped me in about eight different tournaments during 2017, including three Euro Tour finals, but I'd beaten him on the European Tour about four or five months earlier. I trolleyed him 6-2, so I knew I could beat him, and that was a massive confidence boost, but the whole year had been a box-ticking exercise – qualified for this, I can do that, won this, beat him, went toe-to-toe with him – and when I walked in that night, I just felt I was ready to take the next step.

'I think it's still the longest game I've ever played, over two hours from start to finish. It went on until after midnight – I've no idea how all the punters got home because they must have missed the last train. Michael missed six match darts in the deciding set, but don't forget I'd missed two of my own – one at the bullseye, one at double 16 – so it wasn't a total smash and grab. It worked out 27 legs each over the contest, so it was a draw on legs, but I won the war.'

To win the final battle of the war, there was the small matter of sending Taylor into retirement on the back of unaccustomed defeat. 'The Power' had been in 20 World Championship finals and lost only four. Cross knew the script: he was supposed to be the best supporting actor as Taylor scooped up one last Oscar and headed into the sunset in a blaze of nostalgia as the credits rolled.

What unfolded on New Year's Day 2018 was illogical, unfathomable, unforgettable, almost an anti-climax.

'It was a weird experience,' admits Cross. 'Everyone expected Taylor to win his 17th World title, but when I went 3-0 up and then 6-1 up, the crowd seemed a bit nonplussed. They were not hostile towards me because I'd trashed the fairytale ending, they were just in shock. It was only loud when the match-winning dart went in.

'Same as everyone else, I wanted to be respectful and give Taylor the send-off he deserved. How many people can say they've dominated their sport for nearly 30 years? That's insane. Not even Roger Federer or Tiger Woods dominated like Phil. It was his grand farewell, so when the winning dart landed, he didn't need anyone jumping around all over the place or shouting in his face.

'Don't get me wrong, he was my hero. But what are you supposed to do when he was retiring, it was his last-ever game and he was supposed to go out as World Champion? I'd watched Phil dominate his sport and wipe the floor with everybody. He was ruthless, so clinical. But the night before the final, I said to myself, "He ain't bullying me. I can't just let him bully me, even if it makes me the bad guy."

'The hours before the final were the most nervous of my life. I was shaking like a leaf. Before I left the hotel for Ally Pally, I was sat alone in my room for an hour and I didn't know how I was going to get through it. But when I came downstairs, ping! The nerves had gone. I said to myself, "I'm ready for this. I'm going to play properly from the start. If I get in front, I can beat this guy." Before I knew it, bang-bang-bang. I was 3-0 up.'

'Maybe the adrenaline was still pumping through my veins from the semi-final. Darts can be a bit strange – one minute you are on cloud nine, the next you've hit rock-bottom and it takes a lot out of you. But I still had some momentum after beating Michael in such a close finish – it was like going from 120mph to lowering yourself into the bath – and it took me a while to fall asleep afterwards because the nerves were still going haywire, but once I nodded off I slept really well for a block of six or seven hours.

'In a way, I had nothing to lose. It was my first final and I wasn't expected to win it, but for Phil it was different. This was his emotional farewell, and when I walked on stage I looked at the crowd and thought, "Don't get wrapped up in all the emotion." I had watched Peter Wright playing Phil in his last World Matchplay final the previous summer, and from the outside he seemed fine – but if you asked Pete now, he would probably admit he got too involved in the emotion of it. I managed to detach myself from that side of it.

'I remember being in the practice room when Garry Plummer, the managing director of Target Darts, came over and asked, "How are you, son? Everything OK?" We sat there talking for maybe half an hour or 45 minutes and Garry says, "Aren't you going to practise?" I told him, "I don't need to, Gaz

– I'm ready to go." My average didn't dip below 100 in any set and I ended up with 107.67 over the whole match. Phil didn't play badly – he averaged something like 102, which would have been enough to win a lot of finals, but it was a great feeling to take on the greatest player of all time and completely dominate him.

'When I look back, I can honestly say I did it the hard way. If you win a tournament by beating Van Gerwen and Taylor, you haven't fluked it. Those memories will stay with me for the rest of my life. Don't get me wrong, I love the World Matchplay and the Winter Gardens in Blackpool, but there's something special about Ally Pally. No one's chatting backstage, it's strictly business, and when you walk out of there with that trophy, it's life changing.'

To his consternation, Cross found the trappings of success were not confined to a swollen bank balance. The knives of jealousy, sharpened on social media's open sewers, came for him with random brutality and, in one case, forced 'Voltage' to turn off the lights altogether.

At first, Cross concealed the nastiness as the work of lone cranks, but the depravity of some abuse was too much for him to dismiss.

In a revealing interview with the *Guardian*, he said: 'After the final it was like I'd hit rock bottom. It had drained me. I spent January doing interviews and I only got my darts back out when I played the Masters at the end of the month. It's been demanding and I've enjoyed it, even if I don't do social media anymore. I have everything done for me because one guy caused me to come off it. He said he wished all my kids dead. He said I would live but my kids and my wife should die. He said I should live unhappily alone for the rest of my days.'

In what kind of twisted mind should a darts player have to shield his family from arbitrary venom?

Cross took no chances, but it was not the only shock to the system in the lifestyle of a World Champion. His weight ballooned so alarmingly that he ended up fearing he was suffering a heart attack.

'You become set in the routine. I was away playing darts most of the time and I'd finish the night eating the wrong things. You wake up one day and you look down and think, "I didn't want to be 18 stone." The highest I ever went before was 14-and-a-half stone and that was usually when I had eight weeks of easy work, and then we'd go back on the hard graft and get it off. Eighteen stone was a shock.'

Physically, a meaningful acquaintance with the gymnasium has kept the rounded edges in check. But in 2025, a close encounter with the taxman and his revelation that he was diagnosed with attention deficit hyperactivity disorder (ADHD) went some way towards explaining his sketchy performances.

World Champions are not immune to off-stage problems, as other subjects in this book will attest, and Cross – to his immense credit – has shirked away from neither the issues nor their consequences. Out of the blue, following his routine 3-1 win against Ian White in the second round at Alexandra Palace on December 21, he bared his soul about living with ADHD and the side effects of medication to manage it.

The confessional was effectively his release from hiding a guilty secret. Cross marmalised Damon Heta 4-0 in the third round and pushed Littler hard in the last 16, as if the public cleansing of his demons had released the handbrake.

Asked why he had chosen to speak out in mid-tournament, just four days before Christmas, he replied: 'Too guilty to speak out about it, like we do. I just stopped and thought I'd be better off being mates with the person inside instead of trying to shut him off with no emotions, so I stopped taking my tablets before I came here. I feel great. It brings the hyperness out instead of trying to lock something away because that's what they've done to me.

'With the ADHD side of it, it's just probably at a point where I needed a bit of help and I thought that is the way to go because it gets you through it. So now I'm just trying to deal with it, and I tell you what has helped me – having good people around me. It has sorted me to a certain degree.

'I've been on it long enough to actually start to feel a bit better, so I've just tried to keep the good moods going. I'm guilty for not expressing myself to the people that I trust with my own life, so if I can't talk to them, what chance have I got to go and do other stuff?

'But what I would say, having good people around you, anyone that you trust, anyone that wants to help, if you have got that and you do feel like that, you need to speak up. It's going to eat you away eventually and anyone out there that feels like that, they need to try and find a good person.

'I think I can be awkward at times, I'm not much of a talker and I think everyone looks over my shoulder to make sure I'm all right when they know I'm wrong. I'm a lucky person to have that. I'm not an instant person to go: "Oh, I've got this, or me, me, me". I tell you where I am lucky in life, I've got four beautiful kids and I want to steer them down the right path, just as my parents guided me.

'It's OK if you've got good people around you, you always deal with it. At the minute I feel a little bit more in control, so it's probably helped me just to talk about it. I only want to skim it, I don't want to go into major stuff, but that's where I'm at at the minute.

'But just speak up. We all have people in our life and it's important that they're OK. We're all human beings, we all want to be treated well, don't we? Don't get me wrong, we're all guilty for not helping ourselves sometimes, but even then, you need a good Samaritan on your shoulder to get through.

'I'm just so lucky that I've got all these great people around me, I think it puts it all in perspective. I did an exhibition in Germany with PDC Europe and we went to a children's hospital. And when you actually see what other people are going through… it puts life in perspective for people that are OK. And when you've got kids who are OK.

'I know it sounds bad, seeing that, but it really did make me sort of realise how lucky I am in life. There's always someone out there going to go through worse than what you're going through and that's why you need to talk. No matter who you are, whether you're big, small, great, worse off, whatever, I do believe speaking out will help.

'You've got to wipe the slate clean – it's not good just to carry baggage in life, you've got to let go sometimes. I would have had these problems even if it wasn't for darts. I think that's the important bit to understand. It doesn't matter where you come from, what you've got, you can have every bit of money in the world, but if you're not happy, you're not happy.

'We can only wear so much as human beings and sometimes you need that extra help, just with the extra hand.'

As part of his recalibration, Cross has sought the counsel of a therapist to help him navigate the hairpin bends of mental health, and he has learned to discover a renewed purpose on the board when lethargy comes calling.

He was not the first darts World Champion to seek professional advice when mental health rang a few alarm bells and he summoned help from inside the belfry – and, as it turned out, he wouldn't be the last. Throwing darts in front of excitable audiences in rock concert venues can be exhilarating theatre, but for the protagonists it can be a gruelling ordeal.

The pressure, noise, increasingly high stakes and brutal solitude of standing alone on the oche, trying to maintain a precision of aim and stoutness of heart under the punishing TV lights, cannot be underestimated as mere slings and arrows of the profession.

With candour and sincerity, Cross, and others, have addressed the sheer toll of the ultimate sporting tightrope – where the difference between success and failure, between life-changing money and pocket money, often boils down to the width of a wire.

We can only marvel at the fortitude of players who withstand the demands of that pressure. Imagine trying to do your day job on the shop floor with decibels and distractions circling your personal space – let alone the infamous Ally Pally wasp, whose annual buzzing of the stage down the years has added comic value to the hazards of a darts player's workplace.

The Professional Darts Players Association (PDPA) have become increasingly proactive in safeguarding the mental health and general wellbeing of their members. Chief executive Alan Warriner-Little – who won the World Grand Prix in 2001, was runner-up at the 1993 BDO World Championship and a two-time semi-finalist in the PDC's showpiece – was eminently qualified to address the issues generated by pressure.

He says: 'I was a mental health nurse for 26 years, and when my darts career ended, I was fortunate to fall into this job. There is so much pressure on players now, with prize money going through the roof and the abuse swirling around on social media, that they sometimes need our support. In the last ten years we've probably helped 50 to 60 players in different ways.

'When you are up there on stage, you're on your own. You can't lean on team-mates, coaches, psychologists, managers or partners for assistance and there's nowhere to hide. Our service is completely confidential, so when players come to us and say they are struggling, or if they think a mate has a problem, they know where to go. We are here to provide them with a safe space to discuss any challenges they are facing, whether it's an addiction, anxiety, stress or any other branch of mental health.

'We have a partnership with Sporting Chance, founded by former England football captain Tony Adams, and they are absolutely fantastic. They offer counselling for the kinds of destructive behaviour that often exist in sport but which are often overlooked. Whether it's bereavement, anger management, eating disorders, relationship issues or coping with injury, darts players operate in a unique environment and sometimes they feel lost.

'As well as Sporting Chance, we offer seminars for junior players, we have a free, interactive well-being Thrive app which you can look at on a long plane or train journey, or if you're sat alone in your hotel room after a defeat, offering coping mechanisms to manage stress and anxiety.

'We have psychologists, hypnotherapists, and nutritionists – darts players might have been shy of confiding in professional counsellors 20 years ago, but we are trying to cover all bases.'

In the crosshairs of professional sport, when prize money at the top end comes in multiples of your previous annual salary, there are pitfalls best avoided when His Majesty's Revenue and Customs are on the prowl. In 2025, Cross was disqualified from acting as a company director for five years after his firm went into liquidation.

For more than three years, he withdrew funds from the company which should have gone to HMRC and other creditors. But unlike Cabinet ministers who cut and run when their tax affairs are shown to be less than squeaky-clean, Cross took his medicine stoically.

He said: 'It's not the proudest moment in my life. I've done wrong, I hold my hands up to it and going down the route of paying the money back through an IVA (individual voluntary agreement) means I'm not running away from it. We all make mistakes in life, but I'm willing to correct them and do the right thing.

'There's only me to blame, not anyone else around me personally. It's been going on for two years. I wasn't surprised when it came out – I was only surprised it took the best part of two years to come out. I've never had so many texts off people, making sure I'm all right and not suicidal to be honest, but I know what I've done wrong and I'm fine with the outcome.

'I'm sorry to let the fans down, but I'll get back on my feet and hopefully it won't linger over me for the rest of my life.'

Rob Cross will not be defined by financial affairs. He is one of the good guys who turns up to an exhibition for special armed forces, on a detour to a Premier League night 60 miles away, and refuses to vacate the premises until he has played every squaddie who fancies taking on a World Champion. When his courtesy car arrives at 9.30pm, he protests 'I've only just got here' and it's nearer midnight before he has taken on allcomers in uniform.

He is also a family man who recognised the sacrifices made by his wife, Georgia, while he was pin-balling across Europe. The couple separated in June 2026 after 15 years of marriage, a sad punctuation mark in a relationship which began with a chance meeting at the pet shop where she worked and sharing a bag of chips on their first date.

But he remains a committed father who drives hard and late to keep appointments. On the day we meet, he is playing in a ProTour floor competition after hitting the sack at 3am following an exhibition in Ireland and a late-night transit. And he does not complain when crowds cheer for the home-town favourite.

'Whenever I play in Germany against a local player, I get booed and whistled at. You've got to expect it, put your big boy pants on and deal with it,' he told Sky TV documentary *Game of Throws*.

'Ever since becoming World Champion, I haven't had many days off. That becomes very hard on the family. It's a big sacrifice to spend so much time away from them. But I know this won't last forever and you have to make hay while the sun shines. This is the best chance I have of giving my kids a better life than the one I had. You've got to try and grab it while you can.

'I was an electrician and all throughout my first few years, I was working. Eventually I managed to secure some funding which meant I could dedicate myself to the sport and see how far I could go. I knew that I could play the standard of darts that I was seeing in the tournament, but I didn't know if I could do it in front of 4,000 people. Obviously, I've done OK.'

Electricity, as comic genius Tommy Cooper once observed, is a wonderful thing. If we didn't have electricity, we'd all be watching TV by candlelight. Let us give thanks for the electricians who have brightened our lives – especially the one who lit up Alexandra Palace on his debut.

PETER WRIGHT

PDC World Champion: 2020, 2022

ON A grey Monday morning, the Mattioli Arena in Leicester is immersed in sepulchral hush.

The librarian code of near-silence at a ProTour event in the Players Championship is the complete antithesis of bawdy, beer-swilling masses at major darts tournaments on TV.

Clustered around circular tables, 128 hopefuls who have announced themselves before the signing-on deadline sustain a murmur of whispered conversation, their muted gossip punctured only by the gentle tap of darts hitting the 20 boards on three sides of the cavernous venue. Behind a screen, matches on four boards are streamed live on the internet for the sport's obsessive tendency to follow from lunchtime until nightfall.

With the darts providing a soothing arrangement, like a rhapsody of grandfather clocks tick-tocking away, in the middle of the horologists' concerto Peter Wright sits unobtrusively, awaiting his call-up. Recapturing mislaid form is easier said than done at 56, but if the glory of two PDC World Championship titles is still vivid in the memory, he hasn't forgotten that the road to tears of joy and tickertape showers began in spartan, multi-purpose halls like the Mattioli.

Gone, for now, are most of the trappings of Wright's 'Snakebite' alter-ego. Instead of a brazen, nonconformist mohawk, his hair is combed back in an orderly wave, and the artwork of his signature serpent image is partly concealed beneath the half-restored covering of hair above his temple. And this time, neither his laser-blue shirt nor regulation black trousers make him stand out from 127 other contestants.

The old warhorse can still show the young shavers a few tricks, and he clinches victory against rising Dutch prospect Jurjen van der Velde with a rascal 126 checkout – treble 19, single 19, bullseye, see you later – but nobody, bar a handful of intrigued onlookers stood half a dozen paces beyond the oche, was there to see it.

This is plain Peter Wright – the reserved, almost introspective, grand master of his art, still chasing the ranking points before retiring to his budget hotel ahead of the following day's bread-and-butter competition in back-to-back Players Championship events. His 'Snakebite' alter ego is the crowd-pleaser from Brash Street who comes out to play when there are TV cameras around and a gallery of parched ticket-holders to entertain.

'It's like Jekyll and Hyde,' he says. 'Off stage, away from the board, I don't really talk to anyone and I keep myself to myself. I'm just another face in the crowd. But when I put on the warpaint and go into battle up there, I'm a different character called 'Snakebite' who goes prancing across the stage in front of the dancing girls and wearing crazy trousers.

'The first time I wanted to wear the lurid colours and stand out a bit, Matt Porter (the PDC chief executive) said no because black trousers and shoes on stage is the official dress code and he didn't want to set a precedent.

'I appealed to Barry Hearn, who was PDC chairman at the time, and he said yes. So after taking my case from Matt to Barry, the legend of 'Snakebite' was born. We created a monster – and now I've got to keep doing it until my hair falls out.'

With the possible exception of golfer John Daly, whose 'Loudmouth' trousers were easy to spot on the green of a 550-yard par five from the tee box, no champion in any sport has been more famous for his image, or the way he dresses, more than Wright. And even 'Wild Thing' Daly's wacky wardrobe only became his signature when his magic began to fade on the golf course. Wright's chaotic outfits, swirling neon patterns and warpaint became the rocket fuel for his rise to prominence on the PDC. His spiky hair and kaleidoscopic outfits stood out like a hitch-hiker's sore thumb long before his darts. And it seemed the racier the colour scheme, the better he played.

Such was his collection of unlikely garments that, at one stock-take, he had 48 pairs of psychedelic trousers hanging in the wardrobe. His endurance record in the barber's chair, as his wife Jo – a hairdresser by trade and his manager off the board – created another sculpted masterpiece with his hair, is four-and-a-half hours, for a natty popcorn and hot dog number at the World Matchplay in Blackpool. Four-and-a-half hours: long enough for a round of golf, a five-set epic at Wimbledon or waiting for Arsenal to take a free-kick.

Wright's personal favourites were also from his Blackpool range, featuring seagulls in one instance and a pineapple design at the 2017 World Matchplay final against Phil Taylor, where his green mohawk complemented the fruity motif on his shirt as he was serenaded by fans with a chorus of 'He's got a pineapple on his head' – and they weren't bluffing.

'I lost the plot that night because I got wrapped up in the emotion,' he admits. 'I should have gone second on the walk-on because I was the higher seed, but it was Phil's last Matchplay so I asked the organisers to swap it around so he could have the honour. Big mistake. He swarmed all over me. But, hey, at least I looked the part!'

The birth of Wright's 'Snakebite' persona is actually a beautiful love story, fortified as it was by a reunion with his daughter Naomi.

Jo first told it on the *Tops and Tales* podcast hosted by PDC referee Huw Ware, revealing she and Peter had split up for 13 years after the birth of Naomi, their first child, in 1993 and Wright's darts career appeared to be drifting down the road to nowhere.

His mum gave him a set of arrows for his 13th birthday but could not afford a dartboard, so he used to fire them at a makeshift target on a tree, and at 24 he qualified for the British Darts Organisation version of the World Championship at Lakeside, falling in the first round to eventual champion Richie Burnett.

At first, he did not chase his dream of joining the pro ranks, settling for jobs as a builder and tyre fitter until Naomi – whose contact with her father had evaporated – resolved to get in touch with Wright again when she was at secondary school. It led to Jo searching for him on the Professional Darts Corporation website and then knocking on his door, completely out of the blue.

Once they were reunited as a family, Wright's career on the PDC circuit took off like a rocket at the Kennedy Space Center. On *Tops and Tales*, Jo said: 'So, when I was 18 and Peter was 22, we worked in a holiday camp in Lowestoft called Gunton Hall. I was a waitress and Peter worked in the kitchen. I found him sitting under a tree when I came out from work one day, kind of waiting for me.

'We had our first daughter in 1993 and then we split up for 13 years. We had no contact, nothing. I found him when the daughter was on her laptop, she'd been looking for him and searching for him online. Obviously, you keep an eye on your kids, especially what they're doing on social media and stuff like that, although it's nothing like it is nowadays. I thought, well, I'd better go and find him before she did, just in case he doesn't want to see her. It took me four years to find him, and when I did find him, I had my own salon by then.

'So, I was sitting in the salon and I found the players' profiles from the PDC with a picture of him on there, and then there was like some details on, a couple of telephone numbers. I tried the first one, no luck, phoned the second one, which was actually someone in the PDC office at the time, deleting all the old profiles – and he was one of them. If I hadn't have found him on there that night, I wouldn't have found him.'

After managing to trace an address for Wright, Jo eventually plucked up the courage to renew acquaintances – even, as it transpired, if it would complicate both their lives.

'I went and knocked on the door of his last known address,' she said. 'And I'm guessing that was probably the last thing he was expecting.'

Jo had spotted Wright playing on TV in the 1995 Embassy World Championship, when he was sporting his natural brown hair in a conventional fashion and was billed as English – even though he was born in Scotland to a single mother from Livingston who moved to London when he was three years old. But when she turned up on his doorstep unannounced, it turned their worlds upside down.

She continued: 'There was big confusion to go with it all because I was married and Peter had a girlfriend. But a month later, I had no husband and Peter had a new girlfriend – me.

'We knew how good Peter was at darts because I actually did watch him at home with my family when he was at the Lakeside in 1995. Even his daughter was like crawling in front of the TV watching him, and we were all talking about him. That's as close as we actually came to seeing him, but then when we got back together after all those years, it was like, "You could have been so much more if we'd have stayed together."

'But he was a bit defiant back in the day. It was his way or no way, so we kind of look at what we've got now and what we've done, but we missed all those years where we could have had more.'

Wright agrees: 'I could have been challenging Phil Taylor at that time or something like that. I could have been up there with Dennis Priestley and Phil.

'But since then Jo has been my wife, my manager, my hairdresser, my therapist… she's been everything to me. When I've been down, she's the one who's picked me up, encouraged me to start again, and she's always been there when I have turned up and won titles. If I've played well, she's also the one who keeps me grounded and reminds me about the doubles I missed.

'Why Snakebite? I've always been fascinated by snakes, and you know what they are like – they curl up and if you prod them, they bite back. They are usually quiet and shy unless you upset them, and on stage I'm the same: if you make me angry, I'll bite back. Leave me alone in the corner because if you prod me, I'll snap. I often play my best stuff when I'm annoyed.

'I just wanted to be different, to stand out from all the other dart players. I know people thought I was just a novelty act with a weird haircut and I've been called a clown and all that, but there was some calculation involved. When I was young, I used to experiment with some sort of mohican trim. I used to colour the back of my head with food dye from the kitchen cupboard. In the charts back then you had David Bowie with his Ziggy Stardust look, and in the 1980s Boy George and the new wave people all dressed up as well.'

Wright told darts writer Phil Lanning in 2020: 'It was my idea of colouring my hair for darts. It was the Blue Square UK Open and I decided to have blue hair for it, I think that was in 2009. But I always believed in my own ability. The hair and the clothes are just my stage persona. That's what prepares me for matches, my warpaint if you like.'

Once he had made his blue statement in the UK Open at the Reebok, no colours of the rainbow were safe. 'It was me who asked Jo and Naomi, who worked in the salon, if I could colour my hair blue. When I wanted it to be a different colour the following week, Jo had to explain you couldn't just wash it out like that when you're bleaching it, because it makes your hair brittle and fall out, but she found some body spray paint that they used in the film *Avatar*, so we used that. It normally takes a couple of hours to put it on but you can wash it out in five minutes.

'Naomi and Jo came up with the 'Snakebite' nickname and the idea of a snake on the side of my head, although we've done other stuff there for the NHS, *Bullseye*, poppies for Remembrance Day, mistletoe and baubles at Christmas... some of the artwork Jo's come up with has been unbelievable. I wouldn't like to tot up all the hours I've spent in the chair having all that paintwork and hair colouring applied, but it's been worth every second.

'Even Phil Taylor, who has always had an eye for a business opportunity, once told me: "I wish I'd thought of that." And when I started getting my hair done and wearing the Loudmouth trousers, Eric Bristow, God rest his soul, used to scold me and say, "Stop clowning around and remember you're here to throw darts." A couple of years later in Wolverhampton, when I kept losing major finals, mainly to MVG (Van Gerwen), I asked Eric if he would take me on, like he had been Phil's mentor, to help me reach the next level. He told me, "I made a mistake when I said you were clowning around – just carry on what you're doing and the first big one will come. Your game is all there." And he was right, bless him.

'I was about to go on stage at the Premier League in Liverpool when the news came through that he had passed away suddenly. That was my saddest night in darts by a distance. I was literally about to walk on when they told me.

They could have left it and not told me. It's hard enough to hit a target the size of a shirt button without the blur of tears in your eyes.

'Not only that, but I had some idiot in the crowd on my walk-on who wouldn't let go of my hand on the corner. I was already upset, and fighting to hold it together, so I went to the railings, looked him in the eye and squeezed so hard it would have hurt him. Security were jumping in and I was still holding on, giving this bloke the eyeballs and asking, "You still want to hold my hand?" I was on a run of about eight weeks without a win, and that idiot didn't help.'

Wright is no fan of keyboard warriors, whose unsolicited messages in triumph and defeat make him wary of the rapids on social media waters to this day. His breakthrough tournament, reaching his first PDC World Championship final against Van Gerwen in 2014, had a sour post-script. Standing at the bar afterwards, a stranger confronted him and complained that he had lost a £50 wager on 'Snakebite' to win.

The deflated runner-up's riposte brought a swift end to the conversation. 'I turned round to him and said, "I've just lost £200,000 so imagine how I feel, mate",' said Wright.

Yet even in defeat, there was a sense of relief that he had finally proved – to himself, to his family, to the wider public – that he was a genuine contender, not just a novelty act. Wright later revealed that run to his first final at Ally Pally changed his life because he was on the verge of giving up professional darts and returning to blue-collar anonymity as a tyre fitter or mechanic.

He told the *Daily Express*: 'My wife said to me at the beginning of the 2014 tournament, "You have been doing it for five or six years, and not doing very well." I only won £1,200 in my first year, I was losing 6-5, 6-5, every week and it wasn't paying the bills. She said, "If you don't do well in these world champs, we cannot afford it anymore."

'That was the kick up the backside I needed. I knew I had to knuckle down and started to take this game seriously. That could have been it had I lost in the first or second round. I would have been back down the pub and I would have gone back to tyre-fitting and working with cars.

'I came close to packing the game in completely. If I didn't do as well as I did, then I would have packed it all in. It changed my life. Getting to the 2014 final put me in the Premier League and the World Series.

'Until then I had been a little fat man dancing across the stage and it's all part of the show. The crowd want the fantastic darts players, like Michael van Gerwen at a fast pace, crazy stuff. But they also want the entertainment.'

From that moment, Wright realised he could give the fans both elements of the cabaret: a party atmosphere and brilliant darts. His first major would be another three years in the making, but a life-changing three weeks? You bet.

Wright's 'Snakebite' act comes with an excess luggage premium. When he exports it across Britain, all over Europe and worldwide, he never travels light. A whole suitcase is filled with the cosmetics and hairstyling tools required to transform a softly-spoken former garage mechanic into a profusion of colour, plus another case filled with a different outfit for each potential round he plays.

In 2017, he told the *Daily Mail* his excess baggage on a World Series trip to New Zealand set him back £1,700. And extra luggage for a tournament in Las Vegas? That'll be another £600, please.

Each conversion from plain Peter to 'Snakebite' takes upwards of two hours, but it is much more than a makeover. It flicks a switch.

'If you go to work in an office, you might get up in the morning and put on a collar and tie,' he says. 'I go to work in a loud shirt, crazy trousers and my hair in a mohawk. I've got a job to do up on that stage, and those outfits give me the confidence to do it. You need confidence to do this job because if you're meek and timid, your opponents will smell the fear – and if you fear them, they will walk all over you. Getting my hair done and getting dressed for work makes me feel confident and I become that character.

'We created a monster and I have to live up to that image, so when we travel the world, all the paint brushes, sprays, stencils, glitter and hair gel go with us. It's very different from the bloke who turned up to the Lakeside in 1995 in a plain black shirt.

'Snakey isn't to everyone's taste, I get that. Some people say I'm too old to dress up like a jester, but it's put me in the right frame of mind to be a World Champion and take home a pay cheque for half a million quid. Twice.'

To cut back on his marathon sessions in the chair, Wright made a unilateral decision to get a permanent snake tattoo on the side of his head. It didn't go down well.

'I thought I was doing Jo a favour and saving her some work, but she wasn't happy,' he says, wincing at the memory of her reaction. 'Look, it might limit her creative options in future, but next time I'm playing on TV, I'll still be back in the chair and she'll be doing her thing. And when I turn up at Ally Pally in the run-up to Christmas, and all the folks are in full party mode, we'll be giving it the full nine yards. You've got to make en effort. That's why I give it the full Grinch, Elf or Santa Claus, or I dress up as a Christmas tree. As a dart player, I believe you should give the crowd something back – they all come to support us in their fancy dress outfits, so why shouldn't we get in the festive mood? If you can go out and make a memory for somebody, so much the better.

'The World Championship is special. They may not remember how many 180s you hit, or your best finish, but if they go home and tell their mates, "That crazy bloke who was the reigning World Champion went up on stage dressed as the

Grinch" what's wrong with that? Name another sporting world champion who begins the defence of his title looking like he belongs in a cartoon strip? Or who walks on to a Pitbull song called 'Don't Stop The Party' and cavorts across the stage?

'Some people think I'm auditioning to appear on *Strictly Come Dancing*, which is interesting – I have turned down offers to do Strictly, but trust me, this body isn't dancing. I was also offered a place on *Celebrity Masterchef* and that *Celebrity SAS: Who Dares Wins*, but the darts schedule is so packed that there isn't enough time to do reality TV shows. When you're in the top 32, it's a no-brainer when you have to decide whether you want to qualify for the major tournaments or make a nice Victoria sponge. I would have liked to do some of those shows, and I like my cooking, but you can't pull out of the Premier League just to find out if your soufflé rises in the oven or if Paul Hollywood approves of your Pot Noodle for tea.

'Am I glad that I'm now recognised as the dart player who dresses up in crazy outfits? Absolutely. Even when I walk down the street as plain Peter Wright with 'normal' hair, no warpaint, my collar turned up and wearing glasses, people stop me or say "Hello champ" as they pass. I could grow my beard until it's almost caveman length, put a woolly hat on and think I'll be incognito in the street – but whether they recognise me as Pete or as 'Snakebite', they seem to know who I am. I'm not complaining – it's good that people now take such an interest in darts that they know who you are.

'When we played in New York for the first time, they sent special cars to pick us up and as we got dropped off outside the hotel, my feet had literally just hit the ground when a couple walked past with a cheery wave, "How's it going, 'Snakebite?'" I wasn't in darts costume, no mohawk, nothing to give away who I was in the Big Apple, where I thought I would just dissolve among millions of people in this great metropolis. But that shows how far darts now reaches – it's gone global.

'I have enjoyed darts as a career, and the life it has given me, but I wish I'd taken it more seriously. If I took it more seriously, maybe I'd have won more titles.'

What is not in doubt, and Wright has long accepted, is that his rebooted darts career took off because Jo and Naomi launched their search party, gave him the 'Snakebite' moniker and made him stand out from the pack. Now he is recognised for the way he plays as much as the way he dresses – as one of the finest purveyors of tungsten who ever toed the oche.

After his second PDC World Championship win in 2022, just a few days later he walked Naomi down the aisle, in full kilt and Scottish regalia, with the Sid Waddell Trophy proudly placed on the top table in a converted barn. In another break from convention, Jo walked their daughter down the aisle, too. They agreed that a mother who had done 90 per cent of the parenting deserved to share the privilege.

There is a contentment in Wright's family life which was once permeated by guilt at missing his children's birthdays, school proms and landmark dates because darts paid the bills and darts called the tune. By his own admission, he would often be driven home from tournaments late at night announcing he'd had enough, and he didn't want to play at the following week's competition, only to relent when Jo talked him round. 'At the end of the day, we're doing it for them,' he says.

Back home in Suffolk, where the farmstead includes cats, fish, chickens, ducks and geese, the hens lay 50 to 60 eggs a day. Wright often turns up at major tournaments bearing trays of free-range gifts for his rivals and PDC officials, but he doesn't need to court popularity. Long before his throw became poultry in motion, he was well-liked on the circuit.

Being an affable chicken farmer, however, was no substitute for success. Until he conquered Ally Pally in 2020, he had reached ten finals in PDC premier events and won only one – the UK Open in 2017 – with Michael van Gerwen beating him in seven of them. When he became a World Champion aged 49, the emotion came pouring out. The only surprise was that his warpaint was not streaked by all the tears following his 7-3 hammering of Van Gerwen in the final.

'As often seems to be the case with people who go on to win the title, and I don't know why it happens, my biggest scare was probably in my first match of the tournament,' says Wright. 'I got taken to sudden death in the deciding leg by Noel Malicdem, but apart from winning that UK Open in 2017, I had been runner-up in nine major finals, and when you go so close that often, the nerves do kick in.

'I would happily have traded all those finals where I came second for the one where it mattered most. I had lost to MVG (Van Gerwen) in my only previous World Championship final in 2014, so to settle the score meant a lot. Yes, there were tears that night and people said it was an expression of relief or revenge or whatever, but I was more pleased for my family than for myself. After all the rubbish I'd played during the year, and getting my backside kicked in the Premier League most weeks, it was important to let people know I'm still here.

'Jo and my family had seen me go close so often, and you can imagine all those drives home when I'm sat there wondering what might have been. I had set myself a target of being World Champion before I turned 50, and I cracked it with ten weeks to spare so I cut it a bit fine. It didn't matter how I got there, but we did it.'

Within a fortnight of Wright raising the bat for his half-century, the world shut down in the jaws of a pandemic. Instead of taking a bow in front of appreciative crowds, he was confined to his farmstead in Suffolk, taking in the stranded Dimitri Van den Bergh when the Belgian was trapped in Britain by closed borders and travel restrictions.

Van Den Bergh acknowledged Wright's hospitality by winning the 2020 World Matchplay behind closed doors in Milton Keynes, but the following year – with darts still confined to empty arenas – the landlord would prevail over his 'tenant' 18-9 in the final, becoming only the fifth player to win both the PDC World Championship and the World Matchplay crowns.

At first, the lack of spectators did not diminish Wright's pride at landing prizes he had long coveted. 'I didn't feel cheated. Not at all,' he insists. 'I had put a big tick on my list, the most important one of all. I didn't need to be introduced to crowds as World Champion. The deed was done, it's in the record books, you move on. I was happy enough with what I'd done and wanting to do it again. I didn't do many exhibitions anyway, so I didn't miss out on nice little earners parading the trophy around. Why didn't I want to fill the diary with exhibitions? I dunno…that's just me.'

But as a second wave of the COVID-19 plague turned into a postcode lottery, with travel curtailed and parts of the country divided into tiers based on infection rates, Wright's defence of the Sid Waddell Trophy was short-lived and vaguely farcical.

On the opening night, with only 400 fans dotted around the Ally Pally arena in a biosecure environment and with no fancy dress permitted, Wright did his best to enliven proceedings by treating the reduced audience to a gloriously festive Grinch outfit. The spectators' tables were arranged in a pattern reminiscent of a school gym for an A level exam, but the defending champion entered into the sprit of the occasion – even though everyone agreed it was darts, but not as we knew it.

'It's been horrible for me personally,' he said after beating Steve West 3-1. 'At times I've been depressed and I really couldn't be bothered with it all, doing the hair and dressing up. But I have to think about the fans.'

Wright had briefly considered pitching up in civvies to suit the nation's sombre mood, but after a heart-to-heart with Jo they resolved that the show must go on. 'We agreed there might be only 400 people in there, but they bought their tickets in good faith, so I got dressed up for them. I wanted to say thank you for making the effort – they might not have been allowed to put on their costumes as traffic cones, Buzz Lightyear or Scooby Doo, but I wasn't going to sell them short. The following night, the shutters came down and no fans were admitted for the rest of the tournament.'

The Government's cack-handed policing of the Christmas party season was not appreciated by Hearn, who was forced to lock down his blue riband event at point-blank notice. 'I will adapt to any circumstances and I will also follow the rules,' said the frustrated promoter and ringmaster. 'I just need some leadership, I need some consistency and I need some common sense. We've been through this pandemic now for nine months and we should have some idea how we should be dealing with it. Tell me what to do and I will do it, but make it fair. I can't cope with these last-minute knee-jerk reactions.'

Wright was also not inspired by the desolation in an arena where he had thrived on the party spirit 12 months earlier.

He subsided to a shock 3-2 defeat by German giant Gabriel Clemens the day after the Christmas break, admitting he hated the confected 'atmosphere'.

'You're playing in an empty room, with fake noise being piped in like radio interference when you can't find the right wavelength, and it was horrible,' he says. 'It was like white noise, I didn't like it at all. You need the crowd there to make you feel nervous, to feed off them, even when they are giving you some abuse and you give it to them back.

'When you have a real crowd behind you, and your opponent hits a great shot, the fans' reaction cranks up the tension and generates the atmosphere, not a fake wind tunnel noise.'

Twelve months later, with fans readmitted but players still falling by the wayside if they tested positive, Wright – locked away between games with his family in a rented north London house instead of a hotel – completed his Covid sandwich: champion, pandemic, champion.

By the time he came through a close quarter-final against Callan Rydz, the No.2 seed was the man to beat, and his 6-4 triumph over fellow Scot Gary Anderson in the semi-finals was decorated by a tournament record 24 maximum 180s.

He says: 'I had switched my darts in the practice room – same dart, but a longer point – because I knew the key was to match Gary's scoring. If he's hammering that treble 20 bed and you can't keep up, he just disappears over the horizon.

Whenever I managed to get in front, he kept coming back, and it was the same story against Michael (Smith) in the final.

'I didn't play all that well. I changed my points and had a slightly different stem, just to freshen my game up, and thankfully I won nine of the last 12 legs. Like Gary, he just wouldn't go away, but when he was 5-4 up I remember thinking, "You've played your best but I'm still with you – let's see if you can handle my A game, because here it comes." Fortunately I hit my stride when I needed it most.'

Wright's perennial hunt for the ideal combination of flights, stems, points and barrels has earned him a deserved reputation as the No.1 Tinkerman of darts, but the results of his perpetual search for perfection speak for themselves.

Sky Sports commentator Wayne Mardle has sometimes been confused by Wright's change of ammunition in mid-match, but he he admits: 'I don't make him right or wrong – I just imagine what he could have won if he stuck with the same set. But if Peter wants to change his darts, that's his prerogative, it's a personal choice. I would never recommend that anyone takes different sets of darts up there, but if it makes you feel more comfortable, nobody's going to stop you – and Peter Wright is unique.'

Go on the Red Dragon Darts official website and you'll find multiple ranges of Wright's preferred arrows, from Black Mamba to Supa Venom, 50 years Anniversary Limited Edition and Double World Champion (85 per cent tungsten and steel tip) – he's thrown them all, but he is adamant the chopping and changing is not for show: it is a champion's method of making sure his game doesn't stagnate.

'It's not just tinkering for the sake of it,' he shrugs. 'There is a science in making a dart go exactly where you want it to land. Basically, I try and get something that feels comfortable in my hand on any given day, and it may change from one day to the next.

'You might go from hitting 180s and your finishing being spot-on to feeling like you're throwing spanners at the board with the same darts in 24 hours. You go from feeling like you are almost placing each shot in the right bed to wondering, "Where the hell's that one going?" That's why I change – I don't put up with it and wait for my luck to turn.

'If you let it gnaw away at you, and your fortunes don't change, you start over-analysing your throw and next thing you know, it gets worse and dartitis comes knocking at your door. That's why I change to different weights, different stems, different points. As a player, you can become too relaxed and reliant on your dart, expecting it to work instead of making it work for you.

'When I've gone to the Grand Slam, knowing I could be there all week, I might take 20 to 30 different sets with me. That's not showing off – I call it forward planning.'

Another bugbear, sustained only by ignorance of his back-story, has been lazy accusations about Wright's Scottish allegiance, with a poisonous minority on social media dubbing him a 'plastic Jock' who adopted the Saltire as a flag of convenience.

It is true that his elocution is far removed from Sir Alex Ferguson's Govan growl, and on the Red Dragon website it acknowledges his Suffolk tones are nearer East Anglian turkey magnate Bernard Matthews than comedian Billy Connolly's Glaswegian lilt. But Wright's burning passion for Scotland only took root when his young mother, Jean, ran away from West Lothian with him in 1973, when he was still of pre-school age.

Wright had never met his father, who was in prison, when he moved south of the border, and he told Phil Lanning: 'My mum was 16 when she had me and my dad was in jail. Her sisters didn't think she was up to bringing me up at one stage and they were apparently talking about taking me off her, so my mum decided one night to just run away with me to London when I was only three. It was obviously a very difficult time for her but that's the only reason I left Scotland.

'We were in London until I was 18 and since then I've lived in so many places – Suffolk, Norfolk, Cheshire, Ayrshire. I've probably turned out for more counties in darts than any other player – I've represented all the places I've lived in. I've settled in Suffolk now and my mum lives above my wife's hairdressers down with us, but my heart still remains in Scotland.

'My true identity is that I am Scottish – I've got Scottish blood running through my veins. I'm passionate about my upbringing. I was only taken from Scotland so my mum could keep me. I'm happy to tell my story now and hope people realise that I am a true Scot. I hate it when people say I'm not. I'm proud of my country and even prouder to represent it.'

As if to prove his allegiance, Wright partnered Gary Anderson to glory at the 2019 World Cup of Darts and, with 'The Highlander' himself, big John Henderson, as his sidekick, Scotland were champions again two years later.

'You're doing it knowing the whole of Scotland are watching and supporting us,' says Wright. 'It's probably one of the hardest tournaments for a player, because you're not just playing for yourself. If you don't perform, you're not just letting yourself down – you're letting your partner down, your country down.'

It is incongruous that Peter Wright, of all people, should have to explain his identity when he is one of the most recognisable, and most celebrated, players ever to throw a dart.

Sometimes, in sport's twisting kaleidoscope, it is better to be remembered as a truly great character than simply as a great player. And when history judges 'Snakebite' Wright, he will be up there with the great entertainers, not down there among the anonymous chaff.

We shall remember the punk rock hairstyle, the outrageous facial artwork, the loud shirts and the even louder trousers. We shall remember the nearly-man, apparently condemned to a lifetime as runner-up in major finals, who finally cracked the winners' code and became a World Champion twice in three years when he was closer to superannuation than college.

And above all, we shall remember the audacity of a showman who turned darts into the colour of magic, even when the record books tell us others have won more titles and we can't remember a single distinguishing feature among them.

Take or leave his 'bad dad' dance across the stage, take or leave that mohawk, take or leave the pineapples, poppies, popcorn and assorted decorations on those outrageous outfits.

He can make a single pair of trousers look like the Chelsea Flower Show, but goodness gracious: Peter Wright is one of the greatest exponents of his trade, and the tale of his 'Snakebite' incarnation may not rival Rhett Butler and Scarlett O'Hara, but it's a great love story – with more happy endings than Hollywood's star-crossed pair.

GERWYN PRICE

PDC World Champion: 2021

ON THE oche, a 170 'Big Fish' is the holy grail of checkouts – treble 20, treble 20, bullseye, wallop.

But in the close-knit village of Markham, around 20 miles north of Cardiff, the phrase has a different meaning when Gerwyn Price is serving large cod to his customers at Chippy 501, the fish-and-chip emporium he opened in 2024 near the house he built from scratch.

Converted from a pharmacy, Price's takeaway is easy to spot beneath the apex of its charcoal-grey slate roof and the bespoke, snazzy logo. Outside, a couple of picnic benches and parasols stand on guard for those who wish to consume their fish suppers on the spot. And behind the counter, on the rare days when darts' breathless schedule permits, you will often find the former world No.1 preparing the food personally.

There is, as the proprietor himself concedes, an art to producing the nation's signature dish. As any connoisseur of Britain's enduring contribution to world cuisine will tell you, succulent, fleshy cod fillets percolating a maritime fragrance through a waistcoat of light, crisp batter will always trump slabs of frozen breeze block trussed in a soggy bubble-wrap of flour and baking powder. And the best chips are finite cartridges with salt and vinegar dancing on the surface, not saturated, sodden railway sleepers. Price's loyal custom is testament to his skill navigating a fiendishly competitive market and the positive feedback suggests he mastered the art quickly. At £11.95 for fish and chips, The Codfather makes them an offer they can't refuse. Some of his occasional patrons are darts fans who travel hundreds of miles, or make a considerable detour up the valley off the M4, just to sample the grub for themselves.

'It's a small village, only about 1,500 people, and in a place like Markham it's all about footfall,' says Price. 'Some days it earns a few bob, some days it's a little bit slow. January is hard work – people are paying the credit card bills to cover their spending over Christmas after being paid early in December, and you have to work within very tight margins, but there are ways and means of being creative. A little bit of marketing, a special offer, that sort of thing.'

As Price speaks, he is modelling his latest replica kit, as worn on stage at tournaments in 2026, with Chippy 501 among the shirt sponsors. In an antiseptic conference centre, where he is promoting the Bet MGM Premier League, the garment is a source of commercial pride. 'They offered me a gold card, so I took it,' he grins. 'Seriously, I had a spare space on the back of my shirt so I thought, "Why not fill it by promoting my own business?"

'Overall, it's done quite well, especially when you consider that I didn't really know what I was doing when we opened it and I was taking advice off a couple of mates who run fish-and-chip takeaways, asking them for information, pumping them for tips and little bits and pieces of knowledge. I'm not going to lie, the catering and hospitality sector is a difficult market and it's stressful when the staff include your own family and you want to look after them.

'There are so many strands to the business: when you open a fish-and-chip shop, the first thing you need is fish. We try and shop around, because different companies supply different things and you have to barter a little bit. If someone is charging you £40 a box more than someone else, you have to try and make a deal. Every penny counts.

'What hurts us most at the minute is our energy bills. People don't realise how much businesses get hammered for their fuel – we've been paying £1,600 to £1,700 a month just for electricity, let alone gas. We're trying to find ways of saving on energy, whether it's installing solar panels on the roof, cutting down on some of the fridges we use or shutting off appliances unless they are absolutely necessary. I don't want to be one of those sticklers who goes round turning off the lights in an empty room, but when the bills come in you don't feel guilty about doing it.'

Price's previous catering venture in Markham, Cafe 501, was financially crippled by Britain's post-Covid slump and the property was leased out as a dog grooming salon. His sister, niece, nephew, wife Bethan and eldest daughter Emily all helped out behind the counter, and soon became instrumental in running Chippy 501 as a family business, and it's not only cod that makes the tills ring.

There isn't a huge demand for deep-fried octopus or seared scallops in the Valleys on a midweek night, but there is a market for kebab meat and corned beef rissoles (budget-friendly comfort food served as breadcrumbed boulders of corned beef, mashed potato and onion, a staple in Welsh takeaways). Price does, however, get the occasional left-field request.

'We have had the odd person coming in and asking if we sell the cod raw – not grilled, not battered, just uncooked, like you can get in any supermarket – and I've no idea why. Every day is different, but the chippy gives the family work and gives something back to the community. There used to be a decent one in the village a few years ago when my mate ran it, but when he started leasing it out to someone from outside the area who didn't spend enough time there, the place went downhill, so I'm pleased if we're giving Markham something back.

'At first, it probably affected my darts more than I realised. If I was losing and playing rubbish, it's because my mind was elsewhere. I've got cameras in the shop and I was always checking them on my phone to make sure everything was OK.

'It was stressful to get it up and running, and it took up a lot of my time, but I've been able to take a step back and leave the family to run the show more often. If I'm at a loose end, kicking around the house, I'll pop in and help out with the cooking to show my face on the shop floor. It's nice when people wander in and do a double-take when they see me, but I don't do it for recognition. Like I say, it's nice to give a bit back to the place I've always called home.'

Price sets a lot of store by community. He has remained loyal to his roots in the village where he was born and the family house he built, barely a fryer skimming ladle's length from the chippy, was another investment in his roots.

'A lot of people asked me why I built a house bang on a roundabout, but when you shut the front door, you don't hear the traffic,' he says. 'It's hard when people knock on your door and ask for your signature, and not long ago someone came up from another takeaway in Newport and appeared on the doorstep offering me some spicy sauce. Sometimes it's been hard to separate the business from my home life, which is easier said than done when they are so close to each other, but it's probably one of the main reasons why I'm in the process of buying a farm and getting more out of the way. I don't mind interacting with people, but there's a time and a place.'

Price's ambition to become a son of the land and cultivate 185 acres of Caerphilly's rural hinterlands – more than half of it dense woodland – was not so much a project to mark him turning 40 years old but another change in the chameleon's colours. Ever since he quit professional rugby in 2014 to pursue a full-time career in darts, nobody on the sporting landscape has reinvented himself repeatedly with so much success. It took 'Gezzy' just seven years to complete the journey from a fiery hooker on Cross Keys' front row to a PDC World Champion, so why should anyone be surprised he made such a good fist of building his own house, opening a cafe, running a chip shop and answering Wales's agricultural national anthem, Land Of My Farmers?

As a casual player at Markham Welfare Club, where team-mates immediately recognised Price's hand-to-eye coordination was a cut above, he was soon enjoying the challenge of new horizons. Four years after dipping his toe on the oche, he was mixing it with hundreds of prospectors in the annual scramble for a PDC Tour Card at Q-school, after being encouraged to enter by Merthyr Tydfil professional Barrie Bates, the 2006 UK Open runner-up. He took the fast route to the top, as if gliding up the mountain in a cable car where others were digging for a foothold.

'I started up with Markham Welfare on Fridays and then played in the Super League for Aberbargoed on Wednesdays,' he told the *South Wales Argus*. 'It was going pretty well and Barrie (who also reached the PDC World Championship quarter-finals in 2009) encouraged me to have a go at Qualifying School. Day one didn't go well and I lost in the first round, but I managed it on day two.'

Fast forward to the closing overs of 2020, with a second strain of the COVID-19 pandemic killing more people than the original wave nine months earlier, and Boris Johnson's haphazard governance of a crisis was unravelling faster than a knitted jumper's broken stitch. At first, the Prime Minister had promised to relax punitive rules on social distancing and mixed households over Christmas, and the PDC World Championship had been permitted to start, on 15 December, with a reduced audience of 400 spectators dotted around Alexandra Palace's cavernous, 3,300-capacity West Hall.

But after just one night, with reigning champion Peter Wright beginning his defence of the title with a 3-1 win against Steve West and 'Snakebite' admitting he was "a little narked" by the eerie atmosphere where individual hecklers were prominent instead of being drowned out by the party ambience of a full house, Johnson was panicked by the spread of Covid's Delta variant. He ordered the rest of the tournament to continue behind closed doors.

Price picked his way through a sequence of tough matches before a convincing 7-3 demolition of Gary Anderson in the final, where The Iceman's laser-like finishing on tops only deserted him with the chequered flag virtually flapping under his nose, and – having wandered along Ally Pally's improvised runway to within touching distance of the Sid Waddell Trophy to settle his nerves – he sank double five to clinch victory after spurning 11 match darts.

With no dignitaries permitted on stage to hand over the trophy, poignantly Price was left alone to crown his ascension to the summit, emotionally looking towards the heavens in tribute to his mother, who had passed away five years earlier, as he lifted the ultimate prize weighing 22kg with its Eritrean red marble base.

By knocking Michael van Gerwen off the No.1 spot after 2,559 days, and absconding over Muswell Hill with the £500,000 winner's loot, Price became only the fourth player in history to top £1 million prize money on the PDC Order of Merit. And it capped a glorious year for the Welsh, with Price adding the World Cup of Darts (with Jonny Clayton) and the World Grand Prix to join previous British Darts Organisation World Champions Leighton Rees, Richie Burnett, Mark Webster and Wayne Warren as winners of the holy grail.

Darts had its first lockdown World Champion, and it had also been the most tenacious survivor since Bear Grylls in the adversity and emptiness of a viral plague. Back in April 2020, when sport worldwide all but ground to a halt, the concept of world-class players going head-to-head on the internet from their own living rooms, socially distanced by up to 10,000 miles, was supreme innovation. Bonkers, but supreme.

Now Price was lifting the Sid Waddell Trophy in the PDC World Championship's spiritual home – but he had never felt so alone.

'I can't remember too much about it except that it was one of the strangest three weeks of my life, of all our lives. I lived on my nerves a bit and most of my games, right up until the final, could have gone either way,' he says. 'Jamie Lewis, Brendan Dolan, Daryl Gurney, Stephen Bunting in the semi-final, they were all close. Gurney and Dolan went down to last-leg deciders, and I was 3-1 down against Bunting before I hit my stride. The most comfortable I felt was in the final. I'm not sure why it is, but in any tournament I always find the first round is the toughest one and I feel more at ease in semi-finals and finals.

'But when the moment arrived, and I was a World Champion, I had no one there to share it with me. The family were all back home in Wales. I couldn't even drive home that night, with the adrenaline still pumping, because I had to stick around overnight to do the morning-after media interviews. Sure, it's nice when you get back to your hotel room and there's a big trophy sitting on the table, but it doesn't make the running in any conversation. You dream of being a World Champion, the pinnacle of your sport, but when the moment came for me, it wasn't all that.

'Maybe it's because I didn't grow up in darts and I was a late starter, I don't know. But if I had picked up the rugby World Cup with Wales, I'm sure I would have been up there on cloud nine. That wasn't what I felt from winning a darts World Championship. It was weird. When I'd won the World

Grand Prix two or three months earlier, after the winning dart I turned round to see my wife and kids on a live video link from our front room, but this time I was on my own. Even when I got home the following day with the trophy, it didn't feel all that (special).'

Before his reincarnation as a formidable marksman, Price had spent a decade in rugby's professional ranks, a robust hooker who scored a crucial try for Cross Keys in their Welsh Rugby Union Cup final triumph against Pontypridd in 2012. Overturning a 13-6 deficit at the break, Keys turned up the power to run out 32-19 winners at the Millennium Stadium.

On reflection, he drew more satisfaction from the collective achievement than an individual success worth half a million quid (before tax).

He says: 'When you are playing darts, unless it's the World Cup, you are up there by yourself and you're doing it for yourself and your family. In a team sport like rugby, it feels different. It's communal. If you win a cup final, you win together. It's a long journey to the final and you're there fighting with your mates all the way.

'There might be only a few thousand fans rattling around inside the Millennium Stadium, which holds 75,000, but for me scoring a try and winning that cup final against Pontypridd was as magical as I would imagine the winning try in the Six Nations, Grand Slam or a World Cup Final is. You know what's going to happen afterwards – you go out, as a full squad of players, hit the town and have a few beers together. Even for Cross Keys, which is basically a dot on the map, it's a big deal. It's a big deal for the whole village.'

For all his reservations about the emptiness of Ally Pally, or any perceived hollowness of his achievement, in 2026 Price remained the only player to hit No.1 in the charts by winning the World Championship behind closed doors, the only Welshman to plant the red dragon at the PDC's summit and the only 'convert' from another sport who jumped ship to such stunning effect.

Just stop and think about his accomplishment for a minute. Fewer than five years after he resolved to make the oche his workplace instead of the brutal ravages of the scrum's front row, Price won his first PDC Premier event at the Grand Slam. That is an extraordinarily small timeframe for an interloper to gatecrash a circuit where Michael van Gerwen was often unstoppable, Gary Anderson was in his roaring 40s and Peter Wright was about to find his 'Snakebite' venom.

Among modern sporting contemporaries, as a high-end achiever his change of day job has few parallels. Rebecca Romero went from silver medallist in rowing's quadruple sculls at the 2004 Athens Olympics to gold medallist in cycling's individual pursuit in Beijing four years later (not to mention a World Champion's rainbow jersey, also in 2008). But where Romero's versatility was based on raw power exceeding her rivals' capacity, Price was dealing with less quantifiable virtues: precision, accuracy, consistency in an increasingly crowded field.

To become a three-times Grand Slam of Darts winner and add the World Grand Prix (also behind closed doors) in 2020, two World Series Finals triumphs plus two World Cup of Darts victories with Clayton in his first nine years as a professional should never be discounted among the sport's greatest feats.

Over the same period, he was also runner-up in five other PDC majors – the World Matchplay, UK Open (twice), European Championship, Premier League and Players Championship finals. That body of work places him comfortably in darts' top echelon of all time, a serious feat when he only broke into the top 32 on the Order of Merit in 2016.

Clayton, Price's sidekick on international duty for Wales, won four PDC Premier titles in 2021, which persuaded him to give up his job as a plasterer filling in the cracks for Carmarthenshire County Council. For 25 years, his vocation was sweet home alabaster until that gilded run made him throw in the trowel and quit his humble background in property maintenance.

'The Ferret' soon found a kindred spirit on the oche, where Price became both a formidable opponent and a loyal ally.

'We seem to look at the world through the same lens, and it's probably because we have similar backgrounds as former rugby players from a game built around a team ethic,' says Price. 'We never played in the same team because I was operating a couple of leagues above him, and you can put that in the book! I still haven't had a testimonial with Cross Keys yet, so I might set one up and ask Jonny to be our scrum-half and introduce him to our front row! But we are genuine friends off the board and when we play together representing Wales, I think you can see there's a genuine pride in that red shirt.'

Clayton's appreciation of his compatriot is also laced with good-humoured barbs about their rugby hinterland. 'I find it difficult to play against Gezzy – I have enormous respect for every dart player, but with him it's absolute,' he says. 'There's something special between me and Gez which runs deeper than being team-mates at the World Cup of Darts. At the end of the day we're both rugby boys – he was the fearless front row forward, I was a chopsy scrum-half – and there's always banter, taking the mick out of each other.

'Gezzy played a better standard of rugby than I did although I always tell him, "You were the hooker, I was the one with the brains!" Scrum-half is the one who makes the team tick in rugby, so I tease him that I've got more brains, but as a darts player I have nothing but respect for him.

'I'd never actually met him until I started playing darts, but now he's a great mate, a good friend, a great darts player. We're both rugby boys, both have the same banter, both as daft as each other… and if I beat him, I tell him I want free kebabs for a week from his fish-and-chip shop.

'It always made me sad when crowds singled him out. They seemed to pick more on Gezzy. I don't understand why people want to pay good money to watch a game of darts and try to put somebody off. Personally, I'd want to pay good money and see players performing to the best of their ability. By booing somebody, I don't think that happens and I think crowds are dead out of order when they do that.'

Price's relationship with crowds outside Wales became strained for a time after landing his first TV major title at the 2018 Grand Slam, where his £110,000 prize money was trimmed by the Darts Regulation Authority following an ill-tempered final against Gary Anderson.

There is no doubt – and 'The Iceman' readily concedes as much – that Price's fist-pumping, chest-beating, bicep-bulging celebrations when he lands important game shots or 180 maximums can rub opponents up the wrong way like teasing a genie from the lamp.

But it would be unfair to isolate his behaviour as one of a kind or to accuse him of premeditated gamesmanship. Other players can be demonstrative, perhaps not as exuberantly, but a rugby warrior bellowing encouragement to himself or his entourage is not a capital offence, even if it's not everyone's cup of tea.

What cannot happen is physical confrontation, and after Price's first Premier title was sidetracked by a momentary bumper-car collision with Anderson, the DRA hammered him with fines totalling £21,500, reduced to £11,500 on appeal, for bringing the sport into disrepute and social media posts erring towards misadventure.

In short, Price knew how to push his rivals' buttons – but the payback was unhelpful. He was booed by the crowd, even during the trophy lift, and soon he was cast as a pantomime villain at other major tournaments as predominantly English crowds used his Welshness as a flimsy premise for taunting him.

Reflecting on the Anderson incident years later, Price admitted both players were 'a little bit too boisterous', and added: 'On stage, if I hit something good I always like to show my emotions and I probably showed a bit too much in that game sometimes, but you just get caught up in the moment. Once I think Gary pushed me off the oche, but it was one of those games. To a certain extent I don't mind the boos because it can bring the best out of you, but not when you are lining up crucial doubles. That's when it goes too far.'

Behind the scenes, Price's persona has some A-list admirers, including darts royalty Phil 'The Power' Taylor, who sees little harm in his pugnacious demeanour.

Taylor, who never shied away from dissonance if it helped to give him a competitive edge, says: 'He's a difficult player to beat – he's feisty, he's got the scoring power, grit, determination… he's got everything. In fact, he reminds me of myself in my younger days. I used to be like Gezzy, and that's why I like him. If there was a player on the PDC circuit I would have liked to take under my wing, it would probably be him… after I'd wrung his neck!

'You need characters to "sell" your sport, you need rivalries, you want games with a bit of edge. Rivalry puts bums on seats, it drives TV viewing figures, like (Nigel) Benn and (Chris) Eubank when they wanted to knock six bells out of each other. Gerwyn's as fit as a fiddle, he looks after himself and once he's off the stage, he's one of the nicest people you could wish to meet. On stage, he gives it large – but so what? I like that.'

Even Taylor was surprised when Price, trying to drown out the distraction of a large German contingent at Alexandra Palace, resorted to wearing noise-cancelling headphones for a set during his World Championship quarter-final defeat by Gabriel Clemens on New Year's Day in 2023, a traumatic loss which knocked him off the No.1 spot in the rankings.

Struggling to contain his disappointment, Price even threatened to boycott Ally Pally in an emotional outburst on Instagram, posting: 'Not sure I will ever play in this event again. So frustrating, you play all year round preparing for this one tournament. So gutted I wasn't let play but good luck everyone left in.'

The spectacle of a former World Champion, 3-1 down and trying desperately to find his range amid a hostile soundtrack, returning from a break in dustbin-lid ear defenders, was greeted by some as an amusing gimmick, but some of Price's predecessors were less impressed.

In a building swarming with fancy-dress comedians, to see a top player come to the party apparently dressed as one of Doctor Who's feared Cybermen adversaries was a wardrobe malfunction according to John Lowe, who won the world title three times between 1979 and 1993.

'I do not like sitting on the fence,' said Lowe. 'My first reaction when he came out with them on in the fifth set was to smile. A joke, I thought – then I realised he was for real. It was intentional. A bigger smile – he had managed to turn the biggest event in world darts into a pantomime.

'Then it all went wrong: the defenders kept slipping on his head, they only lasted for that one set, and the next set – which was the last – he lost 3-0.'

In the Sky Sports birds' nest above the arena, pundit John Part was also taken aback. He said: 'I was stunned. I was already feeling low with a bit of a bug. That kind of woke me up a little. I thought I'd taken too many drugs. I really didn't know what was going on. I never expected to see anything like that. It was never going to work. I don't think it should ever have happened.'

It would be cruel, and unfair, for that snapshot of Price in his earmuffs to become the enduring portrait of his career. He laughs about it now, as many of us did at first, and ear defenders have since been banned by the Professional Darts Corporation – although he sought their permission, which was granted, to wear them against Clemens.

'I had been practising with them on and you couldn't hear anything,' he says. 'But the moment I walked on stage, my God, you could hear everything. I felt the hairs on the back of my neck standing up and I was like, "What have I done there?" But the thing is, (backstage) Michael (Van Gerwen) was like, "You won't do it", almost egging me on, and I was like, "I will do it." And I did. I wasn't trying to prove a point or anything – it was just something where I thought it might help me.'

Van Gerwen told Sky Sports: 'In his position, with how big he is in darts, I wouldn't have done that, but he was going through a rough period. It has never been done in darts before and also he doesn't need it. He shouldn't put himself in that position but that's darts, unfortunately.'

Happily, crowds eventually swung behind Price and began to spare him the ordeal of provocation. Amid the spectacular commercial success of the PDC, spectator behaviour has been an occasional thorn in the bed of roses, notably when individuals like Price become the lightning rod for fans' ill-mannered tendencies.

When Ally Pally becomes party central, and the PDC World Championship becomes a focal point for declaring Christmas officially open for the fancy-dress legions, normally the mood is overwhelmingly festive. Among the conditions on every ticket is the stipulation 'no football colours' to discourage the atmosphere from being hijacked by tribal rivalry, and at a tournament where more than half a million pints of lager are consumed, there are remarkably few incidents of discord.

Price feels he was singled out, by predominantly English audiences, simply for being Welsh. Others suspect his demonstrative body language on stage, flexing those biceps like Popeye after devouring a can of spinach, was also a factor. Either way, he brings a package of ability, charisma and temperament to the game which is arguably unrivalled. And a reminder: as a darts player, Price went from the foothills to the summit in just seven years.

One of his finest achievements has been to keep all the plates spinning: darts tournaments, exhibition nights, the chippy, house construction, project management and greyhound owner. Gone to the dogs? It's a rite of passage for Gezzy, whose passion for racing greyhounds is reflected in the names of his canine associates: Grandslam Champ (named after his first TV major win), the eponymous Iceman's Girl, Perfect Nine and Double Top.

As a boy, he picked up useful pocket money by walking dogs at his local track, which nourished his love of the sport, and in January 2021, as a newly crowned World Champion on the oche, he became an ambassador for the Greyhound Board of Great Britain, using his profile to promote welfare standards and the care dogs receive during and after their racing careers.

For a Premier League regular from 2018 onwards, the unrelenting schedule tested his powers of multi-tasking, and he coped admirably. Stamina is not an optional ingredient – it's essential.

Price says: 'You might have a Premier League night in Rotterdam or Antwerp, you come home and maybe go straight to a European Tour qualifier or a three-day major like the UK Open, you might have a double-header on the floor in the ProTour and go straight back to the next round of the Premier League. The travel is hard on the players, and even harder on the players' families, but I guess it's a lifestyle choice.

'ProTour events can be lonely places. The venues aren't glamorous. I've been sat in the company of other players who have lost in the early rounds, and they show me messages off partners or from people who should be there supporting them, and it stresses them out, especially if they have got to stick around for another day because it's a double-header.

'If it was just a question of playing in the Premier League – travel on Wednesday, play on Thursday, back home on Friday – it would be easy to cope with that. But if you want to slide in exhibitions, which is our own fault because nobody is forcing you to do them, plus any media days or sponsors' appearances, it's a busy life. Throw in running a fish and chip shop, building a property and buying a farm, and the diary's pretty full.'

Farmer Price has exciting plans for his rustic project. The chameleon's mind was whirling like a windmill from the moment he identified the sprawling estate's potential. It was not his intention to own a substantial expanse of real estate when he first started lobbing darts as a pastime at the Markham Welfare, but agriculture offered his inquisitive nature another avenue to explore. He says: 'Sometimes you're trying to fill a void. When I didn't get into the Grand Slam in 2024 and I had ten days off sat at home, I just didn't know what to do with myself. It's good to have a different focus and some way to just take your mind off the darts and fill that space. We built a property which I thought was our forever home, but it's not. We'd only been living there two years before the farm came on the market and we wanted to be on the move again.'

After the meticulous planning and decoration of his basement man-cave, with its dual-purpose practice area and luxurious lounge, 'The Iceman' simply couldn't resist another Himalayan test of project management. From the cinema with its 100-inch screen and 12-speaker sound system to a stocked bar, planetarium light effects and snooker table – where he has been known to compile century breaks – Price's dream home lacked few creature comforts. He once joked, 'I probably play snooker more than darts, which might be the problem!' But the ultimate man-cave didn't cauterise his creative juices, and the farm has potential to occupy his thirst for innovation on an unprecedented scale.

'The first thing we needed was planning permission effectively to get the farmhouse taken down and rebuilt,' he says. 'After standing empty for 30 years, it needed upgrading so, after building one house from scratch, I wasn't frightened about doing it all over again. What's the bloke who did the documentary about taking on a farm? Jeremy Clarkson? Yeah, that's him – hopefully there will be a new series coming out soon! I wouldn't mind doing some sort of thing where it gets filmed from start to finish. Right now, I could never be a full-on farmer as I just haven't got the time for it.

'I would lease out most of the land because it's quite a big farm – about 85 acres of open fields plus 100 acres of woodland, but I've got a lot of plans I want to do with it. If I retire when I'm 50, I might become a farmer then, but my daughter's already planning to have cats and dogs, mini-pigs, definitely some chickens and other bits and pieces. I want to try and maybe get a barn conversion there as well. Obviously, I want to try and keep somewhere for my daughters to stay around us.

'I've also got ideas about a side business in glamping pods – shepherds' huts, maybe with hot tubs and private terraces – which seem to be popular these days. We'll have the space to do it, that's for sure.

'Maybe, a few years from now, I'll be able to sit back and look at my life – rugby, darts, the chippy, house building, farming – and take some satisfaction from it. But on the darts circuit, you simply don't have time for reflection or patting yourself on the back. I don't know how many motorway miles I do each year, and it would probably frighten me if I did, but I do know every ProTour trip to somewhere like Wigan or Barnsley is at least a 400-mile round trip. The miles soon stack up in all the back-and-forth between airports, exhibitions, ProTours, Premier League nights.

'You have to Google some of the places where we play European Tour events and you need a search party to find the nearest airport. By the time you've found a flight, an onward train to the nearest town and an Uber to your hotel, it can be a bit stressful, but I don't mind. It's all part of the adventure.'

Price still remembers the day, at the end of 2014, when he took the plunge and told Beth he was going to quit rugby, cash in his chips and put the lot on darts – full-time, no cutting corners, all-in. There were no safety nets, no warranties or covenants assuring him of a decent crust by switching codes. Just a hunch that it would all work out.

'It probably took me a couple of attempts to grasp the nettle,' he says. 'I was doing both rugby and darts, Beth was working for solicitors in Cardiff, specialising in mortgage enforcement, so I'd be taking the girls to school before training and picking them up later, but the darts involved more and more travelling as I entered more events. We agreed that she would finish, spend more time with the girls and that would free up more time for me to go and play darts. If we'd hung on for another six months, there was a voluntary redundancy scheme which would have suited us. We probably missed out on 60 or 70 grand there.

'But when I told Beth I was going to jack in the rugby and go full-time on darts, she wasn't sure. It was a big change, and people don't like change, do they? Obviously, there are no guarantees, but I thought I could make a living from it. I think it was a good choice. Being a World Champion? That was a long way off, and world No.1 was even further away. Yeah, starting from scratch and making it to No.1 in the world... that's probably my best achievement professionally. My proudest moment was winning the World Cup with Jonny.

'When you're doing it for Wales, and all the patriotism that goes with it, you walk a bit taller. It's not the most lucrative tournament on the calendar, but it's the only one where you're doing it for your country – and for someone else like Jonny, who's one of the most genuine, down-to-earth guys – it's a bit special.'

Physical fitness has always been a keynote of Price's career, going back to the staple requirements of professional rugby, and occasionally he has been forced to hit the pause button to treat heat edema, a transient condition caused by blood vessels dilating and fluid retention commonly brought on by heat and humidity.

'If I was to sit in the sun or go to a hot place, sometimes it makes my hands swell and you can't grip the darts properly,' he says. 'For some reason your body can't control the temperature, so you can be sat in somewhere boiling hot like a sauna and you don't even sweat. How weird is that?'

In 2025, he also made an impression by shedding around 20kg (three stone) after a strict diet, gym routine and lifestyle changes to help his on-stage performances and mental clarity. He says: 'I wouldn't say you have to be an athlete to play darts, but it's obviously in your own interests if you are not overweight, especially when it gets to the bigger tournaments where it's longer formats. Sometimes in the European events on a Sunday, when you're playing three or four games in a day, it can definitely help.'

In a sport not previously renowned for chiselled shapes and corporal well-being, Price has cut an impressive figure on the Professional Darts Corporation walkway. As an achiever, his journey to the top has few rivals – authentic yet unorthodox. As a player, he is demonstrative and competitive on the oche but easy-going and agreeable in conversation behind the scenes.

And as a chameleon in the outside world, he is a resourceful, intuitive entrepreneur. In a game where the big fish is king, the portions of battered cod at his Chippy 501 serve to remind Gerwyn Price that he has made his mark in more than one vocation. Put his darts and catering ventures together and he's the new Eric Bistro.

MICHAEL SMITH

PDC World Champion: 2023

AS A moment in time, as a commentary box soundbite, it is without parallel.

England's 1966 World Cup triumph will always be synonymous with Kenneth Wolstenholme's conclusive remark, 'Some people are on the pitch, they think it's all over… it is now.'

Botham's Ashes in 1981, when cricket nobility Ian Botham's swashbuckling counter-attack put the Aussies to the sword, would be defined by Richie Benaud's description of a towering six off Terry Alderman's delivery at Headingley: 'Don't bother looking for that, let alone chasing it… it's gone straight into the confectionery stall and out again.'

And Jack Karnehm's whispered three-word message to Cliff Thorburn, as the Canadian snooker star lined up the final black in the first 147 maximum break at the Crucible in 1983, transcended the golden rule of impartiality: 'Good luck, mate.'

But Sky Sports commentator Wayne Mardle's soundtrack, as Michael Smith completed his nine-darter in the 2023 PDC World Championship final, was unprecedented hyperventilation. Mardle's excitable shriek damaged his vocal cords to such an extent that he was unable to continue on the air. Michael van Gerwen had just strayed high on double 12 to miss out on his own perfect leg when 'Bully Boy' stepped up to complete the greatest leg of darts ever set before a television audience.

'One man misses, does the other man get? I have never seen the like,' blustered Mardle. Three darts to go, and the treble 20 lands flush on the lipstick. 'Come on, Bully Boy,' he exclaims. Next up, it's treble 19. 'Yes!' Mardle needs oxygen at this point, and there are no spare canisters in the Alexandra Palace commentary box. Smith is now a single arrow from taking out 141 to turn Ally Pally into the capital of Doolally. 'Double 12...That is the most amazing leg of darts you will ever see in your life,' gasped Mardle. 'I can't spake! I can't spake!'

While Mardle admits his catchphrase was basically a rip-off of Castleford commentator Mick Morgan, who got angry during a rugby league match with Wigan, in a clip widely shared on YouTube, a new generation can now enjoy it.

'Rod Studd (Mardle's Sky Sports colleague) introduced me to it about a dozen years ago and "I can't speak" is something that me and Rod say to each other a lot, and when there are no words, I say it.

'I don't watch rugby league, I have no enthusiasm for it, but it's a brilliant way of saying, "No matter what, you can't add anything so you might as well go quiet."

'Rather than go quiet, I just offer "I can't speak." I do it so often it just came naturally to me, but it is an absolute rip-off of Mike Morgan. I am not claiming it as mine, it just came out.

'Maybe I have introduced it to a new generation. These things just come around, many times people have said "They think it's all over" – we all know where it's come from.

'Many times, things get passed down through the generations and the meaning becomes different. It wasn't scripted, I didn't plan for it, I didn't know what was going to come out when Michael Smith hit the 60 and then 57 and then the 24. And I am not sure it is my commentary that will stand the test of time. Hopefully the leg will.

'I have been involved in darts for 40 years and I have never, ever seen anything like it. I was in the right place at the right time and if anyone thinks I enhanced it, then I am happy to go along with that. I am just a fan with a broadcast microphone in my hand, I was in a privileged position. Unfortunately, my stint in the commentary box was cut short due to a sore throat.

'Of course I was gutted to miss the rest of that final. What was so annoying is that I knew it would be a temporary thing, but I knew I couldn't push it anyway just because the way my throat was. I couldn't help myself. At least I went out on a high.'

It was brilliant television – and probably the highest point, at that time, of darts' inexorable march into a nation's viewing habits. Mardle's shriek was the best thing to decorate a live sporting event since another voice on Sky Sports, football reporter Johnny Phillips, famously went into meltdown in a play-off game between Watford and Leicester in 2013, with a penalty missed at one end and the winning goal scored at the other, 18 seconds later, deep into stoppage time. Phillips soon recovered his composure, but his excitement was christened a 'scoregasm' by viewers.

For Smith, beaten finalist at Ally Pally in 2019 and 2022, the greatest leg was the defining moment of the crowning glory in his career.

'I still get people coming up to me saying it is the best thing they have ever seen, or strangers passing me in the street saying "I can't spake! I can't spake!" It's nice to be remembered for it,' he says.

'It's also a bit annoying that they don't mention I actually won the game. As a Manchester United fan, it's like winning the Premier League 13 times in 20 years but everyone talks about the one they lost in the last seconds of the season and the commentator (Martin Tyler) screams "Aguerrooooooo!!!" when he scores that goal against QPR.

'But I'll take it. As a moment in history, that leg kick-started the most important win of my career. It seemed more people wanted me to win that final than I did myself. I had lost against Michael and Peter Wright in my two previous finals, and I was slowly becoming a people's champion, but I needed to get over the line to justify their support instead of being the nearly-man who everyone pats on the back out of sympathy.

'I'm not bragging, and of course I could be proved wrong, but I don't think anyone will replicate that leg in a World Championship final. When you reach for the sky, you don't expect…' To land on the moon? 'Dead right.'

Smith, lest we forget, had to play out of his skin to break Van Gerwen's spell on that magical night. The nine-darter came at 1-1 in the second set, relatively early in the contest, but even when he was 6-3 ahead, needing to win one of the last four sets to wear the crown, the nerves were jangling for 'Bully Boy'. MVG took the 10th set, and led 2-0 in the 11th, before Smith summoned the resilience to finish the job. At 2-2, he nailed consecutive 180s before double eight sealed the deal.

'I was out in front, but it's not done until it's done,' he says. 'When I was throwing for the match, I had flashbacks to the two previous finals where it got away from me and I'm thinking, "Don't throw it away now – this might be the only chance you get to pick up that trophy." If it had gone to 6-5, Michael would have had the momentum, and you don't want to be giving an opponent of his calibre any more spirit and belief. He had only dropped three sets on his way to the final.

'You could see what it meant to me. I'm glad I remembered to shake Michael's hand – he's an all-time great, and I wanted to make sure I gave him all due respect – before I went off to hug the wife and kids. I think Sky Sports asked me if it was my greatest achievement and I replied, "My two greatest achievements are sat over there – my two kids." There were no over-the-top celebrations, more just a relief that I had finally done it.

'When you are standing there, with a dart in hand to become World Champion, everything you have done before goes out of the window. Like I said, I'd lost to Van Gerwen in one final, I'd lost to Peter Wright in another, and I didn't want my story to become a tale of could have, should have, never did. I had already paid a heavy price for missing out. I wasn't going to do it again.'

Smith had played most of the 2019 final against MVG with a broken left hand.

'During the second break I punched a toilet door out the back because I had darts to win the third set and I needed to get the frustration out of my system. I was careful to use my left hand – not my throwing hand – but that didn't save me. I thought the door would be flimsy and plastic, with a bit of give in it, so I gave it a proper dig… but it was rock-solid.

'My watch dial button dug into the back of my hand and snapped a bone. I knew I had done some damage straight away because I couldn't clench my hand or hold anything properly. When Barry Hearn presented me with the runner-up trophy I had to cradle it under my arm, instead of holding it aloft. I didn't mind losing the first two sets because I was never at the races, but I had a chance to go into the break only 2-1 down and I blew it. That's why I was so annoyed.

'I only had it X-rayed after I got home a couple of days later and it was still throbbing when I woke up. It was getting sorer and colourful bruising was coming out. Three days after the final I got married to (long-time partner) Dagmara and the wedding helped because I had a few drinks and that helped to numb the pain a bit.

'But the trophy was supposed to come down the aisle with me and I couldn't carry it. It was still a perfect day, and I'm not saying the smiles were fake because nobody has to force a smile on your wedding day, but I was grimacing a bit. And there was no way I was going to my wedding with a pot on my arm. I was never going to come back from my honeymoon in the Dominican Republic with half a tan where the plaster cast had been.

'I'm probably the only bloke to play in a World Championship final and get married three days later with a bust hand. Not a good look, but fortunately only a few people knew about it at the time.'

Addressing his close encounter with a toilet door 11 months later, Smith admitted he was a candidate for anger management treatment, saying: 'Well, it's something I've had since I was 14 or 15. If I feel angry with myself, I need to vent my frustration and get rid of it. But I'd never do it in front of kids, it's always behind closed doors.'

When Wright beat him 7-5 in a close final three years later, Smith was barely able to conceal his heartbreak, resting his head against the backboard and dissolving into tears after seeing a 5-4 lead overturned by 'Snakebite' reeling off nine of the last 12 legs. But life-affirming euphoria was just around the corner, garnished with a nine-dart wonder, even if Smith didn't seem to have much time to enjoy scaling Everest at last.

'It must have been 2.30am by the time I left Ally Pally following all my media interviews and got back to the hotel,' he recalls. 'The bar was shut, but I was gasping for a drink and I said, "I've just won the World Championship, is there no way I can get a bottle of lager?" They relented and said if I went to the Games Room, I could order a drink on room service, so my dad and I were sat downstairs until 5am celebrating. I had to be up again at eight o'clock to do the rounds on breakfast news for TV and radio.'

Smith had barely caught his breath before he was off to Bahrain for the first tournament of the New Year, where he took home the unique date palm trophy.

'There was no time to let it sink in. I could identify with the Arsenal footballers who won the title for the first time in 22 years, played in a Champions League final, went straight to the World Cup and had about a fortnight off, if that, before they were back in training when they got home. I needed a bit more time to absorb what I'd done.

'It's beyond most people's wildest dreams to go home with half a million quid in your back pocket – not only that, but as a World Champion your sponsorship goes up, your commercial earning power goes up, you are guaranteed so much more as world No.1 in your profession.

'It didn't change me as a person, but it did change the landscape for us as a family. Two months earlier, I'd been in eight major finals and lost the lot. But after winning the Grand Slam, and now the World Championship, I had financial security like I'd never known before. We could take the kids to places where we wanted to go, not just on budget breaks an hour up the road.'

When Smith eventually dared to let his hair down, and shared the 'postcard' on social media, in some quarters the backlash was po-faced and unhinged. Midway through the 2023 Premier League campaign, where he reached the play-offs, 'Bully Boy' treated himself and Dagmara to a short break in Las Vegas. The reaction, in some quarters, was as if he had defrocked the Bishop of Durham.

Posting on X (formerly Twitter), he published a photo of himself pouring a glass of champagne with the caption: 'Just live like a baller.' Other holiday snaps featured Smith reclining in a jacuzzi and puffing on a baseball bat-sized cigar, saying: 'World number 1, world champion and now life. Completed it mate.'

After counting his chips from a profitable break in Sin City, 'Bully Boy' had resolved to clean up on the oche, saying: 'You know when your luck's in – and it's been a good six months for me since I won the Grand Slam.'

At first, he appeared to be riding the crest of a wave. Marvelling at his run of good fortune, he said: 'I took 12 grand with me to blow it, and on my last night in Vegas I only had four grand left. I decided to blow two grand gambling and spend the rest on shopping – but I ended up winning the jackpot. I put two grand down and ended up taking 22 grand back to my room! I've won the Slam, Worlds, Bahrain, one night in the Premier League and the German Grand Prix.

'I just need to give up thinking. Like the World Championship, if it's meant to be it will happen for me. The pressure is off now that I'm World No.1 and World Champion – but I quite liked the pressure of wanting to achieve that. Now that I've got it, I've lost that little bit of fight, but I'm sure that hunger will come back. I want more world titles than Gary (Anderson). I got to World No.1, which he never did. We are still mates, and when we retire, I want some bragging rights over him.'

When luck, and his form, deserted him, Smith was castigated by the social media hawks. The Las Vegas trip, the railway sleeper cigar, the £750 Don Perignon bubbles and the 'completed it' post became weapons to browbeat him like cavemen's cudgels. His short break on the Strip was an expedient reference point to blame for the downturn in his performances, but when he looks back now, he is defiant.

'If I won another world title, I would go back to Las Vegas and I wouldn't do it any differently,' he insists.

'When I was losing all those major finals, the same people on social media were calling me a bottle job, then when I finally cracked it and landed the biggest prize of all, they were telling me I shouldn't have been giving it large ones. You can't have it both ways.

'I had just got a star on my shirt – why shouldn't I celebrate fulfilling the dream of a lifetime? It's something I had been striving to get since I was at school, but the moment I'm World Champion and reach No.1 in the world I'm supposed to sit in the corner and be quiet about it?

'I gave up five holidays in six months because the schedule was so rammed and I didn't have a spare moment. All I wanted to do was to celebrate properly. Anyone who says they would have stayed at home is having a laugh. If you get promotion at work, and it comes with a big pay rise, you go out and celebrate, don't you? It's human nature.

'I always dreamed of being a darts World Champion, so don't tell me I can't enjoy the moment. If my form tailed off, I've only got myself to blame if I didn't practise enough. But it wasn't down to four days in Las Vegas.'

The down-slope, after the giddy high of that momentous night at Ally Pally, was a reminder for Smith that success is a fickle mistress at the top end of sport. Those who mistake his quickfire delivery for carelessness are wide of the mark. He has never hung around on the oche like a forlorn commuter waiting in vain for a train that's been cancelled. And for those of us who thought it would be difficult to top the nine-dart leg in a World Championship final as a story, 12 months later a 16-year-old lad called Luke Littler came along and disabused us of our restricted horizons.

The journey has, however, vindicated handsomely the intervention of a scout at a Professional Darts Corporation Youth Tour event in February 2011, where the top prize was just £600 and the Barnsley Metrodome was an unlikely setting for future World Champions to audition for visionary mentors.

Smith had beaten Michael van Gerwen, including a nine-darter which turned out to be a harbinger of their famous leg 12 years later, before losing to Shaun Griffiths in the final when he felt a tap on the shoulder and turned round to find Gary Anderson, beaten finalist in the PDC World Championship final seven weeks earlier, making him an offer he couldn't refuse.

Anderson and his manager, Tommy Gilmour, were looking to expand their stable by signing up a couple of likely lads from the under-21 ranks, and Smith's latent promise was by now an open secret on the circuit. The 'Flying Scotsman' invited Smith and Adam Hunt, winner of the year's opening Youth Tour event, to join the band.

'When I started following darts and taking it seriously, Gary, Adrian Lewis and 'Chizzy' (Dave Chsinall) were the people I loved watching because of the way they played and their heavy scoring,' says Smith, who first stepped on to the PDC tour as a shy 17-year-old in 2008. 'When Gary came over, he said Tommy's stable was starting to put a team together and would I consider joining them. I didn't ask any questions. No hesitation, I just dived in. It was too good an opportunity to miss.'

After leaving school, Smith had dropped out of a joinery course at college, with one exam left, to play in a darts tournament and cheerfully described it as the best decision of his life, but hooking up with Anderson as his mentor was on another level.

The day after agreeing to join forces with Anderson, Smith won his first ProTour competition at senior level in a UK Open qualifier, defeating Chisnall 6-5 in the final, and 'Bully Boy' had lift-off. He won the 2013 PDC Youth World Championship with a 6-1 win against Ricky Evans in the final, but his biggest statement by far was to follow on the grandest stage of all.

Smith stunned Phil Taylor, the 16-times champion defending his world title at Alexandra Palace, with a seismic 4-3 win in the second round, taking out 128 on the bullseye to clinch victory. 'The Power' would reach another two finals but never added to his 16 crowns. For Smith, on the other hand, it was time to confront a burgeoning truth: if he could turf Taylor off his throne, the world was at his feet.

He says: 'That was the game that gave me the belief, but working with Gary gave me the momentum. Until then, my mum and dad had been working all hours, several jobs on the go at once, just so they could take me to tournaments which would have been out of reach financially. I remember going to my first tournament abroad – I had never been out of the country before – and we had to drive to Germany because I couldn't afford the air fare.

'When Gary got hold of me, he said, "Instead of being a part-time player, we're going to take you here, there and everywhere. If you're going to be a full-time professional, you've got to be all-in. We can help get you into hotels, but where the darts land is down to you." It was fantastic to live in the shadow of someone who was just arriving at the top.

'For me, having good people around you – in my case, it was parents, extended family and rock-solid influences like Gary – is more important than anything. There's a lot of emphasis on going to Q School, winning your Tour card and it's the golden ticket... but on its own a Tour card won't make you rich. It's a golden ticket to debt unless you win decent prize money on the circuit.

'If you play 35 ProTour events and 15 European Tour events, and you are getting knocked out in the first round every week, you're £250 a week down on hotel bills alone. A lot of the boys starting out have managers taking 30 to 40 per cent cuts, then if you do win some prize money it's taxed at 20 per cent, and when you tot up your net income at the end of the month it's next to nothing. When I was starting out, you won £6,000 if you won a ProTour – but after all the deductions for tax, entry fees and management, you might only walk away with £2,000. That's the harsh reality.

'You can't quit your day job because you still need some income to pay your bills at home. That's why beating Taylor on the big stage was such an important starting block. Overnight I became a household name, or at least my name was in all the papers as the bloke who beat a legend. He didn't play bad, but I absolutely pounded the treble 20 bed that night. Gary told me to make sure I showed the man due respect and said, "You need to kick on now. You need to start taking this forward. You've had a good night but this has got to be your level. From now on, it gets serious." He was right.'

Smith's knockout blow to end Taylor's reign as World Champion – and, it soon transpired, as No.1 in the world rankings – wrongly gave rise to the impression that his 'Bully Boy' nickname was connected with his fondness for checking out on the sweet spot of a dartboard. In fact, it was given to him as a teenager when he worked as a cattle farmhand during school holidays.

It would have been all too easy for Smith to fall into the trap of becoming a layabout, drifting aimlessly on street corners and shopping malls in St Helens with his contemporaries while his mother, Sandra, worked round the clock cleaning pubs, offices and garages to make ends meet. Vacations were scarce, so he would often spend holidays discovering the meaning of the adage that where there's muck, there's brass.

He says: 'I used to work on a cattle farm in Littleborough and I loved it, but it was hard graft and I wouldn't do it for a living. That's where I got my 'Bully Boy' nickname – it was nothing to do with darts. When the cows gave birth, the farm owner, who used to be a bouncer at my auntie's pub, got me to help with tagging the new-born calves.

'It wasn't a slick operation. For half an hour or 35 minutes at a time, I got slammed in cowpats and cow's muck. They didn't always like it and I had one on its back, my fingers in its nose, legs in the air. The farmer called me a bully because I didn't hang about, and that's how the nickname stuck. For the record, I'm not a bully or an aggressive person by nature – far from it – but when I needed a nickname, that's what came to mind.

'From about 13 years old, when I shot up from 5ft 2in to 6ft 1in over a matter of months, I've always been a burly lad. I played rugby a lot for my school and they didn't leave me gathering dust on the wing, put it that way. So, when it came to wrestling cattle, I was up for the challenge – but I wouldn't recommend it if you like pristine white trainers.'

Since the star appeared on his shirt, as he puts it, Smith's toughest opponent has been an insidious, formidable antagonist with no world ranking – arthritis. A freak accident in 2009 left him with a staggering 42 broken bones in his hands and wrists, and it's a wonder he was ever fit to throw darts in the first place.

He tells the story in a remarkably matter-of-fact fashion as if it was as everyday as shopping for bread and milk in the supermarket, but those of a squeamish disposition should look away now or turn the page because it will bring tears to your eyes.

'When you come from St Helens, rugby league is the only game in town,' he says. 'I played rugby as a teenager, but I broke my hip and couldn't do it anymore. I'm not saying I'm glad I got injured, but it led to me putting more emphasis on playing darts, and I've no regrets about skipping my final joinery exam at college to play in a double-header on the ProTour, even though it didn't go well.

'On the day of my exam, I bunked off to play in a PDC floor event instead. I got beat 6-0 in the first round by Phil Taylor, the next day I lost 6-2 against Andy Hamilton and I thought I'd thrown my life away. My parents worked about six jobs to send me to tournaments all over the country and I didn't want to let them down, but I nearly blew it on Christmas Eve 2009. I went out for a few drinks with the lads, slipped on the ice walking home and broke both my wrists. I was in a cast for four months.

'I was sat in my mate's house, in the next road from where I lived, playing *Resident Evil* on the Xbox and drinking too many cans of Stella, just dossing. Although it was only a few minutes' walk home, it had properly iced up outside and I slipped. I put both arms out to break the fall, as you would, and although it hurt the alcohol probably masked the pain. I remember sleeping on my mate's couch, woke at 6am on Christmas morning and when I tried to put my hoodie on, my hands weren't working. I had to ask for help, and as soon as I got home my mum said I needed to go to hospital.

'Although I was told I was a priority case at A&E, and they would get me seen as soon as possible, I was there for seven hours on Christmas Day. Mum had got me a new Xbox as a present and I couldn't play it because there was a plaster cast on one arm and the other was knackered. The only reason they didn't put a cast on both wrists was so I could brush my teeth and perform other daily tasks, if you know what I mean. As a human being, you still have to function.

'I had to put my darts away in a cupboard for about two months, but as soon as the cast came off, I came back and won my first ProTour event, beating 'Chizzy' 6-5 in the final. I had cortisone injections in my wrist because when I first came back, my first dart completely missed the board at home and hit the mural which I'd just painted in my games room, so that was fun.

'I was warned that arthritis might become a factor when I got older, and they weren't lying. It's been catching up with me, especially my right hand, and when I'm playing in cold venues the cold gets to my wrist – but that hasn't been the only problem.'

Another Christmas mishap, in 2024, left him with severe osteoarthritis in his shoulder. This time, it was down to freakishly bad luck.

'I'd bought the kids two e-scooters and I thought I'd race one of them,' he says. 'I went over what I thought was a puddle but it was actually a pothole. I've hit that at 22mph, gone straight over the handlebars and hit my shoulder into the floor. I couldn't pick my arm up for seven weeks. I also had a big cut. Even now, I've still got a bit of bone sticking out in my shoulder.

'Luckily, I had Man City physio Ben Thompson working with me. Dagmara met Ben at the Manchester Premier League meeting a while back. It's mad that he would come over to work on me after doing Erling Haaland or Phil Foden's legs. Ben says AC (acromioclavicular) joint injuries are more common in rugby than footballers or dart players, and I've got a bit of bone that sticks out now, but I'm told that will never go away.

'That scooter is jinxed. It broke my shoulder and then, about a month later, it came out of storage and Junior (Smith's eldest son) hit a stone, came off and broke his hand.

'I've also had problems with my feet. First it was the left one and then the right foot got jealous and started giving me trouble. The pain is manageable, and I'm surrounded by five different painkillers to prove it, but the real battle is in your head. You are always fighting your demons and you have to stay focused, keep doing what you do best. My two strongest suits are how to be a dad and how to play darts, and I'm not going to give up on either of those.

'One thing I'll never do is use it (arthritis) as an excuse. If you want to let it drag you down, it will. I've never feared anything or backed away from a challenge. The pain isn't great but there's nothing that strong painkillers can't help me to get through it.

'I've played a World Championship final with a broken hand, I reached a UK Open final with a hole in my groin due to an infection and I've won ProTours and Euro Tour events despite problems with my ankle. It's a case of mind over matter. I could go and hide in a darkened room, and convince myself that I don't want to do it anymore, or I could quit the PDC, hand in my Tour Card and live off exhibition money for £3,000 a night.

'One exhibition a week means I could do 150 grand a year, but I don't want to make a living out of trick shots – I want to compete, reach finals, win trophies, do it the hard way. If my attitude is right, my luck will change. You will see a burst which will show the magic is still there – 12, 11, 10, maybe even nine-dart legs – what I have been missing is the consistency.

'When you are down in the dumps, you are damaging your brain more than your throw. You can get over pain, but psychologically you are constantly fighting to bring out the best in yourself.

'I might be a moaner, but I've never been a quitter. I know what it takes to reach the top, and whether it's my shoulder, my ankles, my wrist or whatever, I've always just got on with it. There are countless tournaments to shoot for, and if I start winning again, I won't be in pain when I wake up in the morning – I'll be raring to go and get back on the practice board.

'I'm not blaming my shoulder or my ankle – it's my head. I go into matches thinking, "I hope my shoulder doesn't click or my wrist doesn't give out." They're fine, but it's me worrying. That's the real issue.

'Worst case scenario is a shoulder replacement, which isn't great, but that would only be when I retire. A whole new shoulder would be like learning to play all over again. I got scared when I Googled it, but for now injections will keep me going. Hopefully the operation can wait until I'm 45.

'I've never asked for sympathy and this isn't a cry for help, but it annoyed me when I read things online saying that I was finished. This is my reality, and I don't have any problem with sharing it in public. I can still play darts.'

Smith and Luke Humphries joined forces to win the World Cup of Darts for England in 2024, and later that year he was runner-up to Luke Littler in the World Series Finals, but 2025 was a barren year as he tackled his assorted ailments and his first individual title in three years was snatched away, in dramatic style, by Beau Greaves's brilliant 142 checkout to claim the first Players Championship title by a female player at Milton Keynes in April 2026. Greaves beat three former World Champions – Rob Cross, Anderson and Smith – on her path to a landmark victory.

After that near-miss with a winner's cheque, 'Bully Boy' felt his right foot pinching, retreated to his hotel room, removed his sock and watched his ankle swell like a flat tyre being inflated. But any discomfort was pushed into the background by rekindling his acquaintance with the business end of a tournament.

His ambition on the oche is undiminished, and fans who join in with the chorus of his 'Shut Up And Dance' walk-on song have not heard the last of Smith's Walk The Moon anthem yet. As well as being one of the most naturally gifted players of his generation, with a fluid – almost languid – throw, his raw honesty and affable nature preserve him as a crown jewel of the PDC circuit. His glorious, self-deprecating humour may not always have been appreciated by the turkeys among his livestock, with two of his poultry ominously named 'Christmas Day Dinner' and 'Boxing Day Dinner', but he has never been afraid to give it some Paxo in media interviews.

And Smith's lifelong ambition since wrestling young cattle amid the cowpats and agricultural fragrance of the barn as a teenager – to own his own bull as king of the family ranch – still burns bright.

'I need the boys to grow a bit older, and a bit bigger, so they can look after it if I'm away playing at tournaments,' he says. 'They are fine looking after the chickens, turkeys and ducks, but if I'm away or laid up in bed, I can't ask the missus to handle a half-tonne animal. She's only 5ft 5in and it wouldn't be fair. Cows are curious and inquisitive, and you can get close to them, but when a bull's in a bad mood, that's another thing altogether.'

One day, controlling bovine aggression will be for Smith and Dagmara to work out for themselves, but his recollection of how they first hooked up, as recounted to Dutch publication *De Telegraaf*, is pure gold.

'She lived in Ireland and we once played a tournament there for a PDC event. I didn't even remember meeting her. At some point that day, I had managed to lose my coat and phone,' Smith admitted. He had, however, made an indelible impression.

'When I got home I created a Facebook account for the first time in my life, and she was the first one to add me as a friend. I thought, "Who the heck is this?" She asked if I remembered her. "Sorry, but no," was my response. She informed me that she had my coat because I was too drunk to put it on. Then we spent the day together and now look: we're two kids down the road.'

LUKE HUMPHRIES

PDC World Champion: 2024

UP ON the roof, Luke Humphries gained a sneak preview of the scenery from on top of the world.

When he was working for Malone Roofing in Newbury, where the workforce included his father and brother, Humphries knew his way around the tiles, mastic, asphalt, felt layering, leadwork and cladding as well as he found his way around a dartboard.

For the proverbial chip off the old block – his dad, Mark, was a handy darts player himself, playing for Berkshire at county level – the wisecracks and blue-collar banter kept Humphries grounded until, aged 22, he earned a Professional Darts Corporation Tour Card after winning five titles on the Development Tour circuit.

Within six years, 'Cool Hand Luke' was the bad guy who trashed a fairy tale, beating 16-year-old Luke Littler in the World Championship final after the world's media descended on a north London hilltop, and newspapers had cleared their front pages in anticipation of the ultimate boy's own story.

If Humphries reeling off his 19th straight win, or his 26th victory in 27 matches at Premier PDC events, was the director's cut, not the scripted Hollywood finale, he was a model of humility. Diplomatic in victory, and gracious in defeat when the tables were turned by Littler in the Premier League play-off final five months later, Humphries became a role model for sportsmanship in an age when too many cup finals, shoot-outs and prize-fights are tainted by trash talk and sink estate yobbishness.

In short, if your daughter brought a lad of Humphries's basic decency home to meet the prospective in-laws, you'd sink to your knees in thanks for her good taste.

The road to utopia, in January 2024, was not straightforward. Humphries had lived dangerously in earlier rounds, and his third-round 'nipper' against Ricardo Pietreczko had briefly brought out the raging bull in him.

'When I look back now, I keep thinking about how I managed to become a World Champion after so many close calls,' he says. 'More than once I had my back against the wall and I managed to escape so many times. Against Pietreczko I was 3-1 down with the German fans in the crowd getting on my back, staring defeat in the face and I wasn't playing very well – to be blunt, I was being outplayed because I was playing rubbish. From somewhere, and I'm not sure how, I managed to pull that one out of the fire, give it back to those German fans a little bit and you think to yourself, "Is that going to be the great escape that fires you up to win the World Championship?" Even great champions often have a brush with disaster on their way to winning the title.

'Little did I know that I would soon make a habit of it. Going into my next game, against Joe Cullen, I thought I'd already had my fair share of drama for one tournament, but I doubled it and it went down to sudden death. To this day, it's still probably my favourite game of all the matches I've been involved in – you can't manufacture the ebb and flow, the drama, the madness of needing double five to win it and busting your score with double 12 in the next-door bed, as I did.

'When you survive so many close calls, and you're getting away with so much, you do start to wonder if your name is on the trophy. As it happens, I didn't look back – I found my level against 'Chizzy' (Dave Chisnall) in the quarter-final and I was right on it, top gear, in the semis.'

Humphries's 6-0 whitewash of Scott Williams, who had shocked the in-form Michael van Gerwen in the last eight, took him to his fourth final in five PDC Premier events after winning the World Grand Prix, Grand Slam of Darts and Players Championship finals in the previous three months.

Remove all the hogwash about him being the 'bad guy' in the final against 16-year-old Littler, forget about the careless whispers of him being the grinch who sprayed graffiti over a fairytale, and ignore the partisan sniping about him being a 'boring' World Champion. Humphries deserved his crowning glory on 3 January 2024 because he was the best player on the night, and he had lived admirably with the pressure of his pre-tournament billing as favourite.

He averaged 103.50 against Chisnall, a monster 108.74 in his bulldozing of Williams and, where others had been unable to keep a clear mind amid the stardust of Littler's teenage rampage, 103.67 in the final was good enough to get the job done: champion of the world aged 28.

'The long format is more forgiving if you're struggling to find your feet,' admits Humphries. 'If it's the best of 11 legs, like a Premier League night, and you're off the boil for three or four legs, there's no second chances. You're gone. But the World Championship gives you time to grow into your rhythm, and it was effectively a tournament of two halves for me: I was lucky to get away with it in the first half and I had to hold on for dear life to the dream of being a World Champion, but from the quarter-final onwards, that was the real me. I showed the level that was needed, I produced my best darts when it mattered most.

'I'm not going to apologise if it trampled on a few Hollywood scripts, or ruined a few fairytale headlines. The bad guy? Put it this way: I don't think I'd make a very good villain in a James Bond movie.'

Humphries sensed that glory was his for the taking when Littler, 4-2 up and caressing his darts into the board like Liberace playing the piano, crucially missed a shot at double two to go 5-2 ahead. Humphries stepped in to reduce the deficit to just one set by pinning double 14 and never faltered from that reprieve. 'Luke the Nuke' has always looked back in anguish at that turning point, but Humphries believes he could still have gone on to win from three sets down.

'You can look at it both ways,' says Humphries. 'Psychologically, yes, there's one hell of a difference between being 5-2 down and only 4-3 behind, but if it had gone to 5-2, I would have had nothing to lose. Shackles off, no need to over-think things or over-complicate the game, just give it everything and see where it takes you. In a way, I was actually thinking that way when I went into the break at 4-3 because I felt I'd been trying to force it, trying too hard, and I'd been letting Luke run away with it.

'When we came out after the break I said to myself, "It's now or never – let's see if you're ready for this." If I came out and started playing really well, the way I had in the second half of 2023, I was going to win it… and happily for me, that's how it worked out. I started averaging 112 in a set, reeled off five sets on the bounce and even Luke, as good as he is, was always going to struggle when I was posting those numbers.

'Would I have played that well from 5-2 down? It's a hypothetical question now, but the more you keep coming back at someone – even if they have such a good lead – the harder it is for them to break the spell. If he had been 5-2 up and then 6-5 down, his mind would have been in the gutter, especially for a 16-year-old who was relatively new to the best-of-13-sets concept and trying to win a World Championship. I don't often wonder how it might have turned out because I don't really think about it.

'Yes, I was gutted in a way that it was me who ended his fairytale, but I had my own Hollywood script to write and you can't pass up the chance to be a World Champion because you never know when, or if, you'll get another one.

'I'm just glad it was me on that stage with Luke because, at the time, it was probably the biggest game of darts on the planet since the dawn of time – and I was the winner of that game. I was all over the front pages, the back pages and the ten o'clock news because I was part of history. Maybe the outcome wasn't the kind of history they were looking for, but it was the best-ever time to be in the final at Ally Pally and win it because the whole world was watching.

'When it was there to be won, I was just thinking, "For heaven's sake, get this one done because this kid's going to dominate world darts soon and you might not get a better opportunity." On that double eight, my arm was shaking like mad. I'm not sure how the winning dart found the right bed – it just fell in the right place. What made it special is that there was a time in my life when I had been really depressed and I went through a lot of problems.'

It was, and will always be remain, much to Humphries's credit that he decorated his finest hour with humility and exemplary sportsmanship. Where more demonstrative winners might have rubbed a 16-year-old boy's nose in the anguish of defeat by swinging from the chandeliers and ostentatious celebration, 'Cool Hand Luke' was a model of restraint.

A few salty spectators, with little sense of occasion and even fewer good manners, had booed Humphries as he lined up double eight to take the title with Littler gesturing urgently to ask for decorum – a gentleman as well as a phenomenon.

When the arrow landed safely at its destination, Humphries had banished the demons – to use his own word – which had threatened to engulf him, and gone from rock-bottom to cloud nine in the space of four years. It's an astonishing journey worth reliving because it should serve as inspiration to anyone feeling down in the dumps that they can climb the darkest mountain and find salvation in the sunlit uplands.

Back in the closing overs of 2020, with the World Championship banished behind closed doors during the second wave of COVID-19, Humphries had crumbled to a 3-2 defeat, from two sets up, against 66-year-old Paul Lim in the first round, an upset which forced him into a forensic audit of his game: technique, preparation, equipment, lifestyle, diet, the lot.

The brutal honesty of his introspection changed his appearance, his outlook and, ultimately, turned the tide of history in his favour. The pandemic and its suffocating strictures on social distancing afforded him the time and scope to address his weight, and by the time households were allowed to mingle freely again, he had shed four stone in as many months, setting himself a target of losing 4lbs every week, and his fidelity to a punishing fitness regime was soon rewarded on the oche. By the time he faced Lim, now aged 71, again at Ally Pally in December 2025, he had banked eight major titles.

Humphries, addressing his self-loathing with immense candour, said: 'When I looked in the mirror, I didn't like the way I looked, I didn't like the way I felt, I didn't like the way I was feeling tired all the time.

'When you're overweight, you feel tired a lot. There's a lot of things I didn't like about myself, but I changed it all and put it right. It gave me more confidence in myself, not just as a player but as a person as well. That's what definitely helped me become the player I am today.

'Sitting here now, although I lost against Paul on the night in 2020, in a way I think I actually won, to be honest. Sometimes it takes a defeat like that to give you that little bit of a kick up the backside you do need in life. Sometimes a loss like that in any sport can help you in the long run.

'It made me realise that I wasn't at the perfect level that I know I could have been at. I lost the weight because I knew that, after being two sets up, I started to get a little bit jaded, a little bit weary, and it cost me. I just never looked back from that moment. At least I did everything I could to be the best version of myself, so it was a blessing in disguise.

'Obviously, a few months later, I'd lost about four stone, and I was in my first major final at the UK Open. I still speak to Paul about it and kind of thank him for winning that game because it helped to reboot my career.'

Let's get one thing straight: whatever he may have thought of himself, Humphries was never a porker. It is, however, true that he turned the frustration of lockdown into an opportunity for conspicuous body transformation.

Setting himself a nominal target of losing around four pounds (around 1.8kg) per week, his strict regime of pedal power, healthy dieting and diligent practice – in that order – worked wonders.

'Lockdown was a horrible situation for the whole country, and a horrible situation for so many people who lost loved ones and weren't able to say goodbye to them properly,' he says. 'I was one of the lucky ones who was able to turn that negative into a positive during the second one.

'It could have gone the other way – sitting around all day, nothing to do, putting on more weight through sheer boredom because we weren't allowed to mix socially – but fortunately I got on my exercise bike, got myself into a routine of eating well and exercising well, not forgetting about darts but pushing it into the background to some extent. My God, it worked so well. Sometimes you can lose too much weight too quickly and it all piles back on, but losing four stone helped to improve my stamina, my performance and my self-confidence.

'I could walk down the street without wondering if people were thinking, "Look at that fat so-and-so" or muttering under their breath about my weight or appearance. I know it sounds a bit boring, but I was happy just to blend into the crowd... I know that's more difficult now, because sometimes you do get recognised in the street, but at least it's now mainly being "clocked" as the bloke who won a world title, not for being a fatty.

'I've found topping up with energy gels, and electrolytes to keep water retention levels high under the punishing lights on stage, has helped before I go on stage. Look, I'm not running a marathon, and I don't know whether it physically works, but it feels like it works and keeps me feeling energised. There was a time, a few years ago, when I would feel a bit tired if I was involved in a long match on stage and I had to change something. Gels, electrolytes, they just seemed to make a difference. I also noticed that, if I ate any 'bad' food that nutritionists wouldn't recommend, sometimes it would make me feel a bit lethargic.

'When you feel flat and tired, darts is really hard. It's not rocket science – just a bit more exercise, eating healthy and steering clear of the late-night stuff that makes you feel sluggish all helps. Those little one, two, five per cent parts that you put into the system can all benefit your performance. This lifestyle can take a lot out of you, but each player is different. There have been guys who have won major tournaments carrying a lot of weight and there are players on the circuit who are in great shape but they have won nothing, so there's no one-size-fits-all science to it.

'As a rule of thumb, with the demands of the schedule now, you're better off being in good shape, especially when you get into your late 30s and 40s. It's important to look after yourself. When you're younger, maybe you get away with cutting a few corners – but when you reach a certain age, and those joints and muscles are creaking when you get out of bed in the morning, that's when you'll feel the benefit of a sensible lifestyle.'

To emerge from the doldrums, blinking in the pyrotechnic fanfares and tickertape blizzard reserved for a World Champion, was the ultimate vindication of Humphries's recalibration – but the trip wasn't always smooth. Along the way, he had to confront doubts, despair, depression and pangs of distress which, ultimately, required professional intervention to manage them and tether the worst effects.

'There was a time in my life when I was really depressed,' he said after making the acquaintance of the Sid Waddell Trophy. 'I didn't think this was going to be it for me. I couldn't do it up on the big stage. I went through a lot of problems. There were tough times, times when I questioned whether I could do this or be a part of this world because I struggled with anxiety. I've worked hard to overcome things, I had my own battles to face, but I took them head on.

'Anxiety isn't something you can put away in a cupboard and forget about it. I've still got it now, I still get anxious moments – there is no trigger, no single thing which brings it to the surface like a song that makes you cry. I've just learned to manage it better. Dealing with it, and being able to keep performing at a high level, is no mean feat because it's really tough to deal with.

'Your mind is the most powerful part of your body because it can trick you into thinking or believing things that aren't even true, and it can also teach you and train you to do things that you wouldn't normally do. You might be thinking about a problem with your foot, something trivial like a blister if you're getting used to wearing a new pair of shoes, and if you let your mind run away, the next thing you're convinced you need to see a physiotherapist because something's clinically wrong. If you listen to your brain and treat every pain you feel as an emergency, you'll go insane.

'That, in essence, was a big part of my problem when anxiety threatened to take over. My brain wouldn't filter out the small things, so I was having "problems" with my chest when there was nothing seriously wrong with it, and I had to train myself to get over a little bit of tightness which was just the body's natural reaction to excitement or tension. Once I was in control of it, I was more confident, I found more enjoyment playing darts and my life blossomed out more than it ever had. Anxiety was always my toughest opponent, and I'm proud that I managed to evaluate it and keep it in check, even if I couldn't get rid of it.'

Humphries can still recall, with devastating clarity, the night he first encountered the wastelands of anxiety and the realisation that it could seriously derail his career.

If there was a mental tripwire, at first it was not evident in plain sight. He reached the World Championship quarter-finals in consecutive years (in the 2019 and 2020 tournaments), knocking out defending champion Rob Cross in the first instance, and winning the PDC World Youth Championship to underline his abundant promise.

But those demons were lurking in the shadows. In Saarbrucken at the German Open in 2019, Humphries was 5-2 up against James Wade when he suffered a panic attack on stage and went on to lose 6-5. Being able to complete the match, even though he lost, was one of his most important achievements because all his instincts were telling him to get the hell out of there. He knew it was serious because the symptoms were familiar – and now they were becoming repetitive.

He says: 'The first time I can remember it being as problem, like bubbling to the surface, was before I had even played at the World Championship, after an exhibition night where I was playing against Phil Taylor, Simon Whitlock and a few other top professionals.

'I actually beat Phil that night and, for a young kid trying to make his way in the game, that's pretty overwhelming – it sets your pulse racing, in a positive way, and I went to bed feeling pretty happy with myself. But I woke up at about four in the morning with palpitations, as if my heart was trying to punch its way out of my chest and beating like a drum, and I was a bit frightened because I'd never experienced anything like that before.

'I thought something was wrong and it panicked me – I thought I was having a heart attack, although there was no obvious reason why a young man in his early 20s should be going through something so serious.

'The following night I did another exhibition and everything seemed to have settled down, but the next day I started getting a tingling sensation down my arm – which is one of the red flags that you might be heading for a major cardiac event – and it really panicked me again. It stressed me out, and ever since then I've always been more acutely aware of palpitations, my heartbeat racing, that sort of stuff.

'On the whole, I was only aware of it in everyday situations, but then it started creeping into when I was playing darts and it became harder to play my normal game. A lot of people thought I was suffering from anxiety because of darts and the pressure of match situations, or that I had been affected by reaching the quarter-finals at the World Championship and I was suddenly being weighed down by the expectation, but that was nothing to do with it. The issue had already taken root, it was already in my system.'

Clinically, Humphries may have been in good order, but the preoccupation with his heartbeat – listening out for palpitations, racing pulses or irregular rhythms – spiralled towards obsession. Every waking hour he would be checking if his heart was beating normally, and if he sensed any deviation from clockwork patterns, panic attacks would follow.

Nobody could see the battle raging within, but privately Humphries was close to jacking it in and going back to laying felt roofing. He hopes his rise to world No.1 can serve as a template, for legions of people from all walks of life, facing the ghouls of depression and anxiety.

'I've had many, many messages over the years off people saying they look up to someone being so honest and open about it,' he says. 'It's a daily struggle a lot of people go through in their lives, but the important message is that you can overcome it, you can manage it, you can achieve your dreams. I went from a dark place to being a World Champion in three or four years, and I feel very blessed to be sitting here now with accolades against my name.

'Many people have had to go through a lot worse but I want to use it as a positive to say if there are struggles in your life you can still go on and achieve great things. You don't have to be a World Champion to feel like you've achieved something great. If it's just the small things that people are able to achieve, there can be huge positivity in that.

'The anxiety I suffered never goes away, ever, but it's important you learn to identify the signs and how to manage it. It's just a thing that can happen at any moment. You know when you feel it because you start to come over a little heavy chested and faintish, but the important thing I did was to breathe through it.

'There were times when I felt I just wanted to get off stage but you can't do that, so that was the hardest thing for me, but over the last three to four years I've managed to handle episodes of anxiety in a professional way and I try not to let it affect my performances anymore.

'It's important to open up on the subject and talk about it because I feel as if it's not talked about enough, but obviously it's up to people about whether they want to share their experiences and feelings or not. Everybody in life goes through some sort of struggle. Everybody's struggles are different. Life comes at you fast – and you have to be ready for it when it does.

'The thing is, when you are in that position where you encounter it for the first time, you don't know how to react or what you can do to stop it. At first, I didn't know what to do, so I just went into anxious mode and it all spiralled downhill. I didn't know there was professional help available, people who understood the condition and could outline the coping mechanisms.

'So, the two most important factors are, one, recognising there is a problem and, two, seeking help to treat it. Anxiety is a mental condition, not a physiological issue where you are dealing with bones, muscles or moving body parts. Seeking CBT (cognitive behavioural therapy) was probably the best thing I've ever done.

'There was an American coach (New York Yankees legend Yogi Berra) who famously said baseball was 90 per cent mental and the other half is physical – and I can see what he meant. When you are standing on that oche, and there's half a million quid riding on the next dart, it's so important that what goes on between the ears at that moment is calm and rational.

'To be honest, the money side of it and the numbers don't float through your head in those pressure moments. It's more about the feeling of being on the verge of winning a tournament, of being a champion, that's hardest to get over. If I was throwing at bullseye to win £1 million in a non-ranking event or lining up double eight to win the World Championship, there's more pressure riding on that double eight because it could give you a legacy, something for your kids and your family to be proud of.

'Don't get me wrong: the prize money is nice, but there's more to being a World Champion than having a nice sum sat in your bank account. The exhibition dates soon fill up, sponsors want to be associated with the best players and you're a World Champion for life. Nobody can take it away from you. In 100 years' time, my name will still be in the record books.

'And in its own way, that prestige helps you to relax. I won't have to go through my whole career thinking, "I should have been a World Champion" or tormenting myself that I was good enough to win a few majors but never the big one. If I never won that trophy again, I'd always have that moment in time as a reference point. When my son's in the playground and other kids ask him what his dad does, I'd much rather he tells them, "My dad's a World Champion" instead of "My dad's a millionaire." It sounds more cool, less boastful, doesn't it? Money's not the be-all and end-all for me.

'I don't go around spending money like it's going out of fashion anyway, but the buzz I get from winning tournaments will always outweigh the pay cheques that come with them.'

The key to Humphries's stratospheric rise was his brave decision to seek that professional help – namely the cognitive behavioural therapy – instead of soldiering on alone. Where he was once a tortured soul, stressed and distracted on stage and hoping nobody would notice, he reached out for counselling.

'If there's anybody out there who's been going through what I went through, don't suffer in silence,' he says. 'The best thing to do is to seek help because it really did help me as a person – and you'd be surprised how many people identify with your problems. Without naming names, I've had several fellow professionals come up to me saying they had been through the same thing.

'It just makes you realise you are not alone. When I was at a low ebb, I felt lonely because I thought I was the only person going through this and no one else is struggling. That's why I flagged up the idea of giving up darts because I didn't think I could carry on with the burden, thinking I was carrying it alone.

'Once it was out there, public knowledge, so many people rallied around me and helped me deal with it. Fortunately it's not like the bad old days, 30 years ago, where there was a stigma to mental health and people would look down on you or just say, "Come on, pull yourself together." These days you are more likely to find some support – not just a shoulder to cry on but someone who will put the kettle on, make a cup of tea and listen.'

Humphries paraded the Sid Waddell Trophy in front of 36,000 fans at his beloved Leeds United's Elland Road stadium. His father, Mark, had named his son as an acronym of 'Leeds United Kings of Europe' and his subservience to the White Rose of Yorkshire has never wavered – just as his resolve on the oche has served him well.

The morning after his crowning glory at Ally Pally in 2024, speaking to the Professional Darts Corporation's in-house channel after barely three hours' sleep, he said: 'I've always prided myself on being incredibly hard to beat and making the other guy work incredibly hard to win, and now I've achieved everything I've always wanted to, it makes me more hungry and determined than ever to go on and win a lot more in the future.

'In the space of a few years I went from wondering if I was cut out to play darts at the highest level to an aura of feeling invincible. Of course, I'm not invincible – the standard is so high that there's always someone waiting to take aim at that target on your back. You can feel on top of the world, but it can come crashing down at any moment.

'That's why dedication is important and behaving like a champion is important. I have a duty to perform and conduct myself as a world No.1 and prove that I deserve to be where I am. The sport has grown to levels I never thought possible, second behind only football in the ratings, and everybody wants to be part of it. I'm incredibly proud to be a flag-bearer for darts.'

Among the brickbats and barbs aimed witlessly at Humphries after his rise to No.1 in the PDC order of merit was the ludicrous charge that he was a 'boring' champion.

The cheap shots on social media would be amusing if they weren't so preposterous. Dullards don't drive a £200,000 Lamborghini. Losers don't propose to their future wives on the top floor of The Edge in New York, 100 storeys up in the Manhattan skyline. And shambling dolts don't get awarded the MBE for services to darts and charity.

It is not mandatory for superstars to dismantle the television in their hotel rooms like rock stars, nor is it compulsory for successful sportsmen to flaunt their wealth or farm their popularity on a reality TV show. Humphries, based in Cheshire after moving north to be with his partner Kayley – is content to maintain a relatively low profile because it is largely in tune with his unpretentious personality.

'I'm not a boring person,' he insists. 'I know loads of people seem to say it on social media, but what you see on stage is not the person you meet in real life. The comments do not affect me. People can say whatever they want to say – everyone's entitled to an opinion. I'm the one that's doing all the hard work and if I were to create a fake persona, and do things that weren't in my personality, I probably wouldn't be doing the things I do. That's the great thing about darts, there's so many different personalities. A lot of them come out on stage, mine comes out behind the stage.

'A lot of people see me up there and they think I'm miserable and moody – but I'm not not. When I'm on stage, I'm just so dedicated to winning that I don't want to be too happy, too smiley and almost put myself off. You need tunnel vision to win the game, and then you can be happy afterwards. There are moments when you can enjoy yourself and have a bit of fun, but you don't win if you don't put the fear into people.'

Returning to this theme in an interview with the *Guardian*, he said: 'If I've got to be slightly boring to win major titles, like some people say, no problem. No one said it before. But as soon as I won the Grand Prix, one person tagged me and all of a sudden everyone was jumping on the bandwagon. If you're successful, people just want to bring you down.

'Gezzy [Gerwyn] Price got a lot of hate, but for what reason? I get it for not celebrating enough. He gets it for celebrating too much. So, you can't win either way. Darts fans are fickle. You can't win with them sometimes. Everyone's entitled to an opinion and there are some players that do take it to heart. But I've got thick skin. There is nothing anybody could say that would hurt or upset me.'

As for the MBE, there was no disguising the pride behind Humphries's accolade by royal appointment.

After virtually half a century of snobbery largely shunting darts into the long grass, the Kings's Birthday Honours in 2025 recognised Humphries and Littler with MBEs, while first lady of the women's game, Deta Hedman, was awarded the OBE – a distinction she decorated five months later by winning her first world title at the WDF's Lakeside event aged 66.

'I don't think a lot of people realise why it's such a big deal. You don't just get one for being a good dart player – that's only part of the story,' says Humphries. 'I don't blow my own trumpet or publicise some of the things I do off the board for charity or hospitals as well. I don't shout it from the rooftops because I don't need to be told, "Well done for doing this or doing that" or to be rewarded for things away from darts. It's been a privilege to play a part in changing the face of the sport – most of it is down to Luke Littler, of course, but I feel like I've been a part of his success by challenging him and making him work hard for his achievements. In return, he's been making me work even harder to try and keep up with him!

'I know he's done it on a much bigger scale, and from a younger generational part of it, but I think him having someone that can compete with him, compete against him and push him all the way, it's made it really exciting for the sport. Everyone's talking about darts now, and I think that we're two of the pioneering parts of that. We've changed the face of darts over the last couple of years. It's starting to become a younger man's game, and it's nice to be at the forefront of that.

'When I got the letter, I kind of couldn't believe it when I opened it and it's a very proud moment. My mum and dad were obviously incredibly proud as well because their son was getting an MBE, which isn't something that happens every day of the week.

'It usually happens later on in people's careers, but it's happened in mine pretty early and I feel blessed, to be honest. When my son grows up and understands what it means, I'm sure he'd be very, very proud, and it was a great feeling to meet the Prince of Wales (at the investiture) – he knows about darts, which shows just how big the sport has become.'

National allegiances aside, there was a gratifying, satisfying aspect to Humphries and Littler winning the World Cup of Darts for England in 2026 in Frankfurt, where they had endured such a rough ride 12 months earlier on their debut as a pair in the tournament. Drawn against hosts Germany, in a hostile atmosphere they fell by the wayside at the first hurdle. The Lukes of Hazard fared better on their return, the world's two best players living up to their billing as top seeds after their chemistry as a double act had been questioned in 2025.

For conquering Alexandra Palace and mercurial crowds, hobnobbing with royalty at Windsor Castle, confronting the demons of anxiety and carrying himself with a nobleman's dignity, Luke Humphries deserves all the plaudits. Always a class act in victory, his sense of humour in defeat has often served him just as well.

Following his surprise 6-4 loss to Belgian dark horse Mike De Decker in the 2024 World Grand Prix final, fans in Leicester serenaded 'Cool Hand Luke' – to the tune of Joy Division's melancholy gothic rock anthem 'Love Will Tear Us Apart' – with a chorus of 'Leeds Are Falling Apart Again', a reference to his beloved football team's near-miss with promotion earlier that year. Humphries responded by cupping his ear, gesturing to fans that they should crank up the volume, and turned their mocking into appreciative applause.

It's difficult to dislike him. Any hostility towards Humphries feels synthetic or forced at best, and on a professional level he is reliable, the archetypal safe pair of hands.

'He's a very conscientious individual who wants to do the right thing by himself and by the sport as a whole,' says PDC chief executive Matthew Porter. 'Luke always conducts himself in a composed manner – calmness and a mild temperament is sometimes, unfairly, interpreted as a weakness, but with him it's a real strength.

'It's probably reflected in the way he goes about his job on stage. You don't see him lose his rag during a game, and he's not a gloater who tries to get under your skin. He's been a good ambassador for darts.'

Two-time PDC World Champion Adrian Lewis takes it even further. 'Luke is the best World Champion we've had,' he says. 'For the way he plays the game, for the way he represents us as a sport, he's a star. And I'm not just saying that because he lives round the corner from me!'

If there are few horizons left for Humphries to conquer, he has already weighed up his next move beyond the oche.

'First and foremost, I just want to ride the wave and enjoy being a dart player because there has never been a better time to be involved in this sport,' he says. 'But as I get older, and it's something I've always wanted to do but I've never found the time, I'd like to renovate properties. Buy houses going cheap on the market because they need a bit of work, do them up, sell them for a profit.

'I started out working up on the roofs, helping people to improve their properties, but I've always had a wish to get involved in other aspects of maintenance and home improvement. I'd have to wait until I can be fully involved and be a hands-on project manager, but it's something I've always wanted do to – I don't know why, but that sense of fulfilment has always appealed to me since I was 16 or 17.

'Having been up on the roof, putting the finishing touches to a property, I'd like to be there at ground zero when the foundations go in and seeing it through from start to finish. I was in awe of Gezzy (Gerwyn Price) when he built his house from scratch, because you would think there aren't enough hours in the day to do that and become the world's No.1 darts player. Fair play to him.'

LUKE LITTLER

PDC World Champion: 2025, 2026

WE CAN easily forgive a child who is afraid of the dark, surmised the ancient Greek philosopher Plato. The real tragedy of life, he argued, is when grown men are afraid of the light.

Fearless in exalted company, and breathtaking in his release of talent like a genie from the bottle, Luke Littler joined the pantheon of great sporting teenagers by reaching the Professional Darts Corporation World Championship final at 16 years of age and then winning it, 12 months later, to confirm the dawn of a precocious age. Oh, and then he won it again the following year.

In the 21st century, darts has rocketed from pubs to palaces, from working men's clubs to world-class entertainment arenas, from prize money substantial enough to buy a modest house to fortunes vast enough to buy the whole estate.

And nobody has accelerated its affluence more than a kid from Warrington whose mum, Lisa, worked in a candle shop and whose father, Anthony, was a taxi driver. The boy wonder not only turned the soaring ramparts of Alexandra Palace into his own fortress, but among the fancy-dress platoons dressed as Superman, Batman, Spiderman or Thunderbirds characters, he became the real-life superhero who walked among them.

By the time he rung in the New Year by lifting the Sid Waddell Trophy for the second consecutive season in 2026, Littler had captured his tenth major title in 21 attempts. Only Phil Taylor and Michael van Gerwen have dominated the oche to such an exorbitant level. As a teenager, 'Luke the Nuke' was already a generational talent and the closest thing to Taylor's clinical, relentless winning machine since 'The Power' landed his 16th World Championship title in 2013.

Taylor was an obsessive workaholic who left nothing to chance in his exhaustive practice regime; Littler, as he still concedes, only practises when chastised by an unexpected defeat or to fine-tune his competitive sharpness. But it is a measure of darts' stratospheric popularity, and the sums of money now swirling around the game, that when Littler banked the sport's first £1 million payday with his savage 7-1 demolition of Gian van Veen in the 2026 World Championship final, he earned roughly as much in 43 minutes of playing time as Taylor stockpiled in all his 16 triumphs put together.

Darts, as the *Guardian's* Jonathan Liew observed, feels 'like an old house being stripped down and renovated at a furious rate, demolished and rebuilt until it is barely recognisable from its original form.' And the kid from Warrington is at the vanguard of the makeover.

From appearing on prime-time chat shows to an audience with Manchester United royalty Sir Alex Ferguson and receiving an MBE from Prince William at a Windsor Castle investiture, Littler is a certified A-lister now.

But for the boy king who's not afraid of the dark there have already been pitfalls along a gilded path. Capricious audiences, sometimes fuelled by shallow football allegiances and jugs of lager, have occasionally given him a rough ride. And in our rush to learn more about the superstar who was runner-up in the BBC's flagship Sports Personality of the Year poll at the first attempt in 2024, red lines have been crossed.

Littler's adolescence might have been a handicap in other sporting arenas where bullishness, bravado and braggadocio often hold sway against the innocence of youth. Sneers on social media, casting aspersions about his age, even led to certain media outlets reproducing his birth certificate as proof of his tender years. Typically, he batted away the good-natured chants of thirsty crowds serenading him with refrains of 'You've got school in the morning' as saloon-bar humour.

But a World Champion whose adolescence was played out in the public eye should not have to verify his age: it should be venerated.

'What can you do? I was only 12 or 13 when I started growing a little beard,' he says. 'It's just a number, isn't it? If

I'm doing well at a young age, people can like it or not like it. My age is what it is. To be successful, and a two-time World Champion by the time you're 18, isn't normal. I get that. I didn't expect it, the family didn't expect it, but what am I supposed to do? For myself, sponsors have come in and backed me, helped me along, and I appreciate their support.

'But what I am doing is down to me. It's not normal, but I'm not going to apologise for my age or being good at my job. In 20 or 30 years I would like to have more world titles and build on what I've already won. If some people can't handle it, that's their problem.'

One of the most impressive aspects of Littler's ascent to fame is his laid-back nature, and the mask rarely slips. It would have been too easy for him to hide among the massed ranks of sullen, graceless teenagers, but his manners are a credit to his upbringing.

'From a young age, mum and dad just wanted me to enjoy it,' he acknowledges. 'At certain times, at certain tournaments, they have encouraged me as parents who want the best for their son. But telling me, "Come on, Luke, get up and practise" doesn't make them pushy parents. I knew they were right if I was just messing around on my phone or having a laugh and a joke with my mates when a big tournament was coming up and everyone else was on the practice board.

'But that's the only time when they have pushed me. During lockdown, I would be on the board five or six hours a day because there was nothing else to do. During the first seven or eight months of that year (2020), we weren't allowed out of our houses for 23 hours a day. 'That's when I properly kicked on – practising for hours, playing in competitions online. I was playing against friends and a few PDC players at that time, and it definitely paid off.

'When we were allowed back out to play in the pubs, and I was winning straight knockout tournaments, that's when I really started to think I was ready for this.

'To be honest, football was the dream – or at least I wanted to be a footballer – but it's the hardest one to crack. There are so many (broken dreams of) young players who join club academies but they don't go on to get picked as professionals and it's hard to take. My dad told me to focus more on darts than football, and obviously I'm glad that he did.

'Did darts impact my education at school? Well, when I was playing at a tournament three or four hours away, we were getting home around 11 o'clock at night and I was late for school the following morning, at first they were having none of it. But once I joined the PDC Development Tour in 2023, that's when they started to take a bit of care. And when I played at my first World Championship, and reached the final, there was never any question of my going back to school. I guess all those late nights paid off.'

Unlike other freaks of sporting achievement, Littler's success is not based on pursuit of slavish perfection round-the-clock. When it's time to switch on, darts in hand, he is as focused and driven as any of his rivals, but his quality of practice is not measured by hours on the shop floor. He will never champion mechanical, repetitive drills ahead of half an hour picking off combinations. For a 150 checkout, he is not afraid to go treble 20, treble 20, double 15 instead of more prescribed routes.

And he loves a big fish. Littler hit five 170 finishes in the space of four weeks during the 2026 Premier League season. Another one, at a crucial juncture, helped to see off Wales in a tight match at the World Cup of Darts. He practises them like a postman's knock, often engineering the countdown from 501 to leave 170, but it's not a daily routine. 'The Nuke' can go for weeks at a time without committing himself to rehearsals, yet he rarely fluffs his lines.

Phil Taylor used to deny himself a slither of turkey on Christmas Day until he had hit at least half a dozen 180s on the practice board, but Littler's approach is less regimental.

He says: 'Obviously, motivation comes from within, and there will be a few days – although it's comparatively rare – when I think to myself, "You need to go and practice." I don't stay there for hours on end just for the sake of it or to punish myself. Twenty minutes, maybe 25, can make a difference if it's concentrated. But if I go to a tournament and get knocked out, that's when I get in the car and think, "You should have prepared better." When I do practise, I mean business. I like to test myself. Legs of 501, starting with 100 average, then 105, up to 110, going as high as I can. I'm looking to beat myself – not beat myself up.'

If Littler's mastery of combination finishes and turning the dartboard into a funfair ride where others see a maze is a triumph of hand-to-eye co-ordination, his calm authority in the public eye from adolescence is a revelation. He does not freeze on the oche, and he doesn't freeze in the face of a rapacious media. Online channels, YouTubers, TV, radio, newspapers, bloggers… none of it unsettles him.

'I probably learned to face the media in lockdown,' he says. 'I was playing in certain tournaments, like an Australian open, online every Saturday, and games against better players or known players were streamed live on Facebook. You got interviewed if you won and that helped me in many ways not to be shy in front of a camera. I've got better and more confident, which is just as well – there are a lot of people who seem to want to speak to me now!

'Obviously, doing an interview on Zoom is not as intimidating as sitting in front of a whole bank of microphones. But coming on the PDC Tour, with media days before big events, I've just got better at it. And it's just a bit easier if you are sitting there with the world's media camped in front of you, and there's a nice big trophy you've just won sitting on the top table.

'I want to be where I am now, and I'm here on merit, but sometimes I think it would be nice to go back a few years, not be known and it would be better. I'm happy to give anybody a picture – it only takes five seconds of your time, and five seconds for a bit of goodwill is nothing – but there's a time and a place. When I'm eating, just let me enjoy my dinner.

'Plenty of times I've walked into a restaurant and people have spotted me, but they wait until after I've had my meal and I get up to leave. That's fine, and I'm happy to oblige. Manners don't cost anything. Success is nice, but I'm thankful for a bit of "me" time when I go out.'

PDC president Barry Hearn, with half a century of experience in identifying the brightest stars in the constellation, watched Littler announce himself in an elite orbit and knew immediately the boy wonder's feats meant big business. Hearn cheerfully describes himself as a 'benevolent despot' because of his sharp eye for a lucrative opportunity, giving rise to his famous line 'I can just smell the money.'

But he has never seen a kid rise so fast, nor sensed the fragrance of money so readily. 'We should rejoice,' he grins. 'Christmas is a time for rejoicing – not just for Jesus but for the darts as well.

'I thought I'd seen it all when Michael Smith hit that nine-darter in the final and in the commentary box Wayne Mardle is shrieking, "I can't spake! I can't spake!" And then Luke Littler comes along and takes darts to another orbit.'

In that gilded orbit, Sky Sports announced a jaw-dropping deal worth £25 million-a-year as the home of darts on TV in 2025. For Hearn, Littler's fairytale rise was the ultimate bargaining chip.

He said: 'When I took over as Professional Darts Corporation chairman in 2001, Sky Sports were paying us £100,000-a-year for all their darts coverage and I told the broadcaster's head of sport, Vic Wakeling, "It's tough to negotiate with you as I always feel you have one of my testicles in your safe." Wakeling looked at me and replied: "Barry, I've got both your testicles in my safe."

'Luke Littler's story gives me a reason to turn round to my wife and say, "You told me you didn't like darts, but you don't miss a dart when Luke is on the box." He has brought in a new generation of fans and we have to be ready to harness their custom. There's still a look-down-your-nose attitude towards darts in some quarters, but Littler earned over £2 million at 17 years of age, and he bought his mum and dad a nice house. That brings it home what darts can do to change your life.

'It's still too early to say if he will become the greatest phenomenon of my 50 years as a sports promoter because so much depends on those around him and the player himself. But first glances are very optimistic. He seems a very nice young man. He has got frailties, everyone has. But he has an incredible ability. I want to see where Luke Littler is in five years' time. He could be the biggest influence in darts that we have ever seen beyond Phil Taylor, beyond Eric Bristow.

'They were larger than life characters, but this guy has come into it from a slightly different angle because he's retained his ordinariness. "I'll just go and have a kebab." Who says that after a big win at the World Championship? "Did you practice much?" "No, I was on my Xbox all night."

'Before his first game I reminded him about one little thing my best mate in the world, Steve Davis, told me 50 years ago. I asked him how he coped with all the pressure and he said to me, "Barry, when something means the world to you, if you can play as if it means nothing, then you will be a champion." I think Littler has got that little bit of magical ingredient in him along those lines.

'This young man has got his feet on the ground. He's got the right attitude and behind Luke Littler are dozens of other Luke Littlers coming from all over the world, and that's the excitement. Littler took us from a sport to mainstream. All of a sudden, kids were watching, nans and grandads, parents were watching. It became what we always look for in sport – a narrative. It's about the personality and the stories behind the personality.

'There was some feeling within the Professional Darts Corporation, "Is this a bit too early to put a youngster under that type of pressure?" There were going to be 10,000 fans every Thursday night for 17 nights in the Premier League. Can he cope? Will it affect his long-term future?

'Eddie (PDC chairman Eddie Hearn) and I sat down to discuss it and the first thing Eddie said was, "It doesn't matter what age you are, if you're good enough, you're old enough" – our job is to give people a chance and roll the dice and, my word, didn't that pay off in spades?

'I did give him a bit of advice at his second World Championship, when it was clear his success was no flash in the pan. I told him, "Listen, you're going to find you've got a lot of friends now, son – don't listen to anybody. Give yourself a chance. Just put the money in the bank and forget about it." It's the best advice I could ever give anyone. We've got plenty of time to spend money, not necessarily plenty of time to earn money. You don't know what's around the corner.

'Sport is a very brutal world. It is about winning and claiming the high ground. There will be envy around. Luke Littler is the next Tiger Woods for darts, so they'd better get used to it, and the only way to compete is to get better.'

Littler's eye of the Tiger took him to the final in each of his first three PDC World Championship campaigns – runner-up, champion, champion, in that order – and nobody knows how many more will follow, but the potential is frightening.

'There were nights during my first one where I was awake until five o'clock in the morning, just on my phone, refreshing Instagram, watching my followers go up. Before my first-round match against Christian Kist, I had 4,000 followers but with every win, it went crazy. By the time I was in the final I had more than a million followers on Instagram, the most-followed darts player on the planet.'

After his 3-0 whitewash of Kist, with an eye-popping 106.12 average, one of the earnest hacks surrounding the press conference dais asked Littler how a 16-year-old would celebrate a handsome win on his Ally Pally debut. 'I'll probably go out for a kebab,' he replied, little realising that his honest choice of late-night takeaway would earn him an instant reputation as the Pitta Pan of darts. 'Yes, I had a kebab after my first-round win, but after that I didn't have another one for two weeks,' he protested. 'It was almost like they were making out I had kebab for my Christmas dinner.'

Littler did not have to wait long to make his next big statement at Ally Pally. Just 24 hours later, he was taking to the limelight again like a duck to orange sauce. Andrew Gilding, the reigning UK Open champion, was nobody's pushover, even if his body language on the oche was habitual and perfunctory.

'Goldfinger' plays the guitar in his local church band, but behind the kumbaya image there is a headbanger who spends long drives to tournaments assaulting his eardrums with heavy metal rock music. Gilding spent part of his £110,000 prize money from winning his first major extending his collection of replica rock-star guitars, as used by Eric Clapton and Jimmy Page.

'I was hoping to draw some youngster who had never been there before, and that's what I got,' he said. 'But he's something special, that's for sure. I had caught Luke's first-round match (against Kist), and when he averaged 106, I thought "Oh, here we go." When I got up on the stage, there were people booing me and I wondered what was going on.

'I didn't really know much about him until then, I hadn't been following him. But when I was in Blackpool at the World Matchplay, when I went for a kebab after playing one night a couple of people in there were saying, 'Watch out for Luke Littler' and I was saying, "Who's that?" Everyone knows who he is now.'

Before he knew it, the guitar hero was two sets down and Littler was purring again. Gilding eventually went down 3-1 and conceded the boy wonder was going to be the big noise in town, no matter how much he cranked up the volume on his heavy metal racket.

Canadian Matt Campbell, who had made a 7,500-mile dash home from London for Christmas, walked into a firestorm of Littler arrows on his return, shipping the first six legs before the Warrington whizzkid eased home 4-1 to reach the last 16 – and a glamorous tie against former PDC World Champion Raymond van Barneveld, one of his childhood heroes despite the Dutchman's Circus Tavern thriller against Taylor coming three weeks before 'The Nuke' was even born.

Adulation alone could not bridge the 40-year age gap between Littler and 'Barney', and for all his experience of the big stage the former postman fell into the same trap as Kist, Gilding and Campbell: the boy king was three sets up, and disappearing over the horizon, before Van Barneveld knew what had hit him.

Almost lost, amid the marvel of boy wonder schooling the master, was his impressive 105.01 average. Knocking out ton-plus strike rates is the sign of a champion, and there was no let-up in the quarter-final against Brendan Dolan, where a 101.93 going rate was too much for the genial 'History Maker' from Northern Ireland. Now there could be no doubts: Littler was not just a serious contender, he looked a world champion in the making.

In the semi-finals, Rob Cross took the first set, but it was like a red flag to a bull; by the time Littler had romped home 6-2, it was more of a white flag. Of more concern, however, was Humphries's rampant form, and his 6-0 whitewash of Scott Williams to book an all-Luke final, dropping only seven legs, was ominously dominant.

The formbook was not leading us up the garden path. In the final, Humphries prevailed 7-4 and Littler's astonishing run was denied its fairytale ending – but if ever a championship hinged on a single dart, this was it. 'The Nuke' was 4-2 up, and playing like a dream, when he was left with a single dart at double two to go 5-2 ahead after inadvertently landing a treble 18 instead of a single, to leave tops, with 58 remaining. Pin it, and he would have been favourite to go all the way to the winning post.

This time, however, the fine margins went against him. He paused, for the first time, before releasing the dart, which slipped south of the wire on the outer ring, and Humphries – waiting on 28 – seized his chance of reprieve. Instead of being 5-2 down, he was now trailing only 4-3 and the shift in momentum was seismic. He went on to take another four sets without reply to land the title, and Littler would later reflect on the moment the crown slipped away.

'Regrets? Yeah, probably that double two,' he admitted. 'I think that just took a sting out of the game. If I'd hit that... that's the big question, isn't it? If I hit that, do I go on and win it? But I didn't hit it. That was all down to me, not thinking about it, not sure what I had left. That's what happens if you don't take your chance with the best player in the world sat on 28 – he will ping it, like Luke did. That is the one difference I would make because then I'm two sets away and you never know what might have happened... but it wasn't meant to be.'

The agony of defeat was soon outweighed by the realisation that Littler had fired a nation's imagination. He was the talk of the town, and his face was everywhere – including some unlikely bastions of prime-time television.

From the best-kept secret in darts, he was a guest on ITV's prime-time Jonathan Ross chat show, and he was soon appearing every week on current affairs comedy quiz *Have I Got News For You*. Look at the collage of famous faces and headlines behind captains Ian Hislop and Paul Merton on the BBC's long-running hit show and one stood out in the gallery normally reserved for politicians and royalty. Incredibly, larger than life in the backdrop, was a 17-year-old darts player. Have I Got Nukes For You, indeed.

Littler's impact, on his World Championship debut, made his inclusion in the 2024 Premier League cast inevitable, and he celebrated by unfurling a nine-darter against Nathan Aspinall, in the first leg of a quarter-final, on his next appearance at the Bahrain Darts Masters. Aspinall could only laugh at the upstart's grand entrance: 'Who writes your scripts?'

In 2024, His Nukeship would go on to pave the path towards greatness by winning his maiden Premier League campaign, including another perfect leg against Humphries in a re-run of their Ally Pally final – except this time, the momentum shifted in the opposite direction midway through the contest and Littler prevailed.

By the time he returned to Alexandra Palace, after winning the Grand Slam of Darts in Wolverhampton the previous month, Littler was the bookies' favourite and the most in-form player in the field. It was no surprise that he reached the final again, even if he struggled to find any fluency in the earlier rounds, never more so than his opening skirmish with demon barber Ryan Meikle.

The pressure of living up to expectations was almost too much for Littler, who dissolved into tears in his mother's arms by the walkway after grinding out a 3-1 win against Meikle where the margin of victory flattered him. He needed to turn on the power, averaging a tournament record 140.91 in the fourth set, to clinch victory – and he admitted; 'It was probably the toughest game I've ever played. I had to fight until the end. It is the worst game I have played. I have never felt anything like that before.

'It's probably the biggest time that nerves have got to me. Coming into it I was fine, but as soon as [referee] George Noble said, "Game on", I couldn't throw them.'

Ian White and Ryan Joyce were also stubborn opponents in later rounds, 'Diamond' White revelling in the nostalgia of having faced Littler's grandfather, Phil, on the Runcorn pub league circuit during the 1990s – White for the Egerton and Littler for the Albion. 'I used to beat him all the time,' said White. 'Luke hasn't even turned 18 yet, so let's see if he can keep it going. He's got to have a beer, he's got to be with the girls yet. But we have never seen a darts player on the *Jonathan Ross Show* before – now, all of a sudden, Luke's on it and darts is brilliant.'

Never behind in the contest, but never able to shake off Joyce's relentless tenacity until the conclusion, Littler's 4-3 win in the fourth round – where defending champion Humphries came unstuck against Peter Wright – was the last time 'The Nuke' would even give his opponent a sniff in the tournament. He eased past Nathan Aspinall 5-2 in the quarter-finals, blitzed Stephen Bunting 6-1 in the semis after racing into a four-set lead… and then repeated the dose against Michael van Gerwen in the final.

Here was a 17-year-old boy surgically dismantling one of the all-time greats fearlessly, ruthlessly, improbably. In the space of 13 months, destiny's child rose from No.164 in the world rankings to No.2 with a 7-3 win so clinical, so pitiless, that he was 4-0 up inside just 24 minutes. Van Gerwen needed a 132 finish on the bullseye to stop the rot and avert the spectre of a whitewash, but it was only temporary respite.

'Every moment he got to hurt me, he did,' conceded the shellshocked Dutchman afterwards. 'I'm twice his age, and I'm an old b****** compared to him, but every 17 years a star is born and he's one of them. You have to take it on the chin and take it as a champion.'

Perhaps it felt so inevitable that Littler would reach the summit sooner or later, following his near-miss with glory 12 months earlier, but his moment of triumph had the air of a rite of passage. Like a franchise inter-city train, we knew it was coming; we just couldn't be sure when. But at 17 years and 347 days, he was the youngest darts World Champion in history, seven years younger than Van Gerwen when he won his first title in 2014.

Armed with £500,000 pocket money beyond most teenagers' wildest dreams, Littler cheerfully assessed his spending power, resolved to pass his driving test and dreamed out loud of surveying every car showroom to pick his dream set of wheels.

Barely a fortnight after his coronation, he would cross the threshold into adulthood at the bar and ballot box – and his first year as a World Champion was instructive. Ally Pally was the first of six major titles in 2025, but there was also a taste of crowds choosing to place a target on his back instead of a garland around his shoulders.

German audiences, who had greeted him as a kindergarten conqueror in his first year on the PDC circuit in Europe, turned on him for no obvious reason other than being a champion ripe for being knocked off his perch. One defeat, by Gian van Veen at the German Darts Grand Prix, led to him considering a boycott of European Tour events in the Fatherland. 'I had a little head loss moment, as some of us players do,' he admitted. 'I just don't get it, and I can't explain it. Obviously, you do your walk-on, but then as soon as I got on stage, I started getting booed.'

When he did return to Germany, Littler and Humphries's double act representing England at the World Cup of Darts in Frankfurt was short-lived. By a cruel twist of fate, the draw pitted them against the host nation, and they wilted in front of a bellicose crowd backing Martin Schindler and Ricardo Pietreczko.

If he was chastened by the experience, it seemed to infuse Littler with new powers of brinkmanship. At the World Matchplay, he prevailed 13-11 against Jermaine Wattimena after trailing the Dutchman 7-2, squeezed past Andrew Gilding 16-14 in the last eight and edged a classic slugfest with Josh Rock in the semi-finals 17-14, with the help of a nine-darter, after shipping the first five legs. The pair's combined 29 maximum 180s was a tournament record. The final, against James Wade, was almost a carbon copy: Littler, 5-0 down again before he found his range to close out an 18-13 win with a 107.24 average, was almost apologetic afterwards for 'putting my family and friends through it' on his trail of comeback victories.

The World Grand Prix, Grand Slam – where Littler overtook Humphries as No.1 in the world rankings by reaching the final – and Players Championship Finals titles soon followed before he returned to Alexandra Palace as top seed, in top form and looking unbeatable.

But with around 25 per cent of tickets snapped up by German fans, for whom party season at the darts has become a thirsty crusade like the overseas contingent at the Oktoberfest in Munich, he did not enjoy unanimous hero worship. In an expanded 128-player field, after whitewashing Darius Labanauskas (efficiently), David Davies (unconvincingly) and slowcoach Mensur Suljović (brilliantly), he dropped his first sets of the tournament in a 4-2 win against Cross punctuated by pulses of booing.

Littler absorbed the bumps in the road with a torrent of 17 maximums and celebrated several times by asking 'What now?' towards his detractors. 'Am I bothered? Really, am I bothered?! Really not bothered!', Littler told Sky Sports in his post-match interview. 'Can I just say one thing? You guys pay for the tickets and you pay for my prize money so thank you, thank you for my money! Thank you for booing me.'

He would revisit his relationship with hostile audiences in the 2026 Premier League, but where some detected ruffled feathers amid Littler's defiance at Ally Pally, in truth his eyes were still firmly on the prize. The defending champion's eyesight became a hot topic among the chattering classes after *The Sun* and *Daily Mirror* revealed Littler had undergone corrective surgery at Warrington Hospital to repair strabismus – a condition where the eyes do not align – as a child. Asked if his life could have played out differently without the operation, he said: 'Who knows? When I was four or five, I got it sorted. I don't have memories of it now. When I was younger, I didn't really care. But now you look at it, it was a good thing to get done at the time.'

After bulldozing Krzysztof Ratajski 5-0 and Ryan Searle 6-1 to reach his third consecutive final, Littler's opponent at the gates of greatness was Gian van Veen, the rising Dutch star who had beaten him in three of their five meetings in 2025. The match was officiated by referee George Noble, his last assignment before retirement, with stage announcer John McDonald making his final call after being the PDC's master of ceremonies since 2007. Surprisingly, they were treated to a procession.

Van Veen captured the first set, but long before the end of Littler's 7-1 romp – the most one-sided final since Phil Taylor crushed Van Barneveld by the same score in 2009 – he was bewildered and bloodied. During the sixth set, 'The Giant' left a trace of blood on the single five segment when retrieving his darts from the board, later explaining that he had trapped his little finger in a door going to the toilet during a break. It was not as painful as Littler plundering 21 of the last 24 legs in the match to claim the first £1 million payday in darts.

'It felt amazing to go back-to-back at the Ally Pally,' he said. 'I wanted to go into the tournament not for (chasing) the money but to lift the trophy, and I did it again. It's special to join the greats on that list of players who have won the title two years running (Phil Taylor, Gary Anderson and Adrian Lewis).

'As an achievement? I would say it's a bit unappreciated, but then again, I'm just doing my job, and I've had a fair few messages, including one from (Manchester United goalkeeper) Senne Lammens, and of course the support from family and friends has been awesome. The pressure is always on you when you are defending champion and world No.1, and the first game of any tournament is always horrible. You just have to get the job done and get out of there.

'In the final I wanted to put Gian under pressure early, but it didn't happen in the first set. Thankfully the second set was mine and, from then, I just ran away with it, but you can always improve. I saw some stats from the World Championship showing how many legs I'd won and lost, how many sets I'd won and lost in my first three tournaments. I've got a good record, but I was a bit gutted I didn't hit a nine-darter.

'Now I want to extend my lead at the top – Phil was No.1 for more than 3,000 days, and I want to stay on top for as long as I can.'

By now, the Littler effect on darts was more than just a marketing phenomenon. By every commercial measurement, he was the driving force behind record sales of darts, dartboards, replica tops, ticket sales, soaring prize money and TV viewing figures. After-school clubs are now a preferred form of detention if there's an oche and some tungsten available.

Garry Plummer, chairman of Littler's darts manufacturer Target, says: 'Luke is just amazing – what he's delivering, what he's capable of doing. He keeps pushing boundaries, breaking records, and he enjoys that part of it. When we brought out a new Luke Littler shirt, it sold out quicker than Glastonbury.

'I first met Luke at the BDO Youth World Championship qualifier when he was 12, and that day his dad asked if we would sponsor him. We'd never taken on someone so young, but I saw something special in him and saying yes was easy. He never says "How good was I?" But I think he wants to break records and beat Phil Taylor's 16 World Championships and 16 World Matchplay titles. He's young enough to do it.'

James Tattersall, Target Darts managing director, concurs. 'When Luke got to the final of the World Championship all of our metrics went off the scale,' he told *City AM*. 'There's one we watch quite closely, which is the Amazon heat map. How popular is darts on Amazon at a given time? Amazon search data is like, air fryers are No.1, multipacks of loo roll No.2 – common household items that everyone's buying. And in January, darts was No.3 on the whole of Amazon UK, which is astonishing.'

If 2026 dawned as a bed of roses for Littler, however, he would soon encounter some damaging thorns.

First, the bouquets. Dressed up to the nines, he attended an investiture at Windsor Castle to receive the MBE from the future King, whose brother famously enjoyed a soiree at the darts in 2011.

'He said he's been following the journey and we were talking about how big it's got,' Littler told Sky Sports. 'It's a good night out and the offer's there for tickets – I'm sure myself or the PDC could sort some! Turning up at Windsor Castle, it was just like, "How am I here? Why am I here?" It was a crazy experience. Obviously, they don't usually come to people so young.'

Another day out in his glad rags, at the Cheltenham Festival with fellow players Humphries and Aspinall, proved a lucrative excursion. Littler celebrated a £2,500 windfall after placing a £250 bet on 9-1 shot King Rasko Grey. And in the Champion Hurdle, a charity bet he placed on the winner, Lossiemouth, raised £2,500 for The Matthew22 Fund, which supports cancer patients and their families in memory of

Matthew Hollingsworth, who died in 2022 from bone cancer aged just 22.

The sport of kings and rubbing shoulders with royalty suited Littler down to his toe on the oche, but regaining his Premier League crown was a rollercoaster experience which left him psychologically bruised.

After losing four of his first five matches, he was near the foot of the table, but with an improvement in form came mixed receptions from crowds which bordered on bullying. If the noise in Berlin was raucous, and fans in Liverpool and Leeds gave him a predictably rough ride because of his football allegiances to Manchester United, he endured a torrid sequence midway through the league format which would have tested an elephant's thick skin.

In Manchester, ostensibly Littler's 'home' fixture closest to his Warrington base, he made the mistake of making a gesture behind Van Veen's back when the Dutchman missed a match dart. It was a momentary lapse, but hardly the stuff of ambassadors being summoned to explain themselves. Van Veen pulled a face before Littler missed two shots at double seven to win it and made a 'cry-baby' gesture, as if to say he wasn't going to shed any tears over it.

Van Veen later said 'The Nuke' was 'out of order' for what he perceived to be a celebration of the missed match dart – even though it didn't prevent him from edging home 6-5 in the contest.

The atmosphere on social media turned against Littler, and worse was to follow. In Brighton the following week, he was roundly booed and produced his worst TV average, a puny 83.94, in a 6-4 defeat by Stephen Bunting where his body language suggested he would rather be elsewhere. And seven days later in Rotterdam, with Van Veen enjoying the full-throated backing of orange-clad Dutchmen, the din was ear-splitting. Littler reached the final but admitted the reception was 'the worst I have ever experienced' and his mindset was now 'just to expect the worst'.

Behind the scenes, his mood was so dark that Littler could not even bring himself to convey his despair to his family. Only a heart-to-heart with partner Faith Millar, whose loyal support provided an oasis of reassurance amid the antagonism, stopped him from pulling out of the tournament to preserve his mental health.

'It's been a rollercoaster and that's the nature of darts – it's not an easy sport,' he said. 'Rotterdam was the worst, Berlin was OK in patches and at least I won over there, and Liverpool or Leeds is just football banter.'

For his mother, Lisa, and partner Faith, sitting by the walkway listening to the rancour aimed at a teenager, it was even worse. Littler conceded the soundtrack was a tough listen for them.

'I think they find it a bit stupid, but the word they use most is fickle – it's been pointed out there are people cheering for me one minute and booing the next. Cheering, booing, cheering… that's going to happen, but as long as I'm winning, I'm happy and my family are happy.'

Littler regained his Premier League title after a magnificent final against an in-form Humphries, edging home 11-10 before the stress of 17 weeks negotiating the peaks and troughs of a brutal competition caught up with him. Leaning against the backboard, he dissolved into tears – consoled by his ever-magnanimous darting big brother Humphries – and revealed he had been close to pulling up the drawbridge after those back-to-back ordeals in Manchester, Brighton and Rotterdam.

'I'm so grateful for my family and, obviously, Faith,' he said. 'I don't know if my mum and dad were shocked because I didn't really speak to them about it as much as I did to Faith. Maybe I should have spoken to them. But you know us men – we don't want to talk. I had to speak to Faith and tell her how I was feeling. I just kept saying to her, "I don't want to do it, I don't want to do it." (I was) sat at home. I didn't even want to go out. Didn't want to go to the next Premier League night.

'We've all got feelings, not just as darts players. We're just human and we just want to get on with our lives.'

What a way to treat a national treasure. As a nation, we specialise in producing generational talents and then rushing to demonise them. Littler demonstrated extraordinary maturity and good grace in his dealings with the media for a 16-year-old, and his courtesy has not diminished with his assorted feats. Where footballers pretend to talk on their mobile phones, or stare blankly into the distance under dustbin-lid headphones to avoid interaction with fans or journalists, Littler's manner has invariably been impeccable. Give him a break.

All-time great Taylor observed of the booing: 'We've all gone through it. Every professional player has gone through that for years. If it was any other walk of life, people would be arrested for it. The things we used to get called, you wouldn't believe it. I had to get a dictionary sometimes because they were using words I'd never heard of.

'The lad is up there trying to make a living and entertain people. If Robbie Williams was on stage singing and getting abused… it wouldn't be allowed to happen. It can go one of two ways – it'll either ruin his career or it'll make him stronger, but he shouldn't be abused and I do feel for the lad.'

Although his rivals may grow tired of his success, to a man they appreciate the earning power of darts players has been massively augmented by the Littler effect. Even through the crushing disappointment of his narrow 2026 Premier League play-off final defeat, Humphries summoned the empathy to acknowledge the boy wonder's true impact.

'The fans do want to see him play because darts needs Luke Littler – Luke Littler doesn't need darts,' says 'Cool Hand Luke'. 'That's the truth. Everyone thinks he's a robot but he's not. He's a normal person, a good kid as well.'

There was, perhaps, an element of closure when Littler and Humphries joined forces again at the World Cup of Darts in 2026 and lifted the trophy in front of a German audience. This time, any catcalls or whistles bounced off them like raindrops off an umbrella. Littler's big fish 170 checkout in a tight quarter-final against Welsh pair Jonny Clayton and Nick Kenny was a masterpiece, a quantum of solstice in midsummer.

The boy wonder from Warrington looked like a champion with his mojo restored. 'It's not easy at times,' he admits. 'But it's nice to have that winning feeling.'

Give or take its formidable rugby league team, Warrington is the kind of provincial town that would be easy to miss in the unlikely event of traffic flowing freely on the M6. In 1993, it was catapulted into the headlines by two bombs, left in litter bins by IRA murderers, which killed two innocent children on Bridge Street, 12-year-old Tim Parry and Johnathan Ball, who was just three. The wave of repugnance and outrage at such primitive savagery turned the tide against terrorism's agenda irrevocably on both sides of the Irish Sea and effectively started the countdown to the Good Friday Agreement five years later.

The atrocity predated Littler's birth by 14 years, but he has walked past the spot countless times, and he is aware of the tremendous work of the Tim Parry Johnathan Ball Peace Foundation, set up in the boys' memory, in the town.

Now, Warrington is on the map because of a superstar who has turned darts into big business. Look after him, and Luke

Littler could become as synonymous with his hometown as William Shakespeare's link to Stratford-upon-Avon or Robin Hood's to Nottingham.

'I've got plenty of years ahead of me, and obviously if I'm good at it, I want to keep going,' says Littler. 'As Michael van Gerwen said, if there's no fire in your belly, there's no point in carrying on for the sake of it. I don't want to reach a head space where I'm just going up on stage and throwing darts because I can. If you're good at your sport, you should carry on because you're a long time retired.

'Look at Cristiano Ronaldo – he's in a game which takes a real toll on your body, but if you go to a World Cup at 41 as a footballer you must love the game and be really good at it.'

Ronaldo's relentless pursuit of goals and records turned him into one of his profession's all-time greats. It remains to be seen if Littler will attain long-term greatness, but the boy king's potential is frightening. And his 111.04 tournament average, which smashed Taylor's 16-year-old record of 106.31, to land back-to-back World Matchplay titles in July 2026, suggests the real-life superhero who walks among caped crusaders and comic-strip saviours in the fancy-dress garrisons may only just be getting started.